AF770700

Japan's Economy by Proxy in the Seventeenth Century

Japan's Economy by Proxy in the Seventeenth Century

China the Netherlands, and the Bakufu

Michael S. Laver

CAMBRIA
PRESS
Amherst, New York

Copyright 2008 Michael S. Laver

All rights reserved
Printed in the United States of America

No part of this publication may be reproduced, stored in or introduced into a retrieval system, or transmitted, in any form, or by any means (electronic, mechanical, photocopying, recording, or otherwise), without the prior permission of the publisher. Requests for permission should be directed to permissions@cambriapress.com, or mailed to Permissions, Cambria Press, 20 Northpointe Parkway, Suite 188, Amherst, New York 14228.

Laver, Michael, 1973–

Japan's economy by proxy in the seventeenth century : China, the Netherlands, and the Bakufu / Michael S. Laver.

p. cm.

Includes bibliographical references and index.

ISBN 978-1-60497-500-0 (alk. paper)

1. Japan—Commerce—History—17th century. 2. Japan—Economic conditions—17th century. I. Title.

HF3825.L38 2008

382.0952—dc22

2007050647

To Annie Kirk Laver,
my wife and my best friend

Love goes toward love, as schoolboys from their books; but love from love, toward school with heavy looks.

—William Shakespeare

Table of Contents

Acknowledgments

I would be extremely remiss in my filial and scholarly duties if I did not make reference to the considerable support I have received from several people in my life, support that has ultimately made this project possible. I must first extend my deepest gratitude to my parents who have throughout been extremely supportive of my academic career. Having toiled for more than forty years in the steel mills of East Chicago to support his family, my father will probably never truly understand how his son could, in good conscience, spend several years pursuing a PhD. Perhaps that is as good an indicator as any of the unconditional support that my parents have given me; therefore, I offer my humble thanks to my mother and father, without whose support I would certainly not be the person I am today.

Dale Lawrosky has been everything that a true friend should be. He will perhaps never know the influence that he has had on my life, nor just how much he has influenced my early years as an academic. Although not an academic himself, he taught me what it means to be passionate about learning and knowledge and to follow that passion throughout life. For his inspiration and friendship I shall be eternally grateful. At Purdue University, Professor Sally Hastings was a true mentor and a friend, and it is largely her fault that I chose to embark on the path of an historian of Japan. I was fascinated by her ability to relate effortlessly the history of a land that to me seemed (and at times seems) utterly alien.

I would be an ungrateful wretch if I did not acknowledge the considerable support I have received from the Center for East Asian Studies and the East Asian languages and Civilizations department. To Peggy, Linda, and Diane, thank you for your biting humor and your ongoing departmental commentary. Paula Roberts, Assistant Director of CEAS, Frank Chance, Associate Director, and of course G. Cameron Hurst III, director and advisor, have all had unswerving faith in me, and for that I am extremely grateful. Through their generous support and continued friendship, I have been able to pursue my research and writing relatively unencumbered.

I was a visiting researcher at the Center for Non Western Studies at Leiden University, where I was able to work for one year both in Dutch and Japanese sources. Special thanks go to Ilona Beumer-Grill for arranging an office and other amenities that made my experience so wonderful. Thank you also to Professor Willem Boot, a monument of scholarship and the head of the Japanology Department at Leiden, who served as advisor and mentor

Finally, I would like to express my gratitude to my mentors, G. Cameron Hurst III, Linda Chance, and Frederick Dickinson. Cappy has been an unending source of inspiration to me through his first-rate scholarship and easy familiarity with those around him. Cappy Hurst combines the best traditions of academia with an eminently personable nature, and as an advisor he has been nothing but supportive of me in my efforts, and for this as well as for his friendship I shall be forever in his debt.

Professor Chance has been a model of what it means to be an academic in her remarkable command of Japanese language, literature, and commitment to scholarship in general. Despite my obvious flaws as a linguist, she has been patient and kind in her efforts to impart her vast knowledge to me. And I have repaid her kindness with only mediocrity and dull-wittedness, a source of endless frustration for her, I'm sure. Semester after semester she has been a great mentor, and I can only hope to live up to her expectations of me. Professor Dickinson has taught me everything I've ever forgotten about modern Japanese history. As well as being a teacher who commands the adoration of his students, he is a first-rate academic who has been nothing but kind to me and extremely generous with his time. Without the continued support of these wonderful scholars and friends, I would not have had the skills or the means to undertake a project of this magnitude. I owe an enormous intellectual debt to them. Any errors that appear in the present work are the sole responsibility of the author.

Finally, my love and thanks go to Anne Kirk Laver who, as my companion on this journey, has stood by me with the patience and understanding of a saint. I truly hope that I may endeavor to deserve the love she has shown me. This book is dedicated to her, and to Dale Lawrosky who passed away in August 2006; the world is a worse place without him.

List of Foreign Terms and Their Definitions

Bakufu	Literally "tent government." A term that denotes the government of the shogun, which was located in the city of Edo in the Tokugawa Period.
Bawan	The Chinese rendering of the Japanese "Hachiman," the God of War. This term refers to Japanese pirate ships that attacked the coast of China.
Bōeki-ke	Term denoting a merchant family in early modern Japan.
Bugyō	An official in the Tokugawa government responsible for a specific function. For example, the official responsible for governing the city of Nagasaki was called the Nagasaki Bugyō.
Capitão-Mor	A position granted to a Portuguese nobleman by the king which entailed the governance of a Portuguese foreign territory.
Cartaz	A trading pass issued to Asian ships in the Indian Ocean by the Portuguese at Goa. Any ship without this pass was subject to confiscation by the Portuguese.

Chanoyū	Japanese ritualized way of drinking tea. Often called the "tea ceremony" in the west.
Cruzado	A Portuguese gold coin with a weight of 3.45 grams.
Dagregister	The official VOC diaries kept in the trading posts by the chief merchant.
Daikan	A middle ranking official in the shogunal government. Usually translated as "intendant."
Eenhoorn	Early modern Dutch name for a rhinoceros, although it can also refer to a unicorn.
Factorij	A VOC trading post in Asia.
Fudai Daimyo	Daimyo who were either related to or historically allied to the Tokugawa and consequently the most trusted of the Tokugawa vassals.
Generale Missiven	Letters (reports) sent from Batavia to the Herren Zeventien concerning the affairs of the VOC in Asia.
Gulden	A standard unit of Dutch silver currency that was established in 1581. One Gulden is equal to twenty stuivers.
Han	A domain in Tokugawa Japan. Each han was ruled by a daimyo.
Haringbuis	A ship used from the 16th century in Holland that revolutionized the herring industry. It was characterized by three masts and was quite broad in order to accommodate larger loads.
Hatamoto	A rank of samurai retainer in Tokugawa Japan that literally means "bannerman."
Herren Zeventien	The council of seventeen merchants that was responsible for making policy for the VOC. The seventeen directors were drawn from the major commercial centers in the Netherlands, notably Amsterdam and Zeeland.

Hoge Regering	The "High Government" in Batavia, consisting of the Governor General and a governing council, that was responsible for the operations of the VOC.
Hōshojō	A document issued by the shogun's government in Edo in the 1630s that authorized foreign trade; the successor to the Shuinjō.
Hōshosen	Ships in possession of a Hōshojō that traded abroad in the 1630s.
Hyakushō	A land-owning peasant in early modern Japan.
Ikki	A peasant uprising in medieval and early modern Japan, although an ikki could also be a religious uprising as well.
Itowappu Nakama	The official cartel, made up of representatives of the five major Japanese cities, which had exclusive rights to buy and sell imported Chinese white silk.
Jōdaka	A system of trade restrictions placed on foreign merchants in the late seventeenth-century in which goods of only a certain value of silver could be imported into Japan. This was an effort to address what the bakufu perceived to be a chronic shortage of silver because of foreign trade.
Jōkamachi	Literally, "town under the castle," these towns were the places where the daimyo made their capitals and required their vassals to live. These towns quickly became centers of commerce in the Tokugawa period.
Kamer	Literally "chamber," but in this case one of six semi-autonomous subdivisions of the VOC that corresponded to the particular city in which the kamer was located. The two biggest kamers were located in Amsterdam and Zeeland.

Kan	Unit of weight, in this case for silver: one kan is equal to 3.75 kilograms.
Kangō	A document issued to foreign merchants by the Ming government in China. The document had two halves, one kept in China and the other given to the foreign merchant. All legal foreign trade had to be accompanied by a kangō, otherwise it was not permitted.
Kin	Unit of weight in premodern Japan: one kin is equal to 600 grams
Kinsei	"Early Modern." The era in Japanese history between the medieval and modern periods, from roughly 1600 to 1868.
Koban	A standard Japanese gold coin used in foreign trade in the seventeenth century.
Koku	Unit of volume in premodern Japan, usually used in measuring quantities of rice. One koku is equal to 180 liters.
Machidoshiyori	A town official in early modern Japan.
Nihonmachi	Literally "Japan-towns," the settlements consisting mainly of Japanese that were found in foreign countries such as the Philippines and Ayutthaya.
Opperhoofd	The chief merchant of a Dutch trading post in Asia.
Orandafūsestugaki	A report on "world affairs" written every year by the Dutch merchants in Japan for the shogun.
Pancado	Portuguese term for the silk cartel (Itowappu Nakama) that regulated the sale of Chinese silk in the early seventeenth century.
Picol	A Chinese measure of weight; one picol is equal to 125 pounds.
Rangaku	"Dutch studies." Originally referring to Japanese scholars that studied Dutch language and

	medicine, the term came to encompass all scholars of "western learning."
Retourfloot	The return fleet from Asia to the Netherlands.
Rōju	Literally meaning "elder" in Japanese, this was one of the highest positions in the Edo bakufu. There were originally two Rōju before their numbers were increased to four. This served as a governing council of the bakufu.
Rōnin	A samurai who was not a vassal of a daimyo; "masterless samurai."
Sakoku	"Closed country." A term that refers to Japan's period of relative isolation from the 1630s to 1854.
Sankin-Kōtai	Alternate attendance system in Tokugawa Japan. All daimyo were required to spend half of their time in Edo and to leave their wives and children in Edo as hostages at all times.
Sengoku Jidai	The warring states period in Japan from 1467 to 1600.
Shaku	Japanese measure for length: one shaku is equal to 30.3 centimeters.
Shihō Baibai	"Municipal trading" system instituted for a short time in the late seventeenth century. This required that all foreign goods be sold to the Nagasaki officials, who would then sell them to Japanese merchants who would bid for them.
Shuinjō	The document containing the red seal of the shogun, which allowed Japanese to trade abroad.
Shuinsen	Literally "red-seal ships," the term refers to the official shogunal seal that had to accompany all Japanese ships trading abroad in the Tokugawa period.
Staadhouder	The head of a province in the Netherlands. The house of Orange were the traditional Staadhouders of Holland, and thus the most powerful political entity in the Netherlands.

Tael	Unit of weight for silver in East Asia, usually of 1.2 troy ounces, but varying widely over distance and time.
Tōzama Daimyo	Daimyo that were enemies of the Tokugawa at the Battle of Sekigahara, and consequently the least trusted of the shogun's vassals.
Voorcompaniën	Several companies that were established in late sixteenth-century Holland to conduct trade with Asia. Many of these companies merged to form the United Dutch East India Company (VOC) in 1602.
Wakō	Japanese pirates that attacked the coasts of China and Korea in the medieval period, usually from bases in Kyushu or on Tsushima.
Wisselbank	An exchange bank in Amsterdam founded in 1609 for the purpose of dealing in the currencies of several different nations in Europe and backed by the city of Amsterdam.
Yamashi	Literally "mountain master," a specialist in the technical aspects of mining in early modern Japan.

Japan's Economy by Proxy in the Seventeenth Century

INTRODUCTION

One of the most difficult and controversial periods to deal with as a historian of premodern Japan is the *sakoku*, or "closed country," period. Spanning well over two hundred years, from the mid 1630s to 1854, this period for historians represents a profound shift in the role of Japan in the wider world. This era was characterized by major changes in Japanese society itself, most notably in the increasing urbanization of the samurai class (formerly tied to the land that they held in fief), and in the dramatic increase of precious metals within the country that was a direct result of a concerted exploitation of the silver, gold, and copper mines that Japan possessed in such abundance. These changes in Japan's social, economic, and political structure, combined with a policy that severely limited direct contact between the Japanese and foreigners, make this period especially difficult to evaluate accurately. We are particularly prone to misconception because of the latter consideration: direct contact between Japanese merchants and their foreign counterparts was effectively severed in the 1630s, giving rise to the notion that Japan must have somehow withdrawn from the international economy. This, however, was most certainly not the case; rather, the Japanese economy continued to have a tremendous impact on the Asian mainland even after the implementation of the *sakoku* decrees. The relationship between the Japanese economy and the economy of the wider world was somewhat obfuscated insofar as Japanese merchants were no longer the primary agents of this economic activity; and it is this situation that makes it all too easy to overlook Japan's role in the world economy after the "closed country" policies had been set in place.

So much of our traditional understanding of what this period represents—both for Japan as a "country" and the region as a whole—is still subject to misunderstanding. Even the very name by which historians have come to call this period is highly misleading. *Sakoku* literally means "closed country;" the fact that this is by no means an accurate description of Japan's political situation from the seventeenth century has not translated into a more appropriate label for this period, although certainly the term "early modern" (*kinsei*) is becoming more widespread.[1]

The Japanese economic influence on Asia in the seventeenth century was tremendous. Even when the Japanese government resolved to limit its contact with Europeans by expelling first the Spanish and then the Portuguese, as well as deciding to prohibit its own citizens from traveling abroad, the Japanese economy remained a force in Asia and indeed played a significant role in the world economy as well. Recent scholarship has done a good job of demonstrating that Japan, once thought to be isolated from the wider world, was in fact pursuing a careful policy of diplomatic relations with the Korean and the Ryūkyū Islanders. And even though the bakufu had no official diplomatic relations with China and the Netherlands, those two countries maintained a vigorous trade in Japan throughout the first century of the *sakoku* era.[2] The seventeenth-century economy of Japan, however, was an "economy by proxy" since the agents that exchanged Asian and European luxury goods for Japanese products and precious metals were not Japanese, but rather Dutch, Chinese, Korean, and Ryūkyū Islanders. These peoples moved in to fill the economic gap left by the forced exclusion of the native Japanese merchants from an active role in the foreign economy.[3] This book will attempt to show the tremendous impact that this Japanese "economy by proxy" had on Asia and on the foreigners trading in Japan in the seventeenth century.

As a testament to how concerned the Japanese authorities were with maintaining foreign trade, the bakufu repeatedly asked the Dutch if they would be able to import the same amount of goods as the Portuguese did, should the latter be expelled.[4] The bakufu was clearly very conscious of the role of foreign trade in their own economy, and were eager to maintain that role, despite the political restrictions that were implemented.[5] The Dutch, Chinese, and Koreans ensured that throughout the seventeenth century the Japanese economy would continue to have a huge impact on the continent, both through the sheer quantity of Asian goods brought to Japan and in the amount of Japanese precious metals distributed to various ports throughout Asia.

It would be hard to overstate the impact of the early modern Japanese economy on Asia and on the foreign merchants in Japan. With respect to Dutch sources, however, an emphasis has been placed largely on the cultural aspects of the Dutch presence in Nagasaki, with a few obvious exceptions. The influence of *rangaku*, or Dutch studies, has been an especially popular theme amongst western scholars who have demonstrated persuasively that the West interacted with Japanese society in several fields, from art to anatomy, even after the supposed closing of the country. Furthermore, as Marius Jansen has pointed out, because Japan was effectively divorced from direct relations with the West as whole, this period has been labeled one of seclusion, in essence eliding over the fact that the bakufu had simply chosen to orient itself towards Asia rather than towards the West.[6] Similarly, the large body of Jesuit scholarship, by scholars such as Hubert Cieslik, concentrates (understandably) almost exclusively on the Christian persecutions of the Tokugawa period, persecutions that the Dutch, as eyewitnesses, reported quite extensively.

Finally, although Japanese scholars have dealt with Japan's foreign trade after *sakoku* in somewhat more detail, there is still a marked tendency to concentrate on the internal economic development of the country. The establishment of national and domainal rice markets that served to change rice into cash (thereby servicing a growing urban population), the development of a system of credit and a futures market that went hand in hand with these rice markets, and an "industrious revolution" have all been studied rather extensively and have been used to show that Japan contained within itself the "sprouts of capitalism" that allowed it to adjust so rapidly to a radically different world in the nineteenth century.[7]

My purpose is to build on this tremendous body of scholarship and to evaluate the true nature of the Japanese economy in the seventeenth century as it pertained to the wider world, particularly the Asian continent and the Dutch East India Company. Chapter 2 will deal with the role of the *shuinsen* (red-seal ships) in Japanese trade with Asia.[8] Even at the height of Portuguese and Chinese commercial involvement in Japan, the trade carried in Japanese ships dwarfed that of any other party, as Japanese merchants themselves distributed a vast amount of silver throughout Asia. It was of course the sheer amount of Japanese precious metals carried in the *shuinsen* that made Japan such an undeniable economic force in early modern Asia. Chapter 3, therefore, provides a detailed analysis of the technological changes that allowed the Japanese to exploit their mines to such effect, as well as the role of Japanese silver in seventeenth-century trade. Chapter 4 will deal with the function of Taiwan as a convenient meeting place for illicit Chinese-Japanese trade, and later as a strategic link connecting the economies of Japan and Asia that the Dutch were able to exploit to such advantage. Taiwan became a central node in Asian trade after the bakufu banned Japanese merchants from leaving the country, allowing the VOC to move into the lucrative role of middleman between Japan and Asia.

The primary groups to benefit from the trade between Japan and Asia after the institution of the *sakoku* decrees were the Dutch and the Chinese, although the Korean and the Ryūkyū Islanders also shared in the great wealth Japan had to offer. These groups ensured that, in exchange for Japanese precious metals, the Asian luxury goods that were in such demand in early modern Japan flowed uninterrupted. The central role of Japan in the Asian economy becomes particularly evident through an analysis of the quantity and variety of luxury goods imported into the country. That economic role, however, has been obscured by a number of factors, not least of which is the complex nature of the *sakoku* decrees. It is my goal in the final chapter, therefore, to address this phenomenon and to evaluate *sakoku* for what it really was: an effort on the part of the Tokugawa authorities to balance internal security concerns with a genuine desire to participate in the international economy of the seventeenth century.

ENDNOTES

1. It is still somewhat easy to give the impression that Japan was a "closed country," since economic historians have overwhelmingly dealt with Japan's internal development. Certainly scholars such as Ronald Toby, Tashiro Kazui, Arano Yasunori, and many others have dealt with Japan's foreign relations during this period, but the balance of scholarship seems to concentrate on what Hayami Akira calls the "industrious revolution," or at least the internal economic activity that was a precursor to Meiji Japan's "economic miracle." See, for example, Chie Nakane and Shinzaburō Ōishi, *Tokugawa Japan: The Social and Economic Antecedents of Modern Japan*, trans. Conrad Totman (Tokyo: University of Tokyo Press, 1991).
2. *Bakufu* means literally "tent government" and is a reference to a time when the rank of shogun meant simply "barbarian subduing Generalissimo." As "shogun" evolved into a permanent postition more or less akin to that of a military dictator, "bakufu" came to denote his government, located in this case in the city of Edo.
3. Hendrick Brouwer, Governor-General at Batavia, wrote in 1636 that with the Japanese prohibition against travel abroad, the trade of all of Southeast Asia had fallen into Dutch hands. Needless to say, Dutch officials greeted the shogunal edict with a great deal of enthusiasm. See W. Ph. Coolhaas, ed., *Generale Missiven van Governeurs-Generaal en Raden aan Heren XVII der Vereenigde Oostindische Compagnie: Deel I, 1610–1638* ('s-Gravenhage: Martinus Nijhoff, 1960), 522: January 4, 1636.
4. Many of these conversations took place in the form of "interviews" with various shogunal councilors in Edo. One such example is recorded in the diary of Nicholas Couckebacker in early April 1636. See Shiryō Hensan-jo, *Nihon Kankei Kaigai Shiryō. Dagregisters Gehouden bij de Opperhoofden van de Nederlandshe Factorij in Japan, Vol. I* (Tokyo: Tokyo Daigaku Shiryō Hensan-jo, 1974), 217. Hereafter NKKS.
5. The most obvious example of this concerns the Sō house on Tsushima. In order to make it seem that the shogun was placing himself in a position that was akin to that of a diplomatic equal with the king of Korea, the daimyo of Tsushima forged the shogun's signature in a letter. The deception did not stop there, however; to keep from being caught, all signatures on subsequent letters had to be forged as well. The bakufu discovered this subterfuge when Sō Yoshinari's retainer, Yanagawa Shigeoki, petitioned to leave the service of the Sō house and become

a shogunal *hatamoto*. Rather than execute the daimyo for this impropriety, however, he dispensed the relatively lenient sentence of a sharp reprimand, while Yanagawa bore the full brunt of the bakufu's ire. Furthermore, Korean trade was placed under the supervision of Zen monks appointed by Edo, who took up residence in the Iteian hermitage on Tsushima. The Sō family, however, retained their monopoly on trade and diplomatic relations with Korea. This was a remarkably lenient punishment, considering the fact that other daimyo had been forced to commit *seppuku* on less severe charges. The only explanation is that the shogun valued the Korean trade and was not willing to lose it by removing the Sō, the traditional mediator of trade with the peninsula. A description of the end of this affair can be found in the diary of Couckebacker: see NKKS Vol. I, 234–35: April 25, 1635. An English account of the "Yanagawa affair" can be found in Jurgis Elisonas, "The Inseparable Trinity: Japan's Relations with China and Korea," in *The Cambridge History of Japan, Volume 4: Early Modern Japan*, ed. John Hall (Cambridge: Cambridge University Press, 1991), 235–300.

6. Marius Jansen, *The Making of Modern Japan* (Cambridge: Harvard University Press, 2000), 64.
7. For a good bibliographic essay on Japanese scholarship in the field of economic history, see Yamamura Kozo and Susan Hanley, "A Quiet Transformation in Tokugawa Economic History," *The Journal of Asian Studies* 30: 2 (1971): 373–384. This essay is over twenty years old but is still extremely relevant, especially in outlining the shift away from a Marxist approach to economic history that occurred in the 1960s.
8. I have chosen to leave the terms *shuinsen* and *shuinjō* untranslated since the alternative is an unwieldy English term such as "red-seal ship." A *shuinjō* refers to an official document issued by the shogun (or Hideyoshi earlier) and is characterized by his official vermillion seal. Therefore, the ships that were officially sanctioned to trade overseas are called *shuinsen*, or "red-seal ships."

Chapter 1

A World in Flux: Japan and the Netherlands in the Sixteenth and Seventeenth Centuries

The most obvious manifestation of Japanese involvement with the international economy, at least in the first third of the seventeenth century, was the *shuinsen* trade.[1] Although the Ashikaga shogun had sporadically used a similar system of "trade passes" in the early- to mid-Muromachi period, it only came to its full realization as a political and economic tool at the turn of the seventeenth century. We have no surviving documentation to prove that Hideyoshi issued *shuinjō* (trade passes) to his subjects, but it seems clear from later histories that he did in fact issue them to the wealthy merchants of Kyoto, Nagasaki, and Sakai.[2] As a method of political control, however, the *shuinsen* system was only fully instituted in 1604 when Tokugawa Ieyasu followed Hideyoshi's lead and made it a requirement that all merchants trading abroad have a shogunal *shuinjō*. Not only were these permits issued to merchants, but they were also given to daimyo, bakufu officials, foreigners, and even to two women. Iwao Seiichi notes that in the course of the three decades in which the *shuinjō* were used, a total of 355 were issued for trade at nineteen different locations in Southeast Asia.[3] Although the number of ships sailing abroad dropped precipitously as the period drew to a close, seven major families were still allowed to send ships to Tonkin, Cochin, and Siam on a regular basis. The frequency with which the Japanese sent ships to these areas led to the formation of *nihonmachi,* the semi-autonomous enclaves of ethnic Japanese who lived together in a foreign country. The two biggest settlements were located in Dilao (a town just outside of Manila in the Philippines) and in Ayuthia (the capital city of Siam). Dilao, at the height of its prosperity in the early 1620s, had 3,000 Japanese residents, while in 1626, there were 1,700 Japanese who lived in the *nihonmachi* in Siam.[4] These settlements were, in a very real sense, semi-autonomous regions insofar as the Japanese often answered to their own officials and usually lived separately from the rest of the native population. Other areas with sizeable Japanese enclaves included Tonkin, Cambodia, Malacca, Batavia, Macao, Cochin, Burma, and Korea. It is quite clear from this brief introduction that the Japanese represented a significant presence throughout Asia in the early seventeenth century.

Tokugawa Ieyasu exemplifies this outward-looking attitude of the early modern Japanese; to cite a suitably metaphoric example, according to an entry in the *Tokugawa Jikki* for 1611, Ieyasu made a point of studying conditions in foreign countries with the aid of a world map that had, in all likelihood, been imported by Europeans.[5] Even before he assumed the title of shogun in 1603, Ieyasu had sent letters to Southeast Asian rulers in his capacity as one of five regents for the young Toyotomi heir, Hideyori. Upon his assumption of the title of shogun, he began in earnest to work towards peaceful relations with his neighbors. The priest Sūden, Ieyasu's chief foreign policy advisor, included in his *Ikoku Nikki* letters from the shogun to almost every major country in Asia, in which the shogun expressed a desire for peaceful commercial relations.[6] Ieyasu's foreign policy aims included the resumption of relations with Ming China, peaceful relations with Korea, relations with the Spanish empire in Asia including the Philippines and Nova España (Mexico), and commercial relations with the European powers, including Portugal, Spain, England, and the Netherlands. In addition, Ieyasu reached out to such Southeast Asian countries as Siam, Annam, Cambodia, Tonkin, and Cochin.[7] The new shogun was clearly interested in the world outside of Japan; he was interested in learning what the Europeans had to offer, and he was intent on joining the larger world both politically and economically. As Captain John Saris wrote upon receiving a *shuinjō* for the English factory at Hirado, "I have obtained large privileges of the Emperor for trade...Our usage hath been good, and I hope our trade will be no less."[8]

It would be a mistake, however, to view Ieyasu as simply a naïve optimist in a "brave new world." He was rather a consummate politician who had recently gained control of a country, torn by civil strife for over a century, in which there still existed elements that threatened to destabilize the tenuous peace of his infant regime. It is against this background that the increasing restrictions that characterized the next several decades should be seen.

Europeans had already been present in Japan for decades at the time that Ieyasu had vanquished his foes on the field of Sekigahara and consolidated his power. The Portuguese merchants had been importing Chinese silk in exchange for Japanese silver, and Jesuit missionaries had been converting souls to Christ for almost a half century before Ieyasu triumphed over his rivals in 1600. For the Portuguese, at least those not engaged in missionary activity, Japan meant primarily silver, and lots of it. Jan Huygen van Linschotten, a Dutchman in the employ of the Portuguese, wrote of the rich silver mines in the islands and the lucrative trade that the Portuguese drove there.[9] He also wrote of the Japanese "craze" for Chinese products, especially silk; Japan's seemingly endless desire for Chinese silk, combined with a maritime ban on trade between China and Japan, ensured that the Portuguese would be most welcome in Japan.[10]

In addition, the boom in Japanese silver production that occurred in the second half of the sixteenth century made it possible for the Portuguese to realize huge profits from the Macao-Nagasaki connection. The position of captain on this journey, in fact, was consistently the most profitable assignment in the whole of the Portuguese trade empire and was accordingly awarded by the king to a member of the Portuguese nobility.[11] This continued to be the case to the very end of Portuguese relations with Japan, and was the envy of all other European powers in Asia. Dutch merchants in Asia, for example, routinely recorded in their diaries that if only the Dutch East India Company (hereafter shortened to VOC) could find a supply of silk such as the Portuguese had in Macao, they too would be able to tap into the huge profits Japan had to offer.

DUTCH MARITIME SUPREMACY AND THE VOC

The Dutch already had a rather developed seafaring tradition by the middle of the sixteenth century. While the Portuguese were sailing ever farther down the west coast of Africa and eventually around the Cape of Good Hope to India, the Dutch were sailing in the opposite direction. Dutch merchants of the sixteenth century had come to dominate the most lucrative seaborne trade in all of Europe, a trade that always dwarfed other routes, even after the Dutch expanded into the Indian Ocean. The carrying trade between the Mediterranean and the Baltic countries offered tremendous profits for the Dutch commercial apparatus centered on the maritime provinces of Holland and Zeeland.[12] The great strength of the Dutch was that they were able to "undercut" the competition by shipping goods at much lower prices that any other competitor. This was due, in part, to Dutch innovation in terms of shipbuilding; Dutch ships were generally recognized to be the most advanced in Europe. The *Haringbuis*, for example, was able to stay at sea for six to eight weeks, a process being developed in which the herring catch could be salted and stored on the ship, eliminating the need to put in at port.[13] It was this technological advancement, combined with the ability of Dutch merchants to provide cheap shipping, which allowed the Dutch to intrude so successfully on European trade.

The merchants who invested in this trade, many of them Jewish merchants who fled to the United Provinces in order to escape the Spanish Inquisition, specialized in carrying Baltic grain to countries such as Spain and the Italian city-states, areas that were prone to regular famines.[14] In return, they shipped Mediterranean products such as olives and wine north to Scandinavia, the Baltic States, and Russia. An indication of how extensive the Dutch role in this trade was can be seen in the number of ships passing through "the Sound;" Dutch ships outnumbered those of all other countries by a margin of two to one. Merchants at the time referred to the trade with the Baltic as the "mother trade," and by the late sixteenth century the Dutch had as many as 1,200 ships engaged solely in this lucrative business.[15] The cheaper transport rates that the Dutch were able to offer in Baltic grain was so vital to the Spanish that even in times of bitter warfare, Dutch ships were regularly arriving in Spanish ports.[16]

It was this background in the Baltic shipping industry, along with the highly developed Dutch herring and whaling industries, that prepared the United Provinces for an advance into the Indian Ocean. Of the Dutch prowess in the Herring business, Meynert Semeyns wrote in 1639, "The Lord has, through the instrument of the herring, made Holland an exchange and staple market for the whole of Europe. The herring keeps Dutch trade going, and the Dutch trade sets the world afloat."[17] Such an extensive whaling and herring industry naturally ensured that the Dutch would lead the way in technological innovations in the construction of ships and in the ability to operate them cheaply and efficiently. During the years of Dutch supremacy on the seas, 500 ships per year were being constructed in Dutch shipyards, both for domestic use and for sale abroad.[18]

There is a debate among historians of early modern Dutch history as to the true impetus behind the initial Dutch advance into the Indian Ocean. Until the last decades of the sixteenth century, the Dutch received their supply of spices and other Asian products from Antwerp via Lisbon. This market was closed to the Dutch in 1585, however, when a Spanish offensive captured Antwerp and closed the Schelde River, the city's access to the North Sea, to oceangoing traffic. Similarly, with the ascension of Phillip II to the Portuguese throne after the king of Portugal died without heir, Portugal was brought irrevocably into the Spanish war with the rebellious United Provinces. This effectively meant that Lisbon was also closed to Dutch merchants as an entrepôt for Asian goods, especially for such coveted spices as pepper and cloves.[19] The capture and subsequent closure of Antwerp as an international port was a double-edged sword for the Spanish. While it cut the Dutch off from a valuable commodity trade in Asian goods, it also drove a great number of prosperous merchant houses (many of them Jewish) to quit Antwerp and to move to Amsterdam where they transferred their entire operations, along with all of their international contacts.[20] Many historians argue that it was this closure of both Lisbon and Antwerp that provided the impetus for the Dutch to turn their considerable maritime experience towards the Indian Ocean.[21] That contemporary Dutch also believed this to be true is seen in a famous painting by Pieter Isaacz, entitled *Allegory of Amsterdam as the Center of World Trade.* The inscription on the piece reads, "Did you think that, barred from the Spanish west, I would be lost? Wrong: because with God's help I opened the way to Africa and India, to where exotic China stretches out, and to a part of the world that even the ancients did not know. Continue to favor us, God, and pray that they learn of Christ."[22]

This view, however, is challenged by recent Dutch historiography that emphasizes instead the high price and erratic supply of the spices imported by the Portuguese. These historians also cite the influence of Dutch sailors in the employ of the Spanish and Portuguese who brought their knowledge of Asian geography and cultures back home with them. Together, these two factors led the Dutch to seek direct access to the lucrative spice trade.[23] The most famous of these sailors was Jan Huygen van Linschotten, a Dutchman who spent considerable time in Goa and who saw first hand the workings of the Portuguese seaborne Empire.[24] One of his biggest accomplishments, it has been claimed, was bringing to light the fact that Portuguese power in Asia was not the monumental colossus that many Dutch merchants had imagined it to be, but was rather a tenuous patchwork of alliances and monopolies that was very much on the decline. Thus, recent Dutch historiography pays less attention to international political factors such as the war with the Spanish, and instead emphasizes a natural extension of an already quite advanced maritime tradition. The expertise of recently repatriated sailors such as Linschotten and Dirk Gerritszoon Pomp, along with the realization that the Dutch could compete with the Portuguese for power in the "East Indies," prompted the United Provinces to try their luck in the Asian trade.[25]

The Formation of the Dutch East India Company was not the event that inaugurated the Dutch advance into Asia, but rather was the culmination of a process beginning with a number of smaller companies, called *voorcomapnieën*, that were the direct ancestors of the VOC.[26] The first of these companies consisted of nine merchants from Amsterdam who, meeting in the warehouse of Martin Spils, appointed Cornelis de Houtman to lead a voyage to the Spice Islands.[27] Early Dutch captains used Linschotten's *Itinerario* to great effect since it described in detail the trade of the Portuguese in Java and included a number of nautical charts of the Indian Ocean. (The English captain John Saris, who led the first English voyage to Japan, claimed that he found the archipelago using nothing but Linschotten's book).[28] De Houtman's fleet sailed from Texel on April 12, 1595, with four ships and arrived at Bantam after a fifteen-month voyage.[29] While not an overly profitable venture, the earnings were large enough to cover the overhead of the voyage and demonstrate to investors the potential for profit of future Dutch voyages to the Indies. More significant in the long run, however, was that the Dutch had succeeded in breaking the Portuguese price monopoly on spices and were now in a position to challenge their hitherto unrivalled commercial empire.

Ironically, initial Dutch success in challenging the Portuguese in Asia also harmed trade within the United Provinces itself. This was primarily because increased Dutch shipping to the Indies flooded the market in Europe with spices, thereby driving the price down and making their import less profitable.[30] After the initial success of de Houtman's voyage of 1595, several companies were established to undertake a single voyage to Asia.[31] Once the fleet returned home, the merchandise would be sold, the company liquidated, and all profits split amongst the investors. One example of this type of venture was the 1598 expedition of Jacob van Neck who, in the employ of the *Compagnie van Verre*, led eight ships to the "East Indies." Before the formation of the VOC in 1602, in fact, 65 ships in fifteen different fleets sailed from the United Provinces for Asia, most fleets being chartered for only a single voyage.[32] These companies, while generally profitable in and of themselves, quickly created an environment of intense competition that resulted in a drastic reduction of the price of spices. The solution was to form a single company that could somehow consolidate this commercial activity, and thereby foster cooperation among the merchants of the many smaller companies. A major impediment to such a company, however, was that the United Provinces themselves were not a homogenous political entity, but rather a confederation of provinces that had vastly different aspirations both politically and economically, and that were characterized by a great deal of mutual hostility.

The two main centers of maritime commerce in the United Provinces were Amsterdam, the capital of the province of Holland, and Middleburg, the capital of Zeeland in the far south of the country. When a proposal was put forward to combine the efforts and capital of the competing merchants throughout the provinces, Amsterdam was cautiously in favor of the plan while Middleburg, fearful of losing out in such a scheme to the economically more powerful port to the north, rejected the plan. In the end it was the "Landsadvocaat van Holland," Johan van Oldenbarneveld, and the Staadhouder, Prince Maurits (himself a native of Zeeland), who coerced the two provinces into accepting the proposed company.[33] With the consent of the major provinces secured, the fledgling company was able to raise just over six million *gulden* in capital by the sale of stock, and on March 20, 1602, the States General passed a resolution creating the United Dutch East India Company (*Vereenigde Oost-Indische*

Compagnie).[34] In order to mollify various regional demands, the company was divided into six *kamers* (offices) located in the cities of Amsterdam, Middleburg, Delft, Rotterdam, Hoorn, and Enkhuizen. These *kamers* were semi-autonomous in many respects, including being able to send money to Asia and to outfit their own ships; but the company was the final arbiter of overall policy and was also responsible for overall financial matters, such as the payment of dividends to investors.

The new company was controlled not by the investors, who had little say in company affairs, but by a board of seventeen prominent men called the *Herren Zeventien* (Gentlemen Seventeen). The number of directors allotted each of the *kamers* was directly proportional to their contribution of funds to the company, so that Holland and Zeeland naturally had the most, with eight and four directors respectively. The other *kamers* were allotted one member each, with the final member being rotated between Zeeland and the smaller *kamers*. The place in which the directors gathered was also rotated between Holland and Zeeland, the former retaining the privilege for six years straight and the latter two. Directly below the *Herren Zeventien* was a board of directors initially comprising 76 merchants, but soon reduced to sixty, at which level it remained for the rest of the VOC's history. Here again members on the committee were divided between the six cities, and terms were for life.[35] The intimate relationship that existed between the state and the VOC was manifest in the appointment of new directors; when one of the directors either died or retired, it fell to the city government of the outgoing member to appoint a new member to fill the vacancy. Although not as powerful as the *Herren Zeventien*, the board of directors, by virtue of its members having invested at least 6,000 *gulden* in the company, had some say in the operation of the company. The fact that these members comprised the political and commercial elite of the United Provinces also ensured that their wishes would not be entirely ignored.

The VOC was different from previous companies, however, insofar as investors did not simply put their money into a single voyage, but rather invested in the company for a specified period of time, in this case ten years.[36] In other words, rather than liquidating the company after a single voyage and dividing the profits and assets among investors, the VOC used the profits from one voyage to outfit the next one, using the remaining profits to cover operating expenses and, of course, to pay dividends to the investors.[37] The company ostensibly paid a five percent dividend over ten years; very early on, however, it was all but apparent that this would be almost impossible to maintain. This dilemma arose because of the very nature of the company: the VOC was not simply a trading company bent on the pursuit of profit, but it was also a quasi-governmental agency with the ulterior motive of carrying the war for independence against Spain (and Portugal) into the Indian Ocean. Therefore, investing in the VOC, while certainly not unprofitable, did not yield the dividends originally promised; rather, profits were used to support the apparatus of war in the East Indies with the full backing of the state. Furthermore, one of the reasons that the state did not aggressively interfere in company business when it was unable to pay its dividends was that the company was a source of revenue for the state, since in return for having its charter renewed, the directors made a generous "donation" to the coffers of the States General.[38]

In the words of Niels Steensgard, "The formation of the VOC can be regarded as an important activity of war, and in contrast with its predecessors, the United Company soon developed a war-like policy in close cooperation with the States General."[39] In the very charter of the company it was stated that the VOC had the sovereign right to make treaties with foreign rulers in Asia, to build fortifications and recruit soldiers, and to wage war against the enemies of the United Provinces. Undoubtedly this was a reflection of the vast distances involved in the Indian Ocean trade as well as the fact that with the Dutch, Portuguese, and Spanish all active in the Indian Ocean, there were bound to be frequent run-ins with the Spanish. Even so, however, the VOC enjoyed a great deal more autonomy in this respect than did any other European company. The simple fact that the VOC was born in a time of war against an exceedingly powerful sea-borne enemy is the true reason behind these broad powers of war being given the company. A 1629 pamphlet illustrates the dual functions of the East and West India Companies well in the following prayer, "Bless these [companies] with such success and progress that through [them] the enemies' power is broken, [and] the trade and prosperity of these provinces are increased."[40] It is this reason, more than any other, which led the company to renege on its obligations to pay a steady dividend to the shareholders. Dividends were of course paid, but instead of being in the form of cash they were often paid out in the form of some commodity, usually spices. These payments were also much more irregular than was promised in the company's charter. Investors were obviously and justifiably enraged at this "betrayal," but in the structure of the VOC the shareholders had very little influence with the directors of the company, while the company enjoyed the complete support of the States General. Therefore, the VOC was free to use the capital provided by the investors and subsequent profits to exploit the rights given it in its charter.

This extended introduction to the structure of the VOC and its relationship to the state is necessary to understand why, from the beginning, the Dutch were able to create such havoc in the Indian Ocean for both the Spanish and Portuguese, and why the company was able to play the part of sovereign power with local rulers throughout Asia.

The VOC in Asia

The primary trade between Europe and Asia at the beginning of the seventeenth century involved spices. And within the spice trade, pepper (both the black and white varieties) played a leading role in the VOC's attempts to establish itself in the Asian trade.[41] In an effort to facilitate the procurement of spices such as pepper, the Dutch from the very beginning sought to make alliances with influential local rulers, especially in the Spice Islands of what is Indonesia today. Many of these rulers were quite eager to use the Dutch to help them to escape from underneath the oppressive thumb of the Portuguese.[42] The role of silver was in this respect quite important, for VOC officials often presented petty local rulers with *schenkagie* (gifts) of silver, a medium of exchange that was valued even in the most remote of islands.[43] Local leaders also used trade to enhance their own personal prestige, as they were often simply "first among equals" in their kingdoms (such was the case with the ruler of Bantam, with whom the Dutch concluded an agreement whereby the Portuguese would be entirely excluded from the Bantam spice markets).[44]

In 1607 Admiral Cornelis Matlieff signed an agreement with the Sultan of Ternate in which the Dutch gained a monopoly in the export of cloves.[45] This is a particularly good example of the vicissitudes of European and Asian politics, for the Spanish also established a fort on the neighboring island of Tidore after wooing the sultan of that island with offers of military aid against his mortal enemy, the sultan of Ternate. The two European powers were clearly using the rivalry between the sultans to further their own political ends, while the Asian rulers were doing the same. By using mutual European hostility, these rulers were able to extract a number of concessions from the respective companies. This strategy, however, proved to be short sighted politically; in the long run the native potentates always lost out since the Europeans, far from being interested in local politics, were concerned only with the acquisition of spice monopolies and the destruction of their rivals. As soon as these goals were achieved, the local rulers were no longer of much importance to the company and were therefore effectively disregarded, their political ambitions no longer important to the Europeans.

The first fleet assembled by the new company consisted of ten heavily armed ships under the leadership of Admiral Steven van der Hagen. That these ships were, in essence, commercial dreadnoughts illustrates the fact that Dutch aims in Asia were from the very beginning both commercial as well as military.[46] The fleet sailed out of Texel on the 18th of December and immediately set to the task of challenging Portuguese supremacy in the East Indies. Less than two years after van der Hagen's departure, the Portuguese were forced to cede Fort Victoria on the island of Amboina to the Dutch, touching off a string of VOC military victories that would continue throughout the first half of the seventeenth century.[47] In 1607 another fleet left Holland under the leadership of Pieter Willemsz. Verhoeff, this time with orders to destroy Spanish shipping in the Indian Ocean and to set up a commercial base in the Moluccas. Subsequently, on May 22, 1609, Verhoeff established a fort on the island of Banda and became its first president. VOC military activity was strengthened by the establishment of a centralized headquarters in the East Indies, located first at Bantam under the leadership of Pieter Both, and then at Batavia (present-day Jakarta) under the militant Governor-General Jan Pieterszoon Coen.

The establishment of a centralized locus of control was, of course, not an innovation of the Dutch; the Portuguese for almost a century had a similar base at Goa, from which they controlled their commercial empire. The Dutch, following suit, first established a base in the rich spice market at Bantam and appointed Pieter Both as the first Governor-General on November 27, 1609. Both immediately set up a governing council made up of the Governor-General and four additional members, subsequently increased to nine in 1617. Two years later, Jan Pieterszoon Coen conquered the city of Jakarta, and citing a much healthier climate, established it as the headquarters of the entire company in Asia.[48] Batavia became not just a headquarters for the administration of the company, but also a place where goods could be stored in a central location and where ships could rendezvous en route to their respective destinations. This was an extremely important consideration because the power of the Dutch sea-borne commercial empire lay in its ability to exploit the "country trade," in which a complex web of trading patterns rather than a straightforward import trade to Europe allowed the VOC to maximize its profits. Furthermore, Batavia served as a base from which attacks against the Spanish and Portuguese could be planned and executed. It is against the background of both the "country trade" and VOC military policy, in fact, that the initial importance of the company's factory in Japan should also be viewed.

As we have seen, the VOC was committed to the destruction of Iberian trade in the Indian Ocean, in essence, grafting the United

Provinces' wartime aims onto its own commercial goals. Batavia served as a convenient place from which such a unified military campaign could be prosecuted. The Dutch initially used Japan in a similar manner, as a base from which to attack Iberian as well as Chinese ships.[49] This was, first of all, because of the importance of Japan to the Portuguese trading network. The vast amount of silver derived from Portuguese trade in Chinese silk meant that there were richly laden "silver ships" traveling regularly between Nagasaki and Macao; because these ships were built for size rather than speed or defense, they were particularly easy targets for the faster Dutch ships. The Spanish were also active in the China Sea, trading from their base at Manila with both Japan as well as along the Chinese coast, again a fact that made a base in the islands eminently suitable for preying on these ships.[50]

The Dutch faced a major obstacle in establishing a sustained and profitable trade in Japan; the company had no real base from which to acquire Chinese goods that were the mainstay of trade in the islands. The Portuguese, of course, were easily able to obtain silk from their base at Macao, and the Spanish could do the same from the large number of Chinese ships that frequented Manila in search of New World silver. The VOC, however, had no such steady supply, and thus resorted to attacks on Iberian and Chinese shipping to obtain these goods.[51] Katō Eiichi writes, "The increase of trade volume of the Hirado factory from 1615 onward was caused by an increase of captured goods which were temporarily brought to Hirado and then dispatched again."[52] This function of Hirado was only reinforced in 1619 when the Dutch and English signed a joint-defense agreement in which they would cooperate in the capture of Iberian ships.[53] Subsequently, a joint Anglo-Dutch fleet patrolled the seas around Manila in order to intercept Spanish ships. The fleet achieved its greatest triumph in July 1621 with the destruction of an outbound Portuguese ship carrying the new Viceroy to Goa.[54]

The Japanese authorities eventually became rather alarmed at these blatant Dutch attacks on shipping to and from Japan. They were probably more alarmed at the prospect of silk supplies being cut off, but they must also have been concerned with this show of naval strength so close to home. The Japanese had come to regard the Portuguese as the most powerful Europeans, and to suddenly observe their power in decline at the hands of the Dutch must have been more than a little disconcerting, especially considering that Japanese ships, while numerous and often quite large, were not particularly effective militarily.

Whatever the motive, however, the bakufu forbad the Dutch from overt acts of piracy in Japanese waters.[55] The company still regularly attacked both Iberian and Chinese ships outside of Japanese waters, but it was now obliged to respect all ships coming from and going to Japan.[56] Meilink-Roelofsz notes, in fact, that the Dutch continued to enjoy great success in taking Chinese junks off the coasts of both Manila and China.[57] The shogun's edict was less of a blow to Dutch trade in Japan than it might have been, for in 1624 they acquired a foothold on the island of Taiwan after an attempt to capture Macao had failed. After a period of negotiation with Ming officials from Fujian Province, the VOC fleet agreed to leave the Pescadores (Penghu Islands), the islands they initially occupied after the fiasco at Macao, and relocated to Taiwan where Chinese ships would be allowed to come and trade. With the establishment of a factory on Taiwan, the Dutch found a steady supply of silk for the Japanese market, thereby obviating the need to obtain silk from captured Chinese vessels. Not surprisingly, it is from this time that Japan began to play an increasingly important role in the VOC's operations in Asia.

As we shall see in chapter 4, substantial quantities of precious metals could be obtained in the trade with Japan, and this consideration was without doubt the most important in the VOC's activities there.[58] The company's extensive use of the "country trade" gave the Dutch an advantage over the Portuguese, Spanish, and English. It meant that rather than a series of individual trade routes, the VOC utilized a vast network of factories in which goods and precious metals obtained locally were used to maximize profits within Asia.[59] For example, rather than simply send a ship laden with silver from the United Provinces to purchase spices for the European market, the VOC tried instead to buy cloth on the Coromandel Coast and from other Indian factories, using goods obtained from other places in Asia that were in demand in India. The cloth thus obtained could in turn be traded for spices in Java and Sumatra where Indian cloth was in great demand.[60] These spices would only then be sold on the European market for a much larger margin of profit than if bullion had simply been used for spices in a direct two-way exchange. Therefore, rather than simply play a relatively limited role in an already existing, complex web of Asian trade, the VOC was able to effectively superimpose itself onto many of those trade patterns, and in many cases take over native shipping altogether.

The importance of Japan to this system was that the Dutch, by carrying silk and a great variety of Southeast Asian luxury goods to the country, were able obtain a great quantity of Japanese silver, thereby lessening the company's dependence on huge shipments of bullion from Europe. The aforementioned outline is, of course, a vastly simplified example of the "country trade" that in reality involved several destinations and a staggering array of goods. Governor-General Coen was one of the first officials to realize that such a system could be tremendously profitable for the company, and therefore used his term in office to make a number of commercial connections that would enable VOC operations in Asia to operate with as little input from Europe as possible.[61] Such a network, with trade centered on the varying factories in Asia rather than on the commercial cities in Europe, aimed at self-sufficiency as its ultimate goal.[62] In this respect as well, the VOC was truly a "state within a state," using the prevailing theories of mercantilism to foster its own economic development.

THE VOC AND EARLY MODERN JAPAN

The VOC's emphasis on self-sufficiency was precisely why the role of Japan became so important for the company; rather than sending out huge shipments of precious metals from Europe every year to "buy into" the Asian trade, the Dutch were able to obtain the necessary capital locally in the form of Japanese precious metals. This first necessitated that the Dutch obtain a foothold in the Chinese silk market, as silk was the most sought after luxury good in Japan. This was finally achieved with the establishment of Fort Zeelandia on Taiwan in 1624; and when trade with Japan took off in the 1630s, Japan became not only the most profitable factory in Asia (a position it held for several decades), but also served as a "bank" that financed VOC operations throughout Asia. This is illustrated most poignantly by the vast fleets of silver that left Japan for Taiwan, whence that silver would then be redirected to factories as far away as India.[63] When the bakufu, increasingly concerned about a silver drain on society, banned the export of the metal, the VOC turned briefly to the Japanese gold *koban* (a standard coin in Japan, its name literally meaning "small coin"). In many ways the *koban* export was even more profitable than silver since it fetched a tremendous profit on the coast of India, where the gold to silver ratio was quite favorable. This came at a particularly fortuitous time for the Dutch, since in 1673–1674 the shipment of precious metals was temporarily suspended because of war in Europe. Japanese gold shipments to Bengal during these years amply compensated for this deficiency.[64] Governor-General Maetsuyker summed up this situation best when he exclaimed in October of 1668 that there was so much gold in Japan, none needed to be sent from Europe.[65]

Copper was also an extremely profitable metal that the Dutch were able to obtain in Japan, with Japanese copper production rivaling that of even Sweden. Kristof Glamann has calculated that in the 1680s, copper comprised 80.62 percent of all Dutch exports from Japan.[66] In fact, when the VOC decided to ship Japanese copper to Europe because of a war with Sweden, it had a devastating impact on that country's profits from the metal as its monopoly was broken and the price plummeted. Holden Furber states succinctly that "nothing yielded a steadier profit than copper and…when the trade was at its height, no article except cloves was regarded as more valuable to the company's country trade."[67] Although Coen's vision for a completely self-sufficient company in Asia was never fully realized, it almost came to fruition with the profits from the factory in Japan that began increasing in the mid-1630s.[68]

The initial Dutch encounter with Japan came in April 1600 when the ship *De Liefde* ran aground at Usuki. In the words of William Adams, the ship's most famous survivor and an English pilot in the employ of the Dutch, the survivors constituted "no more but nine or tenne able men to goe or creepe vpon their knees."[69] This story is best known through James Clavell's imaginative re-creation, *Shogun*, and while the story is almost entirely the work of Clavell's imagination, it is well documented that Adams did arrive in Japan and eventually become a confidant of sorts to Ieyasu. Of more immediate relevance to the VOC, however, was the survival of a number of Dutch sailors, including Melchior van Sandtvoort and Jacob van Quaeckernack. As already noted, Ieyasu was quite interested in establishing relations with various foreign countries, and in 1605 he allowed van Sandtvoort to sail for Patani in order to bring the Dutch to Japan for trade. It was not until 1609, however, that two Dutch ships, *De Roode Leeuw met Pijlen* and *De Griffoen*, arrived on the island of Hirado.

The two VOC ships that arrived to open a factory in 1609 brought a merchant named Jacques Specx, who was designated the president of the new factory, as well as letters from Prince Maurits for the shogun (to whom the Dutch continued to refer as "the Emperor"). The *Tokugawa Jikki* records that Ieyasu presented the Dutch with a *shuinjō* to trade at "any port in Japan" when they journeyed to Sumpu in order to pay respect to the ruler.[70] From this point until the end of the Tokugawa period, the Dutch were the only Europeans to have continuous relations with the Japanese.[71]

The initial years in Japan, however, did not go well for the Dutch, and there were those within the VOC that believed the factory to be a waste of company resources and advocated its closure. In 1610, for example, not a single Dutch ship arrived at Hirado, and a total of only two came the following year, carrying goods that were of no great value on the Japanese market.[72] Despite this inauspicious beginning, however, the factory remained, and in 1617 the shogun Hidetada issued another *shuinjō* to the Dutch after the death of his father Ieyasu. This *shuinjō* was very similar to the original version, with one important exception: the Dutch, along with all other foreigners, were now confined to the two Kyushu ports of Hirado and Nagasaki.[73] This effective quarantine was a source of great complaint on the part of the company, with VOC officials dramatically prognosticating the imminent ruin of trade in Japan. The true reason for the continued existence of the factory in Hirado, despite its mediocre commercial results, was probably the strategic value that the island represented as a staging area for Dutch attacks against Spanish and Portuguese shipping. The Dutch also hoped that in the future they would be able to establish themselves in the Chinese silk market, and in so doing, tap into the great wealth in silver that Japan represented, as their Portuguese rivals had done before them.[74]

One of the reasons that the Dutch were so successful in Asia was that they exploited the "country trade," incorporating their many factories into a commercial network encompassing the entire Indian Ocean and China Sea regions. This not only helped the Dutch to reduce the large shipments of precious metals from Europe that would otherwise have been necessary, but it also had a tremendous impact on Japanese society.

With the samurai increasingly divorced from the land that they had previously held in fief, and with their removal to either Edo or another of the several *jōkamachi* (castle towns), the Japanese economy became increasingly urbanized and monetized. The economy was still based on rice insofar as land was assessed in terms of its agricultural productivity, and stipends and taxes were calculated in rice; but because of a rapidly expanding urban society from the end of the sixteenth century, a sophisticated market system arose, capable of handling large amounts of rice and exchanging it for cash. Osaka developed the largest of these "rice markets," but sophisticated markets also arose in other cities such as Edo, Kyoto, Nagasaki, and several lesser castle towns.[75]

The process of monetization was also facilitated by a boom in the mining industry that had occurred in the last decades of the warring states period. Several *sengoku* daimyo, in an effort both to strengthen their domains economically and to sustain long military campaigns, promoted the intensive mining of gold and silver.[76] The daimyo that were most successful in exploiting Japan's rich mines were the Takeda, Uesugi, and the Hōjō (and not surprisingly, were also the daimyo that were among the most powerful). When Hideyoshi, and later Tokugawa Ieyasu, succeeded in consolidating their holds over the country, one of their first acts was to confiscate the mines of the various domains and put them under central control. The Tokugawa in particular spared no expense in exploiting these mines; Kobata Atsushi has estimated that Japan produced fully one third of the world's silver during this period, a staggering sum considering the tremendous output of the New World mines in Peru and Mexico.[77] Therefore, intensive silver, gold, and copper mining made it possible to support a rapidly monetizing economy. It was also this abundant supply of precious metals that made Japan such an attractive trading partner for European and Asian merchants.

Increasing monetization of the Japanese economy made it possible for the urban elite—samurai who were made to live in cities as well as the wealthy merchants who catered to their commercial needs—to indulge in luxury goods imported from Southeast Asia, China, and Europe.[78] Chief among these luxury goods was silk in all of its varied forms. The flow of silk to Japan from China, Southeast Asia, and later India in return for silver and copper must be regarded as one of the most pronounced trade patterns in early modern history. By way of comparison, the amount of silk that made its way to Japan, Manila, and other destinations by sea from China dwarfed the amount that actually traveled over the famed Silk Road. In return, the amount of silver that flowed into China from the New World via Acapulco and Manila as well as from Japan was truly staggering. Japanese copper and silver, it can be argued, was a decisive factor in the development of early modern trade in Asia. Not only the Portuguese, but also the Chinese, Dutch, and Koreans (through Tsushima) exported a vast amount of Japanese precious metals throughout the better part of the seventeenth century.

Silk was not the only product imported into Japan; a host of other products from all over Asia was brought by Japanese *shuinsen* merchants, as well as by Chinese, Dutch, Portuguese, and for a time

Spanish and English merchants. The products most in demand were deerskins, ray skins, sugar, spices, sandalwood, and metals (such as lead and mercury). Other exotic goods such as rhinoceros horns and elephant tusks also commanded high prices in Japan and were brought in great quantities. These products were imported from several locations throughout Southeast Asia, including Siam, Cambodia, the Spice Islands, Batavia, Taiwan, China, Tonkin, Manila, and Cochin.[79] As demonstrated by this partial list of direct and indirect trading partners, Japan was an integral part of the Asian economy of the seventeenth century, and remained so even when its own merchants were forbidden to travel abroad.

The VOC offered the Japanese another invaluable service that we shall only briefly touch on here. The Dutch, because of their unique position after 1640 as the only European nation allowed to trade with Japan, provided the bakufu with valuable information on political developments in lands far from Japan, particularly in Europe. The Japanese were able to monitor conditions in Asia through their contacts with the Ryūkyū Islands as well as with Korea; in the case of Europe, however, the bakufu had virtually no knowledge of recent developments and were thus forced to rely on the VOC. Nagasaki has in fact been called Japan's window on the world, because the Dutch provided the Japanese authorities with yearly written accounts of European affairs. These accounts, known as *Orandafūsetsugaki* (Dutch reports), were brought on the ships that arrived yearly at Deshima and were rendered into Japanese by the translators stationed at Nagasaki.[80] They were then given to the Nagasaki *bugyō* who in turn sent them to Edo for the bakufu's perusal.[81] These reports came to constitute the government's main source of information about Europe, until Commodore Perry's arrival in 1854 prompted the shogun to abandon the *sakoku* policies.

Another important role that foreigners played in Tokugawa Japan was that of legitimizing agents for the shogun. This will be touched on only very briefly here, as Ronald Toby has more than adequately examined it in his *State and Diplomacy in Early Modern Japan*.[82] The most obvious example of using a foreign embassy for political means was the 1617 arrival of the Korean embassy in Kyoto. To ensure that the full diplomatic significance of the embassy was not lost on the daimyo, the shogun required that all of them be in attendance at the embassy's official reception.[83] According to Toby, "The ability of the early shogunate to produce ostentatious foreign embassies on Japanese soil, thereby demonstrating international legitimacy, was a powerful propaganda tool in the building of domestic legitimacy."[84] Suffice it to say that the political implications of such lavish Korean and Ryūkyū embassies to the shogunal court ensured that the Tokugawa received a certain measure of international and domestic legitimacy. It is important to note that Korea was an important link in Japan's system of diplomacy and trade throughout the early modern period. Even before Ieyasu established himself as the preeminent political power in Japan, he instructed Yanagawa Shigeoki, a vassal of the Sō family on Tsushima, to make peace with Korea. This mission soon bore fruit in the form of a 1609 treaty, in which the Sō were allowed to send twenty ships annually to Pusan for the purpose of trade.[85] From this date on, Korea remained an important partner in trade and diplomacy, long after the bakufu instituted the series of maritime prohibitions known collectively as the *sakoku* edicts.

The Dutch also sent embassies to Edo in the form of annual visits by the head of the VOC factory. These trips were obligatory and were designed such that the Dutch could pay their respects (and offer gifts from the year's merchandise) to the shogun and his counselors. The gifts were usually quite lavish, and the Dutch presented them in a way that very unambiguously implied a vassal relationship with the shogun. Because the Dutch, obviously quite powerful both militarily and economically, chose to make yearly submissions to the shogun's will, the bakufu derived a valuable source of legitimacy from the Dutch. While the company saw these visits as minor inconveniences performed for the sake of maintaining a lucrative trade relationship, the Tokugawa regarded them as a powerful legitimizing force that served their own political ends. The Dutch, therefore, along with the Chinese, Koreans, and Ryūkyū Islanders, became a powerful political tool used to full effect by the Tokugawa.

The phenomenon of *sakoku* was not a policy that divorced Japan from the outside world. It was rather a process through which the Tokugawa rulers implemented a series of rational measures that would, in their eyes, contribute to the defense and stability of the country. It was also a system in which the shogunate was able to deal with the world on its own terms, effectively removing Japan from a Sino-centric worldview in which counties in Asia were, to varying degrees, vassals of the "Son of Heaven." In considering the first point, twenty-first century observers look back on the Edo period and see a two-hundred-and-fifty-year span of internal peace and security, from Sekigahara to the Meiji Restoration. The Tokugawa rulers themselves, however, did not have the luxury of historical hindsight, and to them the view from "the top" was one filled with possible threats, both internal and external.[86] While this subject will be addressed more fully in the last chapter, let us turn briefly to a few of the restrictions in the *sakoku* policy and the threats to which they were responding.

First and foremost was, of course, the clampdown on Christianity. While modern-day writers might portray this often brutal suppression as a horrible abuse of human rights, the cold, political reality is that the Tokugawa issued these prohibitions in response to what they perceived to be a precarious political situation within the country. Aside from Francisco Sanda's 1596 claim that Christianity was an advance guard for Spanish colonizing efforts, it is not inconceivable that the new religion could represent a threat to the bakufu.[87] First of all, the Christian missionary effort enjoyed its greatest success on the island of Kyushu, with several powerful daimyo families such as the Ōtomo, Takayama, Naitō, and Katō converting to the religion.[88] Significantly, the daimyo of Kyushu also represented the biggest block of opposition to Ieyasu at the Battle of Sekigahara in 1600. Added to this already precarious situation was the idea (popular at the time) that Christianity went against the very nature of the feudal order, advocating rebellion against one's master, and loyalty solely to Jesus Christ and to his representative on Earth, the Pope.[89] While this may have simply been a convenient pretext for the clampdown, the fact remains that Christianity was most prevalent in an area in which an anti-Tokugawa sentiment ran very high, and in which several of the *tozama* daimyo were very powerful. The notion that a coalition of anti-Tokugawa daimyo might use Christianity as a standard around which to gather supporters for a rebellion must certainly have been at least in the realm of possibility for the first few shogun. That several of the warriors who perished with Hideyori during the Osaka campaign of 1615 were Christian only served to reinforce this fear. And finally, the Shimabara rebellion of 1638, although not a Christian rebellion in a true sense, was widely believed to be so, and the fact that the leadership of the rebellion was indeed Christian (as were many of the peasants who flocked to the Hara castle) is well established.[90]

The aforementioned considerations, along with repeated instances of priests violating the ban on missionary activity by smuggling themselves into the country, served to convince the authorities of the necessity of ridding the country of the religion entirely. When it became clear that it would be impossible to ban Christianity while still maintaining commercial relations with the Portuguese, the bakufu did not hesitate to banish them from Nagasaki. The simple fact that the Portuguese were Christian was in all likelihood not the primary issue, for both the Dutch and English were also Christian, albeit of the Protestant persuasion. It is doubtful that bakufu officials had a sufficiently deep understanding of the nuances of the Christian faith to distinguish between Catholic and Protestant, yet the English and Dutch were very welcome to trade in Japan. The real issue was rather one of perceived subversion; Catholicism was perceived as a threat to the internal security of Japan, and as such the Portuguese served as the primary symbol of that threat. Granted, as the Edo period progressed, Japanese fear of Christianity became somewhat irrational, but the initial decades of religious prohibitions were based on rational choices concerning the security of the newly pacified country.[91]

Other restrictions, both political and commercial, were also rational reactions to perceived threats to the security and stability of Tokugawa hegemony. Many of the attacks on Japanese shipping throughout Asia—for example, a Spanish attack on a *shuinsen* in Siam, the Dutch seizure of Japanese vessels and goods in Taiwan, and the destruction of a Japanese ship at Macao at the hands of the Portuguese—were seen as attacks on the prestige of the shogun.[92] Because the very existence of the shogunal government was ostensibly to ensure the military security of the country, attacks such as these demanded a decisive response. Rather than risk the legitimacy and power of his position by responding to every attack of this type, however, the shogun chose simply to curtail Japanese trading privileges so as to minimize foreign scuffles. This did not mean that the shogun was intent on curbing foreign trade; the Dutch and Chinese were allowed to carry on a significant volume of commerce even after the Portuguese were banished in 1640. The Dutch, according to Leonard Blussé, took over Southeast Asian trade formerly carried out by Japanese *shuinsen* merchants, and furthermore served as "go-betweens" between Japan and places such as Siam.[93] In fact, as we shall see in the final chapter, many of the *sakoku* restrictions were simply a means for the bakufu to facilitate the flow of goods within Japan and to ensure their fair distribution.[94]

Finally, the *sakoku* policies must be considered in the context of a Japan-centered worldview, an attempt by the bakufu to remove itself from the perceived vassal status that had formerly characterized Sino-Japanese relations. As Tashirō Kazui notes, "In the whole, *sakoku* represents a constructive policy of foreign relations adopted by Japan in an effort to free itself from Chinese control."[95] Furthermore, the very existence of a system such as *sakoku* was not unique to Japan, but was rather a common feature of East Asian political relationships in the seventeenth century. China and Korea both implemented elaborate restrictions to control not only foreigners but also their own citizens; both countries reserved a single enclave for the carrying out of foreign trade; and both implemented some form of religious restriction.[96] Gaspar da Cruz, a Portuguese Dominican who visited the city of Canton in 1556, in his public edict that was apparently posted for all to heed, states, "under pain of death, none of the country should sail out of the kingdom of China."[97] Likewise,

Captain John Saris, the head of the first English fleet to arrive in Japan, wrote of a rumor in China that the emperor had "put to death about five thousand persons, for trading out of the country, contrary to his edict, confiscating all their goods…"[98] Needless to say, these accounts sound remarkably similar to descriptions of the *sakoku* policy in Japan.

It is interesting that Engelbert Kaempfer, the noted German physician and chronicler of Japan, originally evaluated these restrictions positively.[99] However, regardless of the scope of the *sakoku* decrees, which came into full effect after the eviction of the Portuguese and the removal of the Dutch to Deshima, the Japanese government was in no way signaling its willingness to leave the international system of commerce in Asia. Rather, the exact opposite was true: the bakufu was committed to maintaining a steady flow of foreign goods into Japan by utilizing the Dutch and Chinese at Nagasaki, the Ryūkyū Islanders through Satsuma, the Koreans via Tsushima, and the Matsumae in the far north of Japan.[100] Throughout the seventeenth century, Japan remained a primary player in the economy of not only Asia, but also of the world; the fact that Japanese merchants themselves were not the primary agents of this trade is quite beside the point.

Endnotes

1. Although written almost a half century ago, Iwao Seiichi's study of the *shuinsen* trade remains the most comprehensive study to date. It reads very much like a catalog, which is very useful in terms of ease of reference, but it leaves much to be desired as an integrated history of Japanese trade with the outside world. See Iwao Seiichi, *Shuinsen Bōeki Shi no Kenkyū* (Tokyo: Keibundō, 1958).
2. For the various arguments concerning when the *shuinsen* trade actually began, see Nagazumi Yoko, *Nihon Rekishi Sōsho 60: Shuinsen* (Tokyo: Yoshikawa Kōbunkan, 2001), 3–8. The author sides with Iwao Seiichi in her assertion that the issuance of permits began with Hideyoshi, but takes the view that the"system" itself began in 1604 with Tokugawa Ieyasu.
3. The priest Sūden was Ieyasu's chief "foreign affairs" advisor and was also responsible, along with two other priests, for drawing up the actual *shuinjō.* His *Ikoku Nikki,* ed. Nakamura Tadashi, lists all of the *shuinjō* that Suden drew up, plus a number of letters from foreigners and their responses. See Nakamura Tadashi, ed., *Ikoku Nikki: Konchi-in Sūden Gaikō Bunsho Shūsei: Eiinbon* (Tokyo: Tokyo Bijitsu, 1989). For a more complete analysis of the *shuinsen,* see chapter 2 of the present work.
4. Iwao Seiichi, *Nihon Rekishi Shinsho: Shuinsen to Nihonmachi* (Tokyo: Shibundō, 1966), 182–183.
5. Ayusawa Shintarō, "Geography and Japanese Knowledge of World Geography," *Monumenta Nipponica* 19: 3–4 (1964): 277.
6. See Nakamura, ed., *Ikoku Nikki* for a particularly helpful table of contents in which these letters are listed along with the numerous *shuinjō.*
7. The *Tokugawa Jikki* records in great detail the several letters exchanged between Ieyasu and Southeast Asian monarchs. Just as a single example, on Keichō 9/9/19, Ieyasu replied to a letter from the King of Cambodia allowing trade between the two countries. See Narushima Motonao, *Kokushi Taikei: Tokugawa Jikki, Vol. 38*, ed. Kuroita Katsumi (Tokyo: Yoshikawa Kōbunkan, 1981–82), 396: Keichō 9/9/19 (December 10, 1614). Hereafter KTTJ. The Japanese dates given throughout this text refer to the era name followed by the day/month/and year of that era. Thus the aforementioned date should read: the ninth year of Keicho, nineteenth day of the ninth month. The Japanese used a lunar calendar

to calculate dates so that the nineteenth day of the ninth month does not refer to September 19.

8. Ernest Satow, ed., *The Voyage of Captain John Saris to Japan, 1613* (London: The Hakluyt Society, Second Series, 1967), 201.
9. Linschotten noted that the Portuguese took silk to Japan and "they return nothing but silver, whereby they doe greatly profit." Arthur Coke Burnell, ed., *The Voyage of John Huygen van Linschotten to the East Indies in Two Volumes, Vol. I* (London: The Hakluyt Society, 1885), 147.
10. Kobata Atsushi notes that from the late sixteenth to the first decades of the seventeenth centuries, Japanese silk imports rose to perhaps almost 300,000 kilograms annually. See Kobata Atsushi, "Edo Shoki ni okeru Kaigai Kōeki," in *Nihon Keizai no Kenkyū*, ed. Kobata Atsushi (Tokyo: Shibunkaku Shuppan, 1978), 526.
11. Michael Cooper, "The Mechanics of the Macao-Nagasaki Silk Trade," *Monumenta Nipponica* 27: 4 (1972): 427. Cooper states that the captain of this voyage stood to gain from 150,000 to 200,000 *ducats* for a single voyage (an observation that is first made by Linschotten in his diary; see endnote 9, Burnell, *The Voyage*, 146).
12. M. A. P. Meilink-Roelofsz, "Een Vergelijkend Onderzoek van Bestuur en Handel der Nederlandse en Engelse Handelscompagnieën op Aziëin de Eerst Helft van de Zeventiende Eeuw," *Bijdragen en Mededelingen Betreffende de Geschiedenis der Nederlanden* 91 (1976): 202.
13. Alan Smith, *Creating a World Economy: Merchant Capital, Colonialism, and World Trade, 1400–1825* (Boulder: Westview Press, 1991), 100.
14. The role of immigration in general played a large role in Dutch society in the sixteenth and seventeenth centuries, especially the large scale "exodus" of Flemish merchants and their capital from Antwerp to Amsterdam. Immigration from Scandinavia and Germany was also very important, partly because these immigrants provided a stock of labor for the VOC fleets. In a population study undertaken by Jan de Vries, he notes that one-third of all seventeenth century marriages in Amsterdam involved immigrants. See Jan de Vries, "The Population and Economy of the Pre-Industrial Netherlands," *Journal of Interdisciplinary History* 15: 4 (1985): 667.
15. For a good discussion of Dutch activity through "the Sound" as well as the role of the Baltic in the development of Dutch trade, see Maria Bogucka, "Amsterdam and the Baltic in the First half of the Seventeenth Century," *Economic History Review* 26: 3 (1973).
16. Jonathon Israel, "Spain, the Spanish Embargoes, and the Struggle for Mastery of World Trade, 1585–1660," in *Empires and Entrepôts: The*

Dutch, The Spanish Monarchy and The Jews, 1585–1713 (London: Hamledon Press, 1990), 192. Israel notes that to get around the Spanish blockades of 1585, Dutch ships simply carried papers obtained in German Hanseatic cities. It should be noted, however, that Israel, while conceding that the blockades had serious flaws, maintains that the later blockades in particular hurt the Dutch shipping industry.

17. As quoted in Virginia Lunsford, *Piracy and Privateering in the Golden Age Netherlands* (New York: Palgrave, 2005), 70.
18. Charles Boxer, *The Dutch Seaborne Empire, 1600–1800* (London: Penguin Books, 1990), 29.
19. Jonathon Israel, "A Conflict of Empires; Spain and the Netherlands, 1618–48," *Past and Present 76* (1977): 34–74.
20. Meilink-Roelofsz, "Een Vergelijkend Onderzoek," 203.
21. This is indeed a compelling argument because it has the advantage of a direct cause and effect relationship. Historians such as Gaastra, Bruijn, and Stohls would surely not deny that this must have played some part. They stress, however, that this is a vastly oversimplified explanation and that there were other, deeper causes at play. See Erik Stohls, "De Zuidelijk Nederlanden en de Oprchting van de Oost en Westindische Compagnieën," *Bijdragen en Mededelingen Betreffende de Geschiedenis der Nederlanden* 88 (1973): 33.
22. Kees Zandfleet, *The Dutch Encounter with Asia, 1600–1950* (Amsterdam: Rijksmuseum, 2002), 159.
23. The best-known historians in this camp are Femme Gaastra, Bruijn, and Stohls. While most of their works are in Dutch, there is a monumental three-volume compendium of Dutch maritime activity in Asia, entitled *Dutch-Asiatic Shipping,* edited by Gaastra, Bruijn, and Schoeffer, in which this view is put forth. See J. R. de Bruijn, Femme Gaastra, and I. Schoeffer, eds., *Dutch Asiatic Shipping in the Seventeenth and Eighteenth Centuries, 3 Volumes* (The Hague: Martinus Nijhoff, 1987).
24. Linschotten's *Itinerario* was published first in Dutch in 1596 under license from the States General. It was subsequently translated into English, German, and Latin within three years of its initial appearance. Editions in French and Italian followed a decade later. The version used for this work is the English edition edited by Arthur Coke Burnell for the Hakluyt Society in 1885. See endnote 16 for the full citation.
25. Dirk Gerritszoon Pomp, another Dutchman in the employ of the Portuguese, served as a constable on board a Portuguese ship. He was a friend of Linschotten, but unlike the former, Pomp had actually traveled to China and possibly Japan, although this has never been established

definitively. Although less well-known today, Pomp was almost as famous as Linschotten at the end of the seventeenth century, as the popular nickname "Dirk China" indicates. F. Dekker, *De Betrekkingen Tuschen de Oostindische Compagnie en Japan* ('s-Gravenhage: Boucher, 1941), 8.

26. A history of the *voorcompanieën* can be found in Terpstra, "De Nederlandse Voorcompanieën," in *Geschiedenis van Nederlandsche Indië, Vol. II*, ed. F. W. Stapel (Amsterdam, 1938), 273–475.
27. Leonard Blussé and Jaap de Moor, *Nederlanders Overzee: De Eerste Vijftig Jaar, 1600–1650* (Franeker: Uitgeverij T. Weber, 1983), 101.
28. One of the most useful aspects of Linschotten's journal was not only that it contained useful descriptions of various places in Asia, but that it contained the most up to date Portuguese "sea cards," or nautical maps, used when sailing from Goa to locations throughout the Indies, including Japan. Wim Wennekes, *Gouden Handel: de Eerst Nederlanders Overzee, en wat Zij Daar Halden* (Amsterdam: Uitgerverij Atlas, 1996), 230.
29. P. C. Emmer and Femme Gaastra, "De Vaart Buiten Europa," in *Maritieme Geschiedenis der Nederlanden, Vol. II: Zeventiende Eeuw* (Bussum: De Boer Maritiem, 1976–78), 246.
30. Coolhaas notes that with the proliferation of voyages, profits were becoming ever lower while the risk stayed the same. W. Ph. Coolhaas, "De Vereenigde Oostindishe Compagnie," in *Algemene Geshiedenis der Nederlanden, Vol. 7: Niew Tijd* (Haarlem: Fibula van Dishoek, 1980), 147.
31. Before the advent of joint stock companies such as the VOC and the English East India Company (EIC), trading companies were established for a single voyage before being liquidated after the completion of the journey. Such was obviously the case with the several *voorcompanieën.*
32. Femme Gaastra, "De VOC in Aziëtot 1680," in *Algemene Geschiedenis der Nederlanden, Vol. 7: Niew Tijd* (Haarlem: Fibula van Dishoek, 1980), 176.
33. Jan den Tex, *Oldenbarnevelt, Vol. II* (Haarlem: Tjeenk Willink, 1960–72), 384–420.
34. The entirety of the first VOC contract (chartered for twenty-one years), along with its subsequent renewals, can be found in Pieter van Dam's *Beschryvinge van de Vereenigde Oostindische Compagnie, Deel I, part I*, 43–242. Most of the following details of the formation and structure of the company have been taken from this source. Incidentally, Pieter van Dam was commissioned by the *Herren Zeventien* to produce a history of the VOC, which he presented to them in 1701. I have used F. W. Stapel's

printed version of the work; see Pieter van Dam, *Beschryvinge van de Oostindische Compagnie, 7 Volumes*, ed. F. W. Stapel and C. W. Th. Boetzelaer (Den Hague: Rijks Geschiedenis Publicatiën, 1977).

35. Amsterdam had twenty members, Middelburg twelve, and each of the smaller regions seven each. For a good overview of the workings of the VOC, see Holden Furber, *Rival Empires of Trade in the Orient, 1600–1800* (Minneapolis: University of Minnesota Press, 1976), 185–191.
36. Niels Steensgard called the change that occurred between the previous companies, which were chartered for only a single voyage, and the new VOC a "metamorphosis" insofar as investors still expected to gain a profit in the short term, but were now committed to the company for the long term. Niels Steensgard, "The Dutch East India Company as an Institutional Innovation," in *Dutch Capitalism and World Capitalism*, ed. Maurice Aymard (Cambridge: Cambridge University Press, 1982), 239.
37. Meilink-Roelofsz., "Een Vergelijkend Onderzoek," 210.
38. Ibid., 209.
39. Niels Steensgard, in *Companies and Trade: Essays on Overseas Trading Companies During the Ancién Regime*, ed. Blussé and Gaastra (Leiden: Leiden University Press, 1981), 55–56.
40. Lunsford, *Piracy and Privateering*, 180.
41. W. A. Horst, "De Pepperhandel van de Vereenigde Oostindische Compagnie," in *Bijdragen voor Vaderlandse Geschiedenis en Oudheidkunde* 8:3 (1997).
42. Local rulers apparently believed that once the Portuguese were gone it would be a relatively easy matter to rid themselves of the Dutch. This, however, proved not to be the case. When the Dutch invariably proved every bit as oppressive as their Portuguese forbearers, this led to shifting alliances between the local rulers and several of the Europeans companies.
43. Voskvil-Groenewegen, Leeuwrik, and Titus Eliens, *Zilver uit de Tijd van de VOC* (Zwolle: Waanders Uitgevers, 1998), 12. The authors also note that many local rulers had their own silversmiths who turned this silver into jewelry.
44. Blussé and de Moor, *Nederlanders Overzee*, 106.
45. Coolhaas, "De Vereenigde Oostindishe Compagnie," 155.
46. Meilink-Roelofsz., *Asian Trade and European Influence*, 174.
47. Gaastra, "De VOC in Aziëtot 1680," 189–190.
48. Coen cited the unhealthy climate of Bantam as one reason for moving the capital. He wrote that a total of 32 people died at Bantam because of tropical disease and that this climate made life miserable for the Dutch.

For an account of the war in which Jakarta was conquered, and the subsequent founding of Batavia, see the diary Pieter van den Broecke: W. Ph. Coolhaas, ed., *Pieter van den Broecke in Azië* ('s-Gravenhage: Nijhoff, 1962–63), 179–181.

49. Katō Eiichi sees the primary importance of Hirado between the years 1609 and 1620 as a "strategic base" for Dutch attacks on Spanish and Portuguese shipping. See Katō Eiichi, "Unification and Adaptation: The Early Shogunate and Dutch Trade Policies," in *Companies and Trade: Essays on Overseas Trading Companies During the Ancién Regime*, ed. Leonard Blussé and Femme Gaastra (Leiden: Leiden University Press, 1981), 207–229.
50. In 1623, Coen ordered Dutch ships to try to take the Spanish "silver fleet" that sailed from Acapulco to Manila. This order came after Jan Dirckszoon Lam suffered a resounding defeat at Manila in 1617, prompting the Dutch to abandon the plan to take the Philippines. M. P. H. Roessingh, "Nederlandse Betrekkingen met de Philippinen, 1600–1800," *Bijdragen tot de Land, Taal, en Volkenkunde* 124: 4: 487.
51. Cornelis Matelieff described the desperation that characterized VOC attempts to obtain a supply of Chinese goods when he wrote, "the trade of Japan, since it subsists upon China goods and a few European cloths is not to be entered upon nor thought of, until we have first a firm grasp of the trade of China." Quoted in Derek Massarella, *A World Elsewhere: Europe's Encounter with Japan in the Sixteenth and Seventeenth Centuries* (New Haven: Yale University Press, 1990), 82.
52. Ibid., 220–221.
53. Dutch attacks were by no means limited to Iberian shipping, but extended to the capture of Chinese ships as well. This continued until 1627 when Governor-General van Diemen, acting on pressure from the bakufu, as well as a desire to be viewed favorably in China, forbade further attacks. Furber, *Rival Empires of Trade in the Orient*, 63.
54. Ibid., 44.
55. Coolhaas, ed., *Generalle Missiven, Deel I*, 486.
56. Richard Cocks, in a letter to William Nealson, stated that the Dutch were capturing as many ships as possible; as long as these ships were not involved in trade with Japan, the shogun did not interfere. Edward Thompson, ed., *Diary of Richard Cocks, Cape-Merchant in the English Factory in Japan, 1615–1622, With Correspondences, Vol. I* (London: The Hakluyt Society, 1883), 302.
57. Meilink-Roelofsz notes that in 1622 alone, eighty junks were taken off the coast of China. See her *Asian Trade and European Influence in the*

Indonesian Archipelago Between 1500 and about 1630 (The Hague: Martinus Nijhoff, 1962), 264.

58. Suzuki Yasuko makes this assertion not only for Dutch trade, but for that of the Portuguese as well. She notes that from the end of the 1630s, when trade began to increase rapidly, Dutch exports were consistently 80–90 percent silver. See Suzuki Yasuko, *Kinsei Nichi-Ran Bōeki Shi no Kenkyū* (Tokyo: Shibunkaku, 2004). Suzuki includes an extremely detailed analysis of the many varieties of Japanese silver, as well as of silver's pre-eminent role in Dutch trade with Japan. See chapter I ("Japanese Silver Trade, 1609–1668"), 33–36.
59. Suzuki notes that having a supply of silver within Asia was not only desirable from a purely mercantilist viewpoint, but was also beneficial because the Dutch were at war with Spain, the major provider of silver in Europe at the time. In fact, when the Dutch were briefly at peace with Spain, silver exports from Europe in the form of *reals of eight* increased. When the war resumed, however, the Dutch were again cut off from the Spanish supply, making trade with Japan all the more valuable. Suzuki, *Kinsei Nichi-Ran Bōeki Shi no Kenkyū*, 59.
60. Coolhaas, ed., *Pieter van den Broecke in Azië*, 174–75.
61. This trading network extended to items of necessity as well. For example, Coen originally recognized that Japan could be important as a source of rice for Batavia for and the factories on the Spice Islands. He was also interested in Japan in its capacity as an "arsenal" in the Dutch struggle against the Iberian powers. Furthermore, because Japan was also a source of good soldiers and sailors, Coen was very upset when he learned of the shogun's order forbidding the export of weapons and the use of the Japanese by foreigners. Japan's greatest role in Coen's grand scheme, however, was as a "bank" for the rest of Asia. Coen's vision is borne out in a letter to the *Herren Zeventien* of 1619: see H. T. Colembrander, ed., *Jan Pieterszoon Coen, Beschreiden Omtrent Zijn Bedrijf in Indië, Vol. 5* ('s-Gravenhage: Martinus Nijhoff, 1919–53), 485–86.
62. This was, of course, in keeping with mercantilist theory, which was the predominant commercial ideology at the time in Western Europe.
63. To cite a single example that demonstrates well the role of Taiwan as a redistribution center for Japanese precious metals, Johan Maetsuyker wrote in a letter to the *Herren Zeventien* in 1657 that 1,536,458 *gulden* in silver were sent to Taiwan from Nagasaki. Of this, 920,401 *gulden* were sent to the Coromandel Coast, 723,907 *gulden* to Bengal, 52,106 *gulden* to Surat, 124,549 *gulden* to Persia, 171,000 *gulden* to Siam, 316,350 *gulden* to Batavia, while 190,000 *gulden* remained in Taiwan.

W. Ph. Coolhaas, ed., *Generalle Missiven van Govenaers Generaal en Raden aan Herren XVII der Vereenigde Oostindische Compagnie, Deel III: 1655–74* ('s-Gravenhage: Martinus Nijhoff, 1968), 120: January 31, 1657.

64. Femma Gaastra, "The Dutch East India Company and its Intra-Asiatic Trade in Precious Metals," in *The Emergence of a World Economy, 1500–1914, Part I (Papers of the XI International Congress of Economic History)*, ed. Wolfram Fischer, Marvin McInnis, and Jürgen Schneider (Stuttgart: F. Steiner Verlag Wiesbaden GmbH, 1986), 97.
65. Coolhaas, ed., *Generalle Missiven, Deel III*, 625: October 18, 1668.
66. Glamann's most comprehensive work, concerning trade between the Dutch and Asia, is entitled *Dutch-Asiatic Trade, 1620–1740* ('s-Gravenhage, Martinus Nijhoff, 1958). While it is rather dry and reads somewhat like an inventory, it is immensely helpful in gaining an overall view of these trade patterns. Glamann has also written a number of articles dealing with more localized issues such as copper trade in Japan. See, for example, Kristof Glamann, "The Dutch East Indsia Company's Trade in Japanese Copper, 1645–1735," in *Metals and Monies in an Emerging Global Economy*, ed. Dennis Flynn and Arturo Giraldez (Aldershot: Variorum, 1997), 41–79.
67. Furber, *Rival Empires of Trade in the Orient*, 250.
68. Femme Gaastra notes that between 1630 and 1680 the amount of silver sent from the Netherlands leveled off, whereas the amounts contained in the *retourfloot* [return fleet] increased. This suggests that Asia was essentially "paying for itself." Japanese precious metals, of course, were a major factor in this situation. See Gaastra, "The Dutch East India Company and its Intra-Asiatic Trade in Precious Metals," 97.
69. Thomas Rundall, ed., *Memorials of the Empire of Japon in the XVI and XVII Centuries* (London: The Hakluyt Society, 1963), 38.
70. KTTJ, Vol. 38, 490: Keichō 16/7/17 (September 3, 1611).
71. From the time that the Dutch were moved to Deshima in 1641 until 1728, the factory was profitable every year, and until the late 1680s it was almost always the most profitable factory in Asia. Wennekes, *Gouden Handel in de Eerste Nederlanders Overzee*, 235.
72. Dekker, *De Betrekkingen Tuschen de Oostindische Compagnie en Japan*, 26.
73. Derek Massarella and Izumi Tyler provide an analysis of the various *shuinjō* given to the Dutch (and English) in their article "The Japonian Charters. The English and Dutch Shuinjō," *Monumenta Nipponica* 45: 2 (1990): 189–205. They note that even when the original permit

(granted in 1609 by Ieyasu) was brought to Edo in 1641, the bakufu, although duly impressed, did not repeal the various restrictions imposed on Dutch trade.

74. Coen, in a letter written in 1622, told the *Herren Zeventien* that it was absolutely necessary for the VOC to obtain a steady supply of silk as had the Spanish and Portuguese. Only by so doing would Japan become the source of precious metals that it was for the Iberians. Colembrander, ed., *Jan Pieterszoon Coen, Beschreiden Omtrent Zijn Bedrijf in Indië, Vol. 1*, 718–754.
75. Sydney Crawcour notes that by 1660, the economy of Osaka was based in large part on the "money changers" who changed rice into cash. Furthermore, it was in Osaka that the banking industry developed; from the 1660s a viable system of credit was established in the city when bills, originally used for rice delivery orders, evolved into instruments of a rudimentary credit system. Sydney Crawcour, "The Development of a Credit System in Seventeenth-Century Japan," *The Journal of Economic History* 21: 3 (1961): 347–52.
76. The *Sengolu* Period lasted from the start of the Onin war in 1467 to the Tokugawa reunification in 1600. The term means literally the era of the warring states, and the daimyo of this period are referred to as sengolu daimyo to refer to the fact that these feudal lords were in a state of almost perpetual warfare with their neighbors.
77. Kobata Atsushi, *Kōzan no Rekishi* (Tokyo: Nihon Rekishi Shinsho, 1959). See also Kobata Atsushi, "The Production and Uses of Gold and Silver in Sixteenth and Seventeenth Century Japan," *The Economic History Review* 18: 2 (1965): 245–266.
78. James McClain states that "Japanese urban growth during the years from 1580 to 1700 constitutes one of the most extraordinary periods of urbanization in world history. During that century and a quarter, the population of Japan nearly doubled, reaching a total of approximately 30,000,000. Concurrently, the percentage of persons living in urban settlements of more than 10,000 residents may have multiplied more than tenfold." As McClain goes on to note, this urbanization was a direct result of samurai being required to live in castle towns. A byproduct of this, of course, was the rise of merchants as well as their increasing importance in an urban society. See James McClain, "Castle Towns and Daimyō Authority: Kanazawa in the Years 1583–1630," *Journal of Japanese Studies* 6: 2 (1980): 267.
79. Although quite dated, Murakami Naojirō's work on the Dutch in Hirado is still useful in gaining a picture of early Dutch-Japanese commercial

relations. One drawback, however, is that he does not go into any great detail about other issues, such as the frequent charges of piracy brought against the Dutch by Portuguese and Chinese merchants. See Murakami Naojirō, *Bōeki Shijō no Hirado* (Tokyo: Nihon Gakujutsu Fūkyūkai, 1917).

80. These reports have been translated into Japanese and edited by Iwao Seiichi under the title of *Oranda Fusetsugaki Shūsei, 2 Volumes. (A Collection of the World News Presented Annually by the Dutch Factory at Deshima to the Tokugawa Shogunate, 1641–1857)* (Tokyo: The Japan-Netherlands Institute, 1976). Through them, one can trace a very abridged version of European history, including major marriage alliances and, of course, major European wars.
81. The *bugyō* was the name for a class of officials in the Edo bakufu that was charged with a specific duty. Therefore, the Nagasaki *bugyō* was charged specifically with overseeing the administration of the city of Nagasaki.
82. Ronald Toby, *State and Diplomacy in Early Modern Japan: Asia in the Development of the Tokugawa Bakufu* (Princeton: Princeton University Press, 1984). Toby argues that Japan was not interested in divorcing itself from the outside world, but was rather interested in creating a Chinese-style worldview with the central emphasis on Japan. This was achieved in large part through the embassies of the Koreans, Ryūkyū Islanders, and Dutch, all of whom performed obeisance to the shogun in one way or another. An abridged version of Toby's argument can be found in his article, "Reopening the Question of Sakoku: Diplomacy in the Legitimation of the Tokugawa Bakufu," *Journal of Japanese Studies* 3: 2 (1977): 323–363.
83. Richard Cocks, the head of the English factory in Japan, noted that the Korean embassy to Kyoto comprised five hundred people. Such an embassy certainly made a powerful impression on the daimyo in attendance at Kyoto. See Thompson, ed., *Diary of Richard Cocks*, Vol. I, 255.
84. Toby, "Reopening the Question of Sakoku," 343.
85. James Lewis' important study of the relations between Japan and Korea in pre-modern times provides a detailed description of Korean-Japanese relations from the medieval period through the Edo period. For the resumption of diplomatic relations after the Hideyoshi invasions of the late sixteenth century, see Lewis, James, *Frontier Contact Between Chosŏn Korea and Tokugawa Japan* (London: Routledge Curzon, 2003), 21–24.
86. Iwao Seiichi, in fact, states that this prolonged period of political stability was a result of the *sakoku* policies of the Edo bakufu. In Iwao's

evaluation, there is no discussion of whether the policies were good or bad, only an observation that they contributed to the "Tokugawa peace."

87. Seiichi Iwao, "Sakoku," in *Taigai Kankei to Sakoku*, ed. Fujino Tamotsu (Tokyo: Yūzankaku, 1993), 121.
88. The Jesuit Luis Frois, in his history of Japan, recalls that in the 1570s the church made considerable advances on the island of Kyushu, especially when, in 1566–67, both Amakusa Shigehisa and Arima Harunobu were baptized along with all of their retainers. See Josef Wichi, ed., Padre Luis Frois, SJ, *Historia de Japam, Vol. 2* (Lisbon: Biblioteca Nacional de Lisboa, 1976), 231.
89. Jurgis Elisonas states, "The model of universal truth introduced by Roman Catholic Europeans who came to Japan with a missionary purpose could not be so easily accommodated by a regime intent on refashioning Japanese society in a mold of its own. Hence, the Catholics' mission to Japan was ultimately condemned as subversive to the social order of the Tokugawa, and they were expelled as an alien element from the Japanese body politic." Jurgis Elisonas, "Christianity and the Daimyo," in *The Cambridge History of Japan, Volume 4: Early Modern Japan*, ed. John Hall (Cambridge: Cambridge University Press, 1991), 301.
90. The Tokugawa *Jikki* referred to the rebellion as a Christian *ikki,* and approached the uprising as if it were in fact a religiously motivated rebellion. See KTTJ, Vol. III, 72–91.
91. Elisonas states that "there was no real reason for this elaborate network's existence," in that the religion had been all but eradicated. Yet the bakufu continued to require that all Japanese were able to produce proof that they were not Christian (in the form of temple registration papers) well in to the eighteenth century. See Elisonas, "Christianity and the Daimyo," 370.
92. Kato Eiichi makes this argument most forcefully in his article "Bawansen, Shuinsen, Hōshosen: Bakuhansei Kokka no Keisei to Taigai Kankei," in *Nihon Rekishi 14: Kaikin to Sakoku*, ed. Kamiya Nobuyuki and Kimura Naoya (Tokyo: Tokyo-dō Shuppan, 2002), 41–51.
93. Leonard Blussé, "No Boats to China. The Dutch East India Company and the Changing pattern of the China Sea Trade, 1635–1690," *Modern Asian Studies* 30: 1 (1996): 63.
94. The best example of this is the *itowappu*, or, as the Portuguese and Dutch called it, the *pancada.* This system, although the Dutch railed against it, was designed to ensure a fair distribution of silk within Japan by allowing representatives from the five biggest cities to set

the price at which all raw Chinese silk would be sold. This did not preclude the Europeans from making a tremendous profit on silk imports., and it had the added advantage of promoting an orderly distribution of silk throughout the country at a price that prevented speculation and hoarding.

95. I agree with this statement, but would qualify it somewhat: Japan was never really under "Chinese suzerainty," since periods of even prolonged contact were rare. Although the Ashikaga accepted nominal vassal status under Yoshimitsu, that was a temporary situation and was nearly two hundred years in the past. Kazui Tashirō and Susan Downing-Videen, "Foreign Relations During the Edo Period: Sakoku Reexamined," *Journal of Japanese Studies* 8: 2 (1982): 304.
96. Takeo Tonaka, "Sakoku ni Tsuite," in *Nihon Rekishi 14: Kaikin to Sakoku,* ed. Kamiya Nobuyuki and Kimura Naoya (Tokyo: Tokyo-dō Shuppan, 2002), 39.
97. An account of da Cruz's description of China can be found in Samuel Purchas' *Purchas His Pilgrims* under the heading of "A Treatise of China and the adjoining Regions, Written by Gaspar da Cruz a Dominican Friar, and dedicated to Sebastian, King of Portugal: Here Abbreviated." See Samuel Purchas, *Hakluytus posthumus or Purchas his Pilgrimes. : Contayning a history of the world, in sea voyages, & lande-trauells, by Englishmen and others. ...Some left written by Mr. Hakluyt at his death more since added, his also perused, & perfected: All examined, abreuiated, illustrated w[i]th notes, enlarged w[i]th discourses, adorned w[i]th pictures, and expressed in mapps. : In fower parts, each containing fiue bookes. / [Compiled] By Samuel Purchas, B.D, Volume III* (London: H. Fetherston, 1625), 166–198.
98. Satow, ed., *The Voyage of captain John Saris to Japan*, 1613, 92.
99. Engelbert Kaempfer, *The History of Japan, 3 Volumes*, trans. J. D. Scheuzcher (New York: AMS Press, 1971), 301–336. Kaempfer was not Dutch, but rather German, a fact he was forced to hide in order to be allowed access to Japan.
100. Many Japanese scholars treat the Matsumae clan's trade with the Ainu in Ezo (modern day Hokkaido) as a type of foreign trade. The Matsumae were authorized to trade in Ezo in much the same way that the So clan was in Korea and the Shimazu in the Ryukyu Islands. See Brett Walker, *The Conquest of Ainu Lands: Ecology and Culture in Japanese Expansion, 1590–1800* (Berkeley: University of California Press, 2001).

Chapter 2

Japanese *Shuinsen* Merchants

There is a marked tendency in the historiography of early seventeenth-century Japan to overlook the role of Japanese merchants in the economy of Asia. When writing about Portuguese trade between Macao and Nagasaki, for example, many writers emphasize that the Dutch, the English, and even at times the Spanish were the main competitors of the Portuguese. Similarly, historians of the VOC usually portray the Portuguese as the main source of competition to the company in Japan. This tendency is naturally much more pronounced in the western literature insofar as trade by Japanese merchants was a relatively ephemeral phenomenon, lasting only until the third decade of the seventeenth century. What this Eurocentric picture overlooks, however, is the fact that at any given time until the mid-1630s, Japanese trade by volume as well as by value far exceeded that of any other group, including the Portuguese, Dutch, and Chinese. Arano Yasunori provides us with figures for the quantity of goods imported and exported, as well as the amount of silver taken out of Japan by the Japanese, Portuguese, Dutch, and Chinese between the years 1604 and 1639, and in every category the Japanese far exceeded the other groups, with the most startling figure being the amount of silver exported: a total of 1,053,750 kilograms were transported in Japanese ships to several locations throughout Asia.[1] That this is often overlooked is even more startling because the significance of Japanese foreign trade was certainly not lost on contemporary VOC merchants in Asia. The Dutch at both Hirado and Taiwan repeatedly noted in their diaries that if the Japanese merchants could somehow be limited in their trade, it would redound to the great profit of the VOC.

The Spanish, in an effort to reduce the endemic Japanese presence in the Philippines, requested that the bakufu limit the number of Japanese ships calling at Manila to three per year, claiming that the Japanese merchants represented an unfair source of competition. Because a number of Japanese lived on the island of Luzon and because several Japanese ships called at the island each year, the Spanish found it hard to compete not only in the Japanese market, but also in the Asian market in general.[2] The Dutch were likewise continually lobbying the bakufu to ban Japanese ships from coming to Taiwan in an effort to prevent the Japanese from circumventing the VOC monopoly in deerskins and Chinese silk.[3] Dutch profits in Asia depended heavily on the Japan trade, which in turn depended heavily on the supply of silk; the Dutch were therefore eager to eliminate, as far as possible, Japanese merchants from this trade. By so doing, they would not only improve their prospects in Japan, but also in their other factories in Asia that depended on Japanese precious metals.

Although only a momentary phenomenon in the long history of the Tokugawa period, Japanese *shuinsen* merchants were for that brief time tremendously important within the Asian economy, a fact well documented by contemporary foreign merchants trading in Japan. Not only did the Japanese make frequent voyages to Southeast Asia, but foreign ships also routinely came to Japan since at least the mid-1500s. In 1563, for example, a Siamese ship is known to have arrived in the province of Hizen, and six years later a Cambodian junk made the trip as well.[4] The Spanish, upon establishing themselves in the Philippines in 1570, noted that there were a number of

Japanese already living on the north end of Luzon, at a place called Kagayan.[5] Nor was Luzon in any way a special case; Japanese merchants made regular voyages to ports in Southeast Asia well before Europeans arrived on the shores of Japan. This trend was only accelerated with the increasing political stability at the close of the *sengoku* period. With the reassertion of central control within Japan at the end of the sixteenth century, Japanese commercial involvement with Asia grew tremendously. This growth was facilitated by the role of the trading permits known as *shuinjō*, and of the ships, called *shuinsen*, that carried them. This chapter will deal with the role of the *shuinsen* trade within Japan, and the effect that this trade had on the Asian economy of the early seventeenth century.

Origins of the *Shuinjō*

The extent of Japanese involvement in foreign trade can be seen most clearly through the eyes of Europeans who were making their initial forays into the long-established Asian trading world in the mid- to late sixteenth century. Samuel Purchas, in his celebrated work *Purchas his Pilgrims*, records an encounter with a Japanese junk at Patani that had put to port when their pilot died. He describes the Japanese as "pirating along the coast of China and Cambodia." He further describes them, somewhat dramatically, as "a people so desperate and daring, that they are feared in all places where they come."[6] The noted Dutch mariner Pieter van den Broecke also notes on several occasions the presence of the Japanese in Southeast Asia. At one point, for example, van den Broecke came across a Japanese ship carrying satin cloth, cloves, and significantly, a "pass" from his emperor.[7] Similarly, the Portuguese Governor-General Alfonso d'Albuquerque notes that Japanese merchants often carried great quantities of gold to trade in Southeast Asia. He describes the Japanese thus: "the men are fair; their dress is like a cloak without a hood; they carry long swords after the fashion of Turkish cimeters, but somewhat more narrow, they carry also daggers of two-palms length." Further, "They set out for Malacca in the month of January, and begin their return journey in August and September."[8] This account was written in the mid-sixteenth century, demonstrating that Japanese merchants were active in the Southeast Asian trade a full half-century before the formal establishment of the *shuinsen* system.

The *shuinjō* that were originally issued by Toyotomi Hideyoshi were not limited exclusively to trade, but were in fact used in all official edicts. Elizabeth Berry notes that Hideyoshi was the first ruler to use the vermillion seals to any great extent in routine matters of government:

> We know Hideyoshi's policy primarily through his red-seal papers, or *shuinjō*—documents issued with a vermillion chop containing the characters *hide* and *yoshi*. The first dates from 1583, the last was dispatched not long before his death. Although most of Hideyoshi's correspondence before 1585 concludes with either a monogram (*kaō*) or the more familiar black chop—less formal styles he used occasionally throughout his life—his later preference for *shuinjō* has led historians to describe Hideyoshi's government as the Red-Seal System. Nobunaga, and other warring states lords, and even the Ashikaga had used *shuin* from time to time, yet Hideyoshi was the first routinely to conduct national business with missives bearing his red stamp.[9]

Although references to Hideyoshi's *shuinjō* survive, no contemporary documents relating directly to Japanese overseas trade exists, so we are forced to reconstruct Hideyoshi's policies for foreign commerce indirectly through other materials written shortly after Hideyoshi's death. The *Nagasaki Jitsuroku Taisei*, for example, records that "In the beginning of the Bunroku era, *go-shuinjō* were issued to people from Kyoto, Nagasaki and Sakai to go to Tonkin, Champa, Canton, Cambodia, Patani, Siam, Taiwan, Luzon, and Macao, among other places, in order to trade."[10] Although this account was written considerably after the events described, there seems to be no real reason to doubt it. Further evidence of the Taikō's use of the red seal in matters of foreign trade comes from the Governor-General of Manila, who requested that Hideyoshi issue permits to Japanese ships in order to distinguish legitimate merchants from the pirates who infested Asian waters at the time.[11] Nagazumi Yōko, in her study of the *shuinsen*, includes a discussion of exactly when the "red-seal system" of foreign trade originated, a matter of some controversy. Did Hideyoshi pioneer the system or did it begin with the founding of the bakufu under Tokugawa Ieyasu? The rough consensus that emerges is that Hideyoshi did indeed issue *shuinjō* to merchants who wanted to trade in Southeast Asia and Manila, but that the *shuinsen* system itself did not begin until Ieyasu made it a cornerstone of his foreign policy.[12]

The new *shuinjō* clearly demonstrates that Hideyoshi was quite interested in the resumption of formal trade, particularly with China. In fact, one of the main items of the proposed peace agreement between the two countries during the wars on the Korean peninsula was the resumption of trade.[13] Furthermore, as justification for his attempted invasion of China, Hideyoshi claimed that he wanted to re-establish trade with the Ming Empire. And finally, although Hideyoshi's assumption of direct control over Nagasaki and his employment of *bugyō* to oversee the city was the result of policies aimed more at control than trade, we nevertheless see, through his interest in foreign goods such as clay jars from Manila and silk from Macao, that Hideyoshi was in fact highly interested in commerce.

Probably the main impetus behind Hideyoshi's use of the *shuinjō* was an attempt to control the piracy that was endemic in the waters between Japan, the Korean peninsula, and the Chinese coast. The issue of piracy, however, is a complicated one since it is bound up in popular conceptions of what constitutes piracy and who pirates were. In the West at least, our image of piracy has usually been associated with swashbuckling sailors who lived and died by the sword, and whose sole aim was to wreak destruction and havoc in the pursuit of "treasure." While this sort of activity certainly took place in Asian waters, and indeed the destruction brought about by pirates along the Korean and Chinese coasts was often considerable, the definition of piracy must be greatly expanded.[14] The task of defining the concept is not made any easier by the recognition that, in the words of Phillip

Curtin, "the Japanese could shift back and forth between plunder and trade. They could trade with or attack the Chinese mainland as the opportunity presented itself."[15] In a discussion of Japanese and Chinese piracy, therefore, "secret" or "hidden" trade must be considered, along with the more conventional conceptions of piracy such as armed attacks on foreign ships and coastal villages.[16]

Because of the Ming maritime ban on trade with Japan, Japanese merchants were excluded from direct trade in such high-demand luxury goods as raw silk and porcelain. One way to get around this ban was to use the relatively neutral harbors of places such as Taiwan and Siam as bases in which these ships could meet and conduct business. Taiwan, in particular, came to serve this function very well in the sixteenth and early seventeenth centuries.[17] Another way to circumvent the Ming prohibitions was to simply resort to smuggling and secret trading along the Chinese coast.[18] The Chinese coastline is extremely long and consists of thousands of tiny uninhabited islands lying just offshore. It was impossible to guard the entirety of the coast, and, as James Geiss notes, "such bans were not easy to enforce, for local civil and military authorities were themselves involved in the conduct of illicit trade."[19] We know from European sources that a great deal of trade by both Europeans and Asians occurred quite regularly in these remote places.

To be sure, there were a number of Japanese coastal raids that often entailed a good deal of violence and pillaging. However, a great deal of Japanese piracy was in fact secret trade conducted illegally in ports in southwestern China. This illicit trade was, as much as coastal raids and attacks on Chinese ships, considered piracy by the Ming authorities, and as such was strictly censured.[20] Jurgis Elisonas also notes that illicit trade worked both ways; not only were Japanese ships traveling to the coast of China to trade, but Chinese merchants also came to various ports in Kyushu in defiance of the Ming authorities. An example of this type of merchant was Wang Chih who, in the mid-sixteenth century, set up bases at Hirado and the Goto Islands from which he conducted a great deal of illicit trade in Chinese goods. Pirate leaders such as Wang Chih, and later Li Tan and the

Zheng family, established connections with Kyushu daimyo such as the Shimazu and Matsuura, and in conjunction with them carried on an extremely lucrative trade that represented the forerunner of the semi-official Chinese trade that occurred at Nagasaki during the Edo period.[21]

Japanese piracy in all of its forms was rife in Asian waters when Hideyoshi consolidated his control over the Japanese archipelago in the last decades of the sixteenth century. Joao Rodrigues states in his history of Japan that Europeans originally called Japan the Island of Robbers "[b]ecause at that time, many pirates usually came from Japan with large crews in their fleets to rob and infest the coast of China."[22] Along with his policy of demilitarizing the peasantry in what has come to be known as the "sword hunt," Hideyoshi also moved to control the activity in Japanese waters as well. Nagazumi Yōko calls this policy the "*umi no katana-gari*," or the "sword hunt at sea."[23] This move toward centralization inherent in the increasing control of Hideyoshi and later the Tokugawa shogun represented a new era for Japan not only internally but also internationally, as the government began to concern itself with international relations, including the control of piracy. The *shuinjō* system, symbolic as it was of legitimacy and central authority, played a large role in both spheres.

Upon his "pacification" of Kyushu in the late 1580s, one of the first decrees that Hideyoshi issued to the western daimyo concerned the elimination of the *bawan* ships.[24] *Bawan* is the Chinese pronunciation of the Japanese *Hachiman*, the god of war in the Shinto pantheon, and was the Chinese name for Japanese pirate ships that were endemic off the coast of China. Beginning in 1588 Hideyoshi ordered western daimyo such as the Shimazu, Katō, Matsuura, Mōri, Kuroda, and Nabeshima to prevent these pirates from interfering with Chinese ships coming to trade at western ports such as Hirado.[25] Not only were the pirates an obstruction to legitimate trade in Japanese ports, they were also a source of friction in other countries as well. This was most evident in Manila where Japanese ships consistently came into conflict with the newly settled Spanish colonizers. The Spanish Governor-General tried in 1581–1582 to control the Japanese who were using Manila as a base for piracy, but when they resisted, there was a pitched battle and the Spanish were obliged to retreat.[26] In the end, however, the Europeans prevailed and the Japanese relocated to a site north of Manila called Dilao where they established a *nihonmachi*.

Incidents such as these prompted the Governor-General at Manila to demand that Hideyoshi issue permits to legitimate trading vessels so as to distinguish them from pirates, and implicitly to restrict the number of Japanese ships trading at Luzon.[27] Therefore, the two major reasons for licensing Japanese trade are in reality two sides of the same proverbial coin: control. By licensing Japanese trade with Southeast Asia and Manila, the authorities were sanctioning and regulating the western daimyo's means of revenue and in the process establishing the central government as the sole arbiter of international relations. Furthermore, by suppressing piracy and normalizing trade with foreign countries, the central government was in fact extending its authority beyond simply its own domains and into the arena of what can at this period plausibly be called "international politics."

Toyotomi Hideyoshi died in 1598, leaving the regency of his young son in the hands of five of his most trusted vassals. Of these five, Tokugawa Ieyasu quickly established himself as the dominant force in Japan and, after defeating a coalition of rival daimyo, received the title of *Sei-i tai shōgun* in 1603 from the emperor. Ieyasu's story is, of course, well established, but what is less commonly known is that even before the decisive Battle of Sekigahara in 1600, Ieyasu was dealing with the issues of foreign relations and piracy, a consideration that may be taken as an indication of his far-sighted ambitions. In the fourth month of Keichō 4 (1599), Ieyasu, in his capacity as regent for Toyotomi Hideyori, ordered the Shimazu family of Satsuma to put an end to the activity of *bawan* ships in the waters around Kyushu. He also answered a letter from the King of Patani in the seventh month of the same year, and shortly thereafter ordered the Sō house of Tsushima to begin negotiations with

Korea for a resumption of peaceful relations.[28] These activities may be construed as simply the normal activity of government, but in the context of Japan, a land that had been torn by war for over a century and a half, this represented the beginning of a new era of stability in its history. Ieyasu was in effect signaling his intention to create a government able to regulate affairs both within the country as well as internationally. His policy of establishing friendly relations with his Asian neighbors and his implementation of the *shuinsen* system are a testament to that intention.

Iwao Seiichi, in his analysis of the *shuinsen* system, calls Ieyasu's attitude toward the outside world a "goodwill policy."[29] As we have seen, even before he established his own hegemony at Sekigahara, Ieyasu was exchanging formal letters with a number of Asian countries and was at least considering the restoration of diplomatic relations with the Ming Empire and Korea.[30] Indicative of his "internationalism" is the number of letters that Ieyasu sent to foreign countries between his assumption of the title of shogun in 1603 and his death in 1619. According to Fujii Jōji, there were no fewer than eighty letters addressed to the sovereigns of twelve separate countries, most of the early letters reversing Hideyoshi's policy of intimidation and stressing that Japan was interested in friendly diplomatic and commercial relations.[31] In addition, many of the correspondences contained *shuinjō* for merchants who wished to trade with Japan.[32]

In 1600 Ieyasu further ordered Shimazu Yoshihiro to go as an ambassador to the Ming Empire in order to reestablish commercial relations with China. According to Fujii, this mission was successful, and the Ming promised to send two vessels to Satsuma the following year (it was no accident that Satsuma was chosen as the port of call, since the Shimazu family was the daimyo of that province). As it happened, however, these vessels were attacked by pirates en route and turned back without fulfilling their mission.[33] The Japanese also attempted to use their relations with both Korea and the Ryūkyū Islands to establish commercial ties with the Ming.[34] In fact, the bakufu's effort to bring the Ryūkyū Islands into the Japanese tributary system was most likely an effort to establish indirect trade with

China.[35] Although the amount of silk imported into Japan from the Ryūkyūs was never very large, it did serve as a check on the silk monopoly that the Fujianese merchants tried to maintain.[36]

The great number of correspondences that Ieyasu sent to foreign countries suggests that, in contrast with the later *sakoku* era, we should consider Japan in this period as an "open country."[37] Nothing illustrates this fact more than Ieyasu's policy towards the Europeans in which the Portuguese, English, Spanish, and Dutch were all given *shuinjō* to trade freely within Japan and were encouraged to set up factories for that purpose. Moreover, cordial letters were exchanged with Prince Maurits, the *Stadhouder* of the United Provinces, King James I, King Phillip II, and the lesser officials at Goa, Manila, and Batavia. In 1610, for example, Suden records in the *Ikoku Nikki* that "Minamoto no Ieyasu" entrusted a letter to the Dutch envoys at Sumpu to be delivered to Maurits, "King" of Holland. Similarly, three years later, Dutch officials presented letters from both Prince Maurits and Peter Both, Governor-General of the VOC, to Ieyasu.[38] As for the Spanish, in 1604 Ieyasu received a letter from Don Pedro Acuña, Governor-General of Manila, and in the following year Ieyasu responded.[39] These letters were generally warm in tone, with Ieyasu promising free trade as well as the eradication of piracy in Japanese waters so as to facilitate that trade.

The story of Ieyasu's warm reception of the English and the Dutch is a familiar one and need not be repeated here. Suffice it to say that the shogun was extremely welcoming of the newly formed East India companies, in spite of the dire warnings by the Portuguese Jesuit fathers.[40] These priests, in an effort to exclude the English and Dutch from trade in Japan, accused them of the most heinous crimes, claiming that they were nothing but pirates and that they were from countries in which the rule of law had no meaning (a shrewd accusation in light of Ieyasu's fervor for establishing order in Japan).[41] Ieyasu was politically astute enough to recognize that these were accusations based not necessarily on reality but rather on political and religious hostility, and therefore paid scant attention to them. Rather, in their initial *shuinjō*, the English and Dutch were not only allowed to trade in Japan, but were allowed to trade freely in any harbor throughout the country. The Spanish, for their part, were given leave to survey the coast of Japan for suitable harbors, despite the warnings of William Adams that they would use this as a pretext to gather military data. Ieyasu was interested not only in trade with the Spanish in the Philippines, but also with Nova España, a position he made abundantly clear in his letters to the Governor-General in Manila. Therefore, in stark contrast to the later policy of the bakufu, Ieyasu was initially well disposed towards the Europeans and the possibilities of foreign trade that they represented.

When Hideyoshi began to issue *shuinjō* in the early 1590s, the phenomenon was by no means a new one. Trade permits that insured protection for ships bearing them were issued in Japan by the Muromachi bakufu. The Ashikaga shogun issued such permits to the Shimazu family authorizing them to trade with the Ryūkyū Islands; and although these passes were both physically and conceptually different from the later *shuinjō*, the fact remains that the central government took upon itself the responsibility of authorizing the foreign trade of several western daimyo.[42] Nor was the phenomenon of trade permits a particularly Japanese one; the Ming Empire issued them to Chinese junks trading to ports in Southeast Asia as early as 1567.[43] Furthermore, the Ming Emperor, before the maritime restrictions imposed on trade with Japan, issued *kangō* to Japanese vessels that wanted to trade in Chinese ports. Not a system of trade permits per se, the *kangō* was a trading permit, of which one half was given to a foreign merchant while the other half was kept in China. This system of commerce, generally translated into English as the "tally trade," stipulated that only ships bearing the corresponding half of a Ming *kangō* could lawfully put to port and trade.[44] This was the Chinese trade that Hideyoshi and the Tokugawa were interested in reviving.

The Japanese *shuinsen* system was different from the "tally trade" system of the Ming Empire in many respects, not the least of which was that even during the height of the Chinese emperor's power, the *kangō* were more or less local initiatives in which the highest authority involved was the provincial official. The system operated with the implicit consent of Beijing, but because of its local nature, instances of bribery and collusion were relatively frequent. Therefore, the Japanese, Portuguese, and at times the Dutch, were able to carry on an irregular trade along the coast of China even though they did not possess the required *kangō*. The *shuinsen* system, on the other hand, was from the beginning used as a means of extending bakufu control into the domains of even relatively powerful daimyo in Kyushu.

When the Europeans arrived in Asian waters seeking trade and beginning to establish their respective commercial organizations, they did not institute particularly innovative policies, but rather grafted their activities on top of preexisting Asian trade patterns.[45] Holden Furber notes, for example, that the European companies adopted existing Asian practices when establishing their "trade empires" in Asia, including the use of trade permits. The Portuguese established the *cartaz* system whereby ships, for a fee, were issued permits that guaranteed safe passage throughout the Indian Ocean.[46] The Dutch also tried to implement such a system to license Asian (mainly Chinese) merchants who arrived to trade in places such as Batavia.[47] Therefore, not only was the use of trading permits not particularly new, but it was adopted wholesale by the European companies who moved into the Asian trade in the sixteenth and seventeenth centuries.

The bakufu's decision to issue *shuinjō* to both Japanese and foreign merchants, therefore, was born out of a long tradition in Asian trade and as such should not be seen as particularly innovative. The important thing to note is that early modern Japanese rulers, by using such a system of trade permits, were in the process of establishing a unified state and the effective control of a fairly centralized government. Many historians will object to the notion of a centralized government, given that individual *han* were in effect semiautonomous domains responsible for such fundamental administrative policies as the collection of taxes, the minting of money, and a host of other governmental policies. While this was certainly true, there is no denying that the bakufu repeatedly worked for the increase of central power at the expense of the daimyo domains. Nowhere is this more evident than in the conduct of foreign policy, a policy dictated increasingly by the shogun and his councilors in Edo.

By 1606, Ieyasu had sent at least one letter to every major kingdom in Southeast Asia, beginning with Annam and the Philippines in 1601, followed in quick succession by Cambodia, Siam, Tonkin, and Cochin.[48] Included in these letters of goodwill were usually *shuinjō* for the merchants of those countries, effectively declaring that the Japanese were making an effort to control the endemic piracy that plagued Asian waters, and that it was safe to trade with Japan. The bakufu also issued *shuinjō* to several people within Japan, which served to demonstrate that the Tokugawa were firmly in control and that they were the legitimate rulers of Japan.[49]

The *Shuinsen* System

In his landmark study entitled *Shuinsen Bōeki Shi no Kenkyū* (*A Study of the Shuinsen Trade*), Iwao Seiichi details in great depth the people who received these permits, how many ships they sent, where they were sent to, and the cargo that was transported. Between 1604 and 1635, an estimated 356 ships sailed to a total of nineteen different locations, with Siam being the kingdom most frequented, followed very closely by Luzon.[50] This number may not seem all that large to our modern sensibilities, but when the expense, risk, and duration of a single voyage are taken into account, it is a rather remarkable achievement. Among the factors that those who wanted to trade abroad had to consider were: the process of applying for the *shuinjō* in the first place, obtaining a suitable ship, finding the manpower to sail the ship, obtaining sufficient goods to trade once the ship reached its destination, making the perilous voyage from Japan to Southeast Asia, selling the goods obtained in the foreign country in question, giving suitable presents to the shogun and his councilors after the completion of the voyage, and of course waiting approximately one year for this huge investment to pay off. Needless to say, this was a long and often arduous process that was for all practical purposes limited to the very wealthiest stratum of society. A telling indictor of this is the fact that most people who applied for a *shuinjō* did so only once. Only the extremely wealthy merchants of Kyoto, Nagasaki, and Sakai were able to afford the outfitting of multiple ships. The Suminokura, Chaya, Suetsugu, Funamoto, Sueyoshi, Nishi, Araki, and Hirano families were the only groups able to send more than four *shuinsen*, with the Suminokura sending a total of at least sixteen ships over the course of the period.[51]

Although the *shuinsen* trade came to be limited almost exclusively to wealthy houses with close connections to the bakufu, there was originally a great deal of variety in terms of who was applying for and receiving these permits. According to Kawajima Genjiro, there were five distinct categories of people who received *shuinjō*: daimyo, bakufu officials, Japanese merchants, Chinese merchants, and Europeans. Of these, perhaps not surprisingly, merchants received the most with a total of fifty. A striking aspect of the *shuinjō* is the fact that there were fourteen foreigners who received permits, a group that included familiar figures such as the Englishman William Adams. Several Spanish merchants involved in trade with Manila also received *shuinjō* from Ieyasu. In addition to these, eight daimyo (all of them from western Japan), four bakufu officials, and six Chinese merchants received *shuinjō*.[52] Therefore, in the early years of the Tokugawa period, foreign trade in Japan was by no means an isolated phenomenon, but was rather a prominent feature of Japan's upper stratum of society, as demonstrated aptly by the sheer number of *shuinsen* that were approved by the bakufu.

Although we do not have extensive evidence that the *shuinsen* system was circumvented, illicit trade must certainly have occurred to a certain extent; however, how widespread it was must of necessity remain unknown. Dutch sources refer to a number of Japanese ships "without the Keizer's pass." Governor-General Specx notes, for example, that in 1632, two Japanese junks were trading in Manila unlawfully. In fact, not only did these ships not have a *shuinjō*, but they were also flouting the shogun's order that no trade be carried on with the Spanish, a restriction that will receive more attention later in this study.[53] The Dutch factory on Taiwan also reported that unlicensed Japanese junks were often trading with the natives as well as with Chinese merchants, activity that was proscribed by both the bakufu and the VOC.[54] Incidents in which Chinese ships arrived at Taiwan with a *shuinjō* that was several years old also occurred, another violation of bakufu law, as *shuinjō* were ostensibly valid for only a single voyage.[55] And finally, there were instances in which Japanese ships arrived on Taiwan with *shuinjō* after the bakufu had suspended this trade.[56] The VOC had a vested interest in reporting this illicit commercial activity because it was a source of unwanted competition. It was a huge victory for the Dutch when the shogun banned Japanese ships from traveling abroad insofar as the *shuinsen* were consistently the major source of competition in the Japan trade, far more than even the Portuguese trade from Macao. In short, incidents of flouting shogunal regulations seem not to have been many compared to the rampant piracy that characterized Asian trade previously, but there were evidently those who did circumvent the system.

When those interested in foreign trade wanted to obtain a *shuinjō*, the first step was to contact one of the shogunal councilors at Edo, almost always through an intermediary. Therefore, from the very beginning one had to have relatively good connections to even consider undertaking such a venture. In the early years of the bakufu, Honda Masazumi was the main avenue by which prospective investors received *shuinjō*, although other officials such as Hasegawa Zaemon, the Nagasaki *bugyō*, or Gōtō Mitsusugu, the head of the Ginza, also played a major role.[57] A "gift," usually a small amount of silver or gold or some other suitably valuable commodity, naturally accompanied this request.[58] Who this gift was intended for is not entirely clear, but most likely at least a part of it was for the Zen priest responsible for drawing up the documents.[59] A gift was also required at the end of the journey, and this usually took the form of luxury goods obtained in the destination to which the *shuinsen* was sent. There are several references in the *Tōdaiki* and the *Sumpuki* to *shuinsen* merchants presenting these types of gifts to Ieyasu. In 1612, for example, Suminokura Yōichi returned from his voyage to Annam and presented Ieyasu with red silk, scarlet damask, spices, medicinal herbs, and oddly enough, a litter of cats.[60] These gifts were mandatory for those who wished to stay on good terms with the bakufu, and in modern terms can be seen as a sort of "luxury tax" on foreign trade since the government did not attempt to tax this trade.

From 1612, a Zen priest by the name of Suden was Tokugawa Ieyasu's chief advisor for foreign affairs, and as such was responsible for many of the documents that were issued under the shogun's name (he lived in a sub-temple called the Konchi'in and was therefore often referred to as Konchi'in Sūden). He was also responsible for drafting some of the most important documents of the period, which would set the tone for the entire Tokugawa shogunate. For example, Sūden's brush was responsible for the *Buke Shohatto*, *Kuge Shohatto*, as well as the *Ji-in Shohatto*.[61] These three documents regulated the activity of the warrior class, the nobility, and temples and shrines respectively. In addition, he also composed the work entitled *Bateren Tsuihō no Bun*, an order to root out the existence of priests in Japan. These documents, and the ideology behind them, extended the authority of the bakufu into virtually every major facet of Japanese life, from the secular to the religious. Suden was also responsible for drafting many of the early *shuinjō*.[62] Although drafting these documents was one of Sūden's main responsibilities, he was in fact much more than a scribe. While it is true that the government in Edo had little power in exclusively domainal affairs, this vestige of semiautonomy became increasingly limited. It is obvious, therefore, that in setting the tone for an increasingly authoritarian central government, Sūden was one of the most important figures in the early bakufu, although his name is often obscured by those of the senior councilors and *fudai* daimyo who were close intimates of Ieyasu.

Once the *shuinjō* was procured and the requisite gifts given, the physical reality of a *shuinsen* voyage set in, and the investor was now confronted with the prospect of obtaining a suitable ship. According to Iwao, there were five considerations when obtaining a vessel for trade: the cost of the ship, repair costs, the cost of the actual voyage, the cost of the cargo, and, of course, the cost of the human labor involved.[63] Most daimyo did not have oceangoing ships in their harbors even before the bakufu decreed in 1609 that no daimyo have ships of more than 500 *koku* in size, and so were forced to either build a ship or contract one, usually from the Chinese at Nagasaki. After this prohibition, powerful daimyo such as the Shimazu and Date families, although previously able to furnish their own oceangoing vessels, usually resorted to chartering suitable ships in Nagasaki.

A good example of the process of outfitting a foreign voyage can be seen from the instructions that the Shimazu family, daimyo of Satsuma, gave to the merchant Tōda Gorōzaemon. He was ordered to purchase a "Fujianese" ship of 20,000 *kin* capacity to be sent to both Luzon and Annam under the direction of a merchant from Chikugo named Yatsugu Zaemon. In another example, the Kamei family purchased a ship costing "several tens of *kanme*" to be sent to Siam. After the ship was bought, it was loaded with a cargo of precious metals, swords, Japanese screens, and other miscellaneous goods from Kyoto and Sakai. The Kamei then hired a crew which was, according to these instructions, made up of *hyakushō*, a term that literally means peasant.[64] Surely these "peasants" had some knowledge of seamanship, but perhaps to a powerful daimyo there was little distinction between those people of lower status who tilled the fields and those who plied the seas.

Rather than bear the high cost of purchasing a ship, some *shuinsen* merchants chose instead to build their own. These ships could be as large as six or seven hundred tons, although the average size was two to three hundred tons, especially after the shogunal edict limiting the size of daimyo ships to a 500-*koku* capacity or less. Katō Kiyomasa, for example, built a ship in 1604 that was 36 meters long, 10 meters wide, and had a berth of 650 tons.[65] Date Masamune also built a ship in his domain of Sendai that was capable of taking an embassy to Europe and back. It is clear when studying Japanese trade in this period that there was a long tradition of shipbuilding and seamanship that, combined with a staggering quantity of precious metals, enabled the Japanese to compete successfully in international trade.

Because outfitting a ship for the kind of voyage that international trade entailed was incredibly expensive and risky, it became the norm for this trade to be dominated by *bōeki-ke*, or "merchant families." This term did not imply that all of the families were of the merchant class, but rather that the particular family in question was involved in foreign trade. The Shimazu were considered *bōeki-ke* because of their extensive commercial activities, although they were among the more powerful daimyo families of Kyushu.[66] One of the major reasons why trade came to be dominated by these families was that a *shuinsen* voyage was a long-term investment involving a great deal of capital. Ships took almost a year to complete their journey, and this does not take into account the time spent organizing the journey and liquidating the merchandise at the completion of the venture. Therefore, if a single person were to finance this type of trade, that person would not realize a profit for more than a year, while at the same time bearing the tremendous risks inherently involved in such journeys; the unusually rough seas around Japan, the prevalence of piracy, and the natural capriciousness of the weather made the risk in investing in a *shuinsen* quite high.[67] It should come as no surprise, therefore, that individual merchants eschewed direct foreign trade and chose rather to invest capital in a voyage undertaken by one of the wealthier *bōeki-ke*. The formation of wealthy *shuinsen* families was further facilitated by the fact that even though each *shuinjō* was ostensibly good for only a single voyage, they eventually came to be kept in wealthy merchant families for years and were in some instances inherited or passed on to other families.[68]

The financial burden that necessitated the spreading of risk in the *shuinsen* trade makes it difficult to define exactly how this trade was conducted. Iwao Seiichi has identified five distinct methods of organizing a voyage, and in so doing has recognized that there is no single "model" to hold up as the ideal of what a *shuinsen* venture looked like. These five patterns are as follows:

1. One party invests all of the money in the voyage. (This was not a very widespread practice given the cost and the risk of the voyage).

2. A single party invests all of the money for a voyage but uses a ship owned by a second party.
3. Two or more parties cooperate in a single voyage, including the purchase of a ship.
4. A number of merchants invest money in a ship owned by another party.
5. Several merchants in a given locality participate indirectly in a voyage, using an outside party's ship.[69]

One aspect of international trade in this period that emerges from these patterns is that the purchase of a ship was a major expense that merchants often chose to avoid.[70] By renting ships for a single voyage, the *shuinsen* merchants disentangled themselves from the considerable financial burden of maintaining and repairing the ship after each use. With regard to investment in a *shuinsen* voyage, investors were able to loan money at a rate of interest—usually around fifty percent—that reflected the risk involved as well as the potential profits to be made. The attractive part of this investment scheme, however, was that if the voyage somehow failed, the merchant's debt was cancelled, therefore shifting much of the risk onto the lender, again reflected in the high rates of interest.[71] Naturally, only wealthy families were able to lend under these somewhat onerous terms, but the returns on such investments could be extremely high: usually 40 to 50 percent, but often as high as 80 percent.

Another consideration that makes it difficult to define the *shuinsen* trade with any precision is that it was rarely conducted solely by Japanese merchants; rather, foreigners were often involved in almost every stage of the process. The most conspicuous case of foreign involvement in the *shuinsen* trade was when a foreigner petitioned the bakufu for a *shuinjō*. The *Ikoku Nikki* records several foreigners who lived in Japan and engaged in foreign trade, individuals ranging from survivors of the Dutch ship *De Liefde* (such as William Adams and Jan Joosten) to Spanish merchants (such as Andre Rodriguez) who generally lived in Nagasaki. Adams in particular availed himself of Ieyasu's favor to send ships to Siam and Cochin, while Rodriguez was naturally interested in the Manila trade.[72] It was on board such foreign-owned ships, in fact, that Japanese mariners became proficient in western methods of sailing and navigation. An invaluable account written by the Japanese pilot Ikeda Kōzaemon (Kōun), who served as a sailor on a *shuinsen* owned by a Portuguese merchant named Emanuel Gonsalo, has survived and records in detail many western innovations in navigation. Gonsalo obtained a *shuinjō* to trade with both Siam and Cochin, and on these journeys taught Ikeda such western nautical arts as how to located the ship's position by measuring the sun and how to navigate using the stars as a guide.[73] Ikeda recorded this information in his *Genna Kōkai-ki*, undoubtedly influential in the spread of the new sailing and navigational techniques in Japan.[74]

Apart from such *shuinsen* merchants, a number of foreigners played a role in the technical operation of Japanese-owned ships, especially in the early years of the *shuinsen* system. Most notable of these were the foreigners who served as pilots on Japanese vessels. The practice of employing foreign pilots began almost immediately after the Portuguese arrived in Japan and was extended when the Dutch and English set up factories at Hirado.[75] It was also common for Japanese junks to have a number of Chinese sailors aboard, including at times a Chinese pilot. The president of the VOC factory on Taiwan, for example, often recorded the arrival of Japanese junks piloted and operated by Chinese. Finally, foreign merchants occasionally sent goods on Japanese-owned *shuinsen*. In at least one instance, the English sent merchandise to Hirado from factories at Bantam, Siam, and Patani aboard Japanese ships. This was because the English, not having as extensive a trade network as the Dutch (nor as many ships in Asia), often had trouble supplying their factory in Japan using their own ships, and thus were forced at times to use local ships.[76]

Even though the *shuinsen* trade was a Japanese system in competition with the European companies, there was usually some foreign element involved. In fact, there seems to have been very little concern on the part of the Japanese about foreign competition in international trade. Rather, the great majority of the grumbling in this regard came from the foreigners, especially the Dutch and the English who found themselves in stiff competition with the Japanese *shuinsen* merchants. It should be remembered that the purpose of the bakufu in establishing the *shuinsen* system was not to further the interest of native merchants at the expense of foreigners, but rather to centralize the control of foreign relations and to facilitate the flow of goods into the country.

One aspect of the *shuinsen* trade that continually vexed foreigners (especially the English) was the Japanese custom of allowing sailors a measure of private trade while serving on board. The owner of a *shuinsen* generally allowed each sailor, according to his rank, goods that he could trade privately in Southeast Asia. In the same way, space in the ships on the return voyage was allotted to the goods that sailors had obtained in their private trade and that would be sold in Japan on their own initiative.[77] Cargo space was also often rented out for a fee to Japanese merchants, not associated with the *shuinsen*, who would load their own goods and be responsible for their own trade.[78] The English in particular, because they were forced to rely on Japanese sailors more so than the Dutch and Portuguese, were extremely annoyed by this practice and often felt that the private trade was more profitable than official company business. The issue was a source of continual friction between the English and Japanese sailors, and often led to feelings of ill-will between the EIC and Will Adams—the latter, understanding and generally tolerant of Japanese customs, was judged to be overly "Japanized by his English colleagues."[79]

Nihonmachi and Japanese Foreign Trade

Japanese trade with Southeast Asia was greatly facilitated by enclaves of Japanese merchants in many of the major trading ports across the region. Phillip Curtin characterizes this "expatriate" Japanese population in the beginning of the seventeenth century as a "Japanese trade Diaspora."[80] Although there were undoubtedly those who chose to live abroad for reasons other than trade, for the most part these enclaves seem to have been economic in nature. It has been estimated that in the three and a half decades spanning the establishment of the Edo bakufu to the final *sakoku* edicts, over 71,000 Japanese spent significant periods of time in Southeast Asia.[81] Known to historians as *nihonmachi*, or "Japan-towns," these enclaves were used by merchants within Japan to ease relations with local rulers and officials, and were a reflection of local demand for Japanese goods and precious metals.

The first true *nihonmachi* sprang up on the northern part of the island of Luzon in what came to be known as the towns of Dilao and San Miguel.[82] Japanese settlements in Cochin, Cambodia, Siam, and Burma followed in quick succession. There were also smaller settlements located in Taiwan, Tonkin, the Celebes, and Jakarta, but because of their small size they are usually considered separate from the larger *nihonmachi*.[83] The two main characteristics of the larger settlements were the existence of a headman who acted as the representative of the Japanese population within the larger native political structure, and the existence of a separate space in which the Japanese community lived.[84] In Cambodia, for example, there were five of these types of leaders representing the major group of foreigners in the country: one Japanese, one Portuguese, one Javanese, and two Chinese. The example of Cambodia was not unique and is a testament to the cosmopolitan nature of many port towns in Southeast Asia.[85] Unfortunately, as we shall see, the *nihonmachi* were also characterized by a certain amount of friction with the local authorities, indicative perhaps of the prosperity of the trade that occurred between these Japanese enclaves, Japan, and the rest of Asia.

For our purposes we shall examine briefly two of the largest and most documented *nihonmachi*: those located in Siam and Luzon (the Philippines). In the case of Luzon, Japanese, along with a number of Chinese, were already living on the island at the time of the Spanish conquest.[86] The Chinese and Japanese came into conflict with the Spanish early on, resulting in a series of armed clashes. The Japanese eventually moved (or were moved, depending on the version one accepts) outside of the main Spanish settlement of

Manila to what became known as the town of Dilao. This seemed for a time to put an end to the armed conflicts, but the Spanish were still irritated by the number of Japanese ships coming to the island and they therefore petitioned Hideyoshi, and later the Tokugawa, to limit them. The Spanish were successful in their petition with Hideyoshi and Ieyasu, the bakufu eventually establishing a limit of three Japanese ships per year to the island. This order, however, seems to have been violated quite regularly.

The Japanese population on Luzon rose dramatically when two daimyo families from Kyushu began to send ships there regularly. The Ōmura and Matsuura families both concentrated their *shuinsen* trade at Manila, and consequently many of the Japanese living on the island were from the domains of these daimyo.[87] The population of the Japanese settlement at Dilao fluctuated with the fortunes of trade with the Spaniards, the high point being from 1621–1623 when more than three thousand Japanese lived there. This number soon decreased, however, after the shogun severed relations with the Spanish.[88] Even after this ban, however, there were still roughly eight hundred Japanese living in Dilao, many of them choosing exile when the bakufu's enforcement of its anti-Christian policy became increasingly strict.

There was also a sizeable Japanese population living at Ayuthia, the capital of the kingdom of Siam. This *nihonmachi* is much more documented in the Japanese sources because of a man named Yamada Nagamasa, a merchant who rose in the Siamese bureaucracy to become one of the king's chief advisors.[89] It was in this capacity that he sent a letter in 1621 to the bakufu requesting official diplomatic relations between the two countries. Along with the letter (which was ostensibly from the Siamese king), Nagamasa included a present for Hidetada of two shark skins and two hundred *kin* of pepper, two items to be found in Siam that were quite valuable on the Japanese market. The real reason for the letter seems to have been much more than simply an interest in commercial ties; the Siamese monarch was, in fact, attempting to purchase Japanese weapons for his interminable wars with the neighboring kingdom of Cambodia.[90]

Doi Toshikatsu and the Zen priest Sūden, writing on behalf of the shogun, granted the Siamese request for an official embassy to the shogun's court. This embassy arrived at Nagasaki in the eighth month of 1621, and in the first month of the following year was granted an audience with Hidetada. The bakufu replied favorably to a resumption of ties with Siam, sending the embassy back with sumptuous presents for the king. This promising start, however, was not to last. Internal Siamese politics caused the Japanese, and Nagamasa in particular, to lose favor at court, and the entire Japanese population at Ayuthia was driven out of the country.

While Nagamasa's favorable position within the Siamese court lasted, and because there was a sizeable *nihonmachi* at Ayuthia, trade between Japan and Siam flourished.[91] Of the 356 *shuinsen* sent to foreign countries, Siam was the most popular destination, accounting for a total of fifty-six ships. The Shimazu family was especially active in the Siam trade; they received several *shuinjō* over the course of the period, and because the Ryūkyū Islands were vassals of theirs, they actively incorporated these islands into their trade with Southeast Asia in general, and Siam in particular.[92] Likewise, the Hosokawa profited in the trade with Siam; the *Tōdaiki* records that in 1611 they sent a junk to Ayuthia in order to procure elephant tusks and raw white silk, a portion of which they offered to Ieyasu as a present upon completion of the journey.[93]

The end of the Keichō and the following Genna periods represented the high point of relations between Japan and Siam. A Siamese junk arrived at Nagasaki in Keichō 17 (1612), and in a replay of a scenario so familiar to the Europeans, the captain was escorted to Sumpu to offer his respects (and of course a gift) to Ieyasu.[94] This embassy was received very cordially, and the Siamese returned to their own country having attained favorable trading privileges. The Siamese king, perhaps because of this warm reception, later sent another official embassy to the shogun, this time consisting of more than twenty people. This group proceeded to Edo to pay its respects to Hidetada, and was again favorably received.[95] Thus, for a while it appeared that the Siamese would enjoy the same commercial privileges as the Chinese, Dutch, and English. This expectation, however, soon faded as internal developments in Siam took a decidedly anti-Japanese turn.

Yamada Nagamasa, as foremost advisor to the Siamese king, had a great deal of influence in Siamese politics, and was also prominent in the Japanese trading community. The Japanese population as a whole was well integrated into Siamese society and politics, as evidenced by the existence of an entire army division comprising three to four hundred Japanese soldiers.[96] Upon the king's death in 1630, however, the new monarch, Prasart Thong, resented this Japanese influence, and that of Nagamasa in particular. The king drove Nagamasa out of the court and, on October 26, 1630, sent a large army to burn down the Japanese settlement, causing the Japanese to flee into Cambodia.[97] The *nihonmachi* in Ayuthia never really recovered from this blow, and in the following year the bakufu retaliated by suspending relations with Siam.[98] Soon thereafter, however, the new Siamese king attempted to revive trade with Japan by using the Dutch as middlemen, but this attempt came to nothing (and one suspects that the Dutch welcomed this failure since they were surely not eager for Siamese competition in Japan).[99] For all practical purposes trade between Japan and Siam was suspended indefinitely. Chinese junks based in Siam, however, continued to arrive throughout the Edo period and were allowed to trade with the same privileges as other Chinese merchants.[100] This indirect Siamese trade was not inconsiderable: between 1651 and 1700, a total of 130 ships arrived at Nagasaki from Siam, operated largely by Chinese crews.[101]

One of the most remarkable aspects of the *shuinsen* system is that it worked as well as it did. If one of Ieyasu's primary goals in setting up the system was to offer protection to ships carrying shogunal passes, then we must conclude that it worked splendidly.[102] There is copious evidence in Western sources of the respect shown to ships in possession of *shuinjō*. This of course did not mean that the Europeans were pleased with the system, as it inevitably offered stiff competition to their own interests; but they rarely interfered with the ships, much less attacked them outright.

A Spanish observer writing from Manila has left us an account of the respect shown by the Dutch to Japanese ships armed with *shuinjō*. In 1618, as part of a VOC policy of intercepting Portuguese and Spanish shipping, the Dutch were patrolling the mouth of the harbor at Manila. When this fleet encountered a Japanese vessel bound for Manila, they stopped it and asked if it had a pass from the "emperor." When the Japanese ship produced the *shuinjō*, it was allowed to proceed into Manila, even though the Dutch were blockading the harbor. According to the Spanish chronicler, "…the Hollanders respect the emperor's license insofar as it concerns them, and they give free passage in every part of these seas to all Japanese ships bearing it."[103] Furthermore, the joint Anglo-Dutch fleet that was formed in the 1620s to disrupt Spanish and Portuguese trade was "scrupulous about not molesting *shuinsen* or Chinese vessels with a pass from Dutch factories elsewhere in the Indies."[104]

The Spanish and Portuguese also respected the shogunal authority inherent in the *shuinsen*, although a Spanish attack on one of these ships at Siam led to great complications between Portuguese merchants and the Japanese authorities. In May 1628 a Spanish ship seized a *shuinsen* sent to Siam by the Nagasaki *machidoshiyori* Takaki Sakuzaemon, then confiscated its cargo, and (more seriously) took the ship's *shuinjō*. This was, according to Francois Caron, an extremely serious offence insofar as an attack on a *shuinsen* was tantamount to an attack on the shogun's authority.[105] Although this may have been a relatively minor incident, it had serious repercussions both for Japanese merchants, and more immediately for Portuguese commercial interests.

Although it may not be entirely obvious why an attack by a Spanish vessel should redound to the harm of the Portuguese, it was in fact because the two countries were united under a common monarch when, in 1580, Phillip II ascended the Portuguese throne after the previous Portuguese king died without a viable heir.[106] And although one of the stipulations attached to Phillip's claim on the throne was that Portuguese possessions in "India" were to remain independent of Spanish control, the Japanese were not interested in these subtleties of European statesmanship and did not hesitate to punish the Portuguese for the crimes of the Spanish.[107] Part of the explanation for this is that it was undoubtedly easier to place sanctions on Portuguese trade (the Spanish were barred from trade in Japan) than to mount a punitive expedition against the Spanish at Manila. And since an attack on the shogun's authority absolutely demanded a response, the bakufu resorted to this relatively easy (and safe) expedient. The result was that Portuguese trade with Japan was suspended for two years.[108] This temporary ban on their shipping, however, did not prove to be of lasting damage to the Portuguese since trade was eventually restored upon the dispatch of a suitably lavish embassy, after which Portuguese trade continued to flourish until the final expulsion decree of 1639. This incident did, however, have a lasting impact on the institution of the *shuinjō* itself.

THE DECLINE OF THE *SHUINSEN* SYSTEM

As Francois Caron astutely observed, the attack on a *shuinsen* was perceived as an attack on shogunal prestige; the bakufu therefore decided that it was no longer proper for the shogun to be directly involved in the issuing of trade permits. The system was consequently changed so that the ultimate responsibility for issuing the *shuinjō* no longer stemmed directly from the shogun, but rather from his chief councilors.[109] In recognition of the change, the permits were no longer called *shuinjō*, but *hōshojō*.[110] This new policy was made public in 1631 by the Nagasaki *bugyō*, although it was apparently only loosely enforced until the bakufu began to seriously restrict overseas travel in the first of the *sakoku* edicts.[111] This seemingly minor change in bakufu procedure heralded the beginning of a general clampdown on Japanese overseas activity that would soon culminate in the end of the *shuinsen* system, followed shortly thereafter by Japanese travel abroad in general. These so-called *sakoku* decrees will be dealt with more fully in chapter 6, but suffice it to say that the end of the *shuinsen/hōshosen* system was a direct precursor to the decrees that put an end to direct Japanese involvement overseas. Let us now turn to an examination of the last few years of the *shuinsen/hōshosen* system, a period that witnessed a sharp drop in direct overseas trade followed, of course, by its prohibition altogether.

Overseas trade came to be increasingly monopolized in the late 1620s by a small number of wealthy families with relatively close ties to the governing elite. Whereas there had previously been several individuals who sent at least one ship to places such as Siam, Cambodia, Manila, and so forth, the harsh reality of the financial burden for such a voyage soon deterred all but the wealthiest from engaging in them. During the Keichō era (1596–1614) more than seventy-five families sent 169 ships to nineteen locations in Southeast Asia; by the succeeding Genna period (1615–1623), however, only thirty-one families had sent ships abroad, and of these only eleven were first-time participants in the *shuinsen* system.[112] Clearly, the volume of *shuinsen* trade was in rapid decline throughout the first two decades of the seventeenth century. Furthermore, whereas the early years of the system saw the participation of several powerful western daimyo, by Keichō 17 (1612), not a single Kyushu daimyo was still involved in foreign trade. The reasons for this precipitous decline are manifold, but most important perhaps was the increasing pressure that the bakufu brought to bear on the powerful daimyo of Kyushu, still perceived as a threat to Tokugawa supremacy within Japan. An increasing fear of Christianity and its propagation within Japan also led the bakufu to more tightly control the flow of goods and people into and out of the country, especially in the distant domains of Kyushu, which had historically been the nucleus of Christian missionary activity.[113]

In 1622 a combined English-Dutch fleet patrolling the Indian Ocean for Iberian ships captured a Japanese ship sailing from Manila and brought it to Hirado.[114] There was nothing particularly special about this ship, except that in the cargo hold, beneath a pile of deer skins, were two Spanish priests, Pedro Zuninga and Luis Flores, who were obviously trying to smuggle themselves into Japan. Ever vigilant for a means of turning bakufu sentiment against their Portuguese and Spanish enemies, the Dutch and English turned the ship (along with the two Spaniards) over to the authorities. After a long and arduous trial in which Zuninga and Flores insisted that they were merchants, they were found guilty and in 1623 executed at Nagasaki.

In the immediate wake of this incident, the bakufu became ever more vigilant for the possibility of priests entering the country disguised as merchants. The English and Dutch used Japanese anxiety about Catholicism to impress upon the authorities that as long as the Spanish and Portuguese were allowed to trade in Japan, they would continue to smuggle priests into the country.[115] This, along with Spanish attempts to limit the Japanese presence in Luzon, proved to be a major consideration in the bakufu's 1624 decision of to suspend all *shuinsen* to Manila. Subsequent Spanish delegations were of no avail in restoring trade, and the ban remained in place for the remainder of the Edo period.This in and of itself was a considerable blow to the *shuinsen* trade because Manila was second only to Siam in terms of the number of ships sent there each year. Furthermore, Siam itself would soon fall prey to bakufu reprisals when the new Siamese king destroyed the *nihonmachi* at Ayuthia in 1630 and forced the Japanese inhabitants to flee to Cambodia. After the bakufu discontinued formal relations with Siam in 1631, only one Japanese ship was sent there in the years leading up to the suspension of the *shuinsen* system, a severe blow to a system in which Siam played such a prominent part.

Another factor that contributed to the greatly diminished role of the *shuinsen* was the bakufu decree banning Japanese ships from calling at Taiwan.[116] Frequent clashes between the VOC and Japanese merchants culminated finally in the Nuijts affair of 1628, the result of which was the suspension of Dutch trade in Japan for four years.[117] Although trade was restored when VOC officials turned Nuijts over for punishment, the company was increasingly concerned that stiff Japanese competition on Taiwan would make their entire Japan trade less profitable. This was the rationale behind repeated VOC petitions in which the Dutch asked the shogunate to prohibit Japanese merchants from sending ships to Taiwan.[118] When the bakufu finally granted these petitions, they were in essence renouncing previously vague Japanese designs on the island and confirming that Taiwan was in fact a Dutch possession.[119] With this latest decree, the bakufu fundamentally banned trade with the three areas with which Japanese merchants were most intimately involved.

With the trade in Siam, Manila, and Taiwan now forbidden, only less profitable destinations such as Tonkin, Cochin, and Cambodia were viable destinations for Japanese *shuinsen* merchants. Trade in all of these areas combined, however, could not yield the profits that the Japanese realized in Siam alone. Furthermore, the most profitable items for import into Japan, namely deerskins, raw silk, and sugar, were found mainly in areas in which it was now prohibited to trade. The Japanese therefore relied increasingly on foreigners for the import of Southeast Asian luxury goods. One important factor to note, however, was that even with a decrease in Japanese shipping, the demand for foreign goods never diminished, but rather came to be satisfied mainly by Dutch and Chinese merchants.

The diminished role of the *shuinsen* is highlighted by a visit that Francois Caron received in 1634 from Joseph Adams, the son of the English pilot William Adams. Adams mentioned to Caron that the bakufu had recently limited the issuance of *shuinjō* to a mere seven families, his own family included.[120] The other six families were the Hirano, Sueyoshi, Chaya, Suetsugu, Hashimoto, and the Suminokura. The Hirano, Sueyoshi, and Suminokura families were given *shuinjō* to trade with Tonkin, the Suetsugu and Chaya families sent their ships to Cochin, and the Adams and Hashimoto families traded in Cambodia.[121] It is important to note that all of these families had important connections with the bakufu, three of whom had served as shogunal councilors.[122] It is also not a coincidence that none of these families had relations with powerful daimyo families in Kyushu, such as the Shimazu. This is indicative of the bakufu's desire to reserve for itself the conduct of foreign affairs as well as to limit the power of the western daimyo. The limiting of *shuinjō* to these seven families, however, was only the penultimate step in the bakufu's effort to control foreign trade; within two years, even these well-connected families would be deprived of the right to engage in foreign commerce, however limited.

In the first of the *sakoku* decrees issued by the bakufu in 1633, we see that the *hōshosen* were still allowed to trade, a reference to the special privileges of the aforementioned seven families. The first article of the edict clearly states, "The sending of ships other than *hōsho* ships is strictly forbidden," an official acknowledgement that the *shuinsen* system as it had existed previously had come to an end.[123] Furthermore, article three of the same edict allows for the return of Japanese who had been living in foreign countries for fewer than five years, "following an official investigation." These two clauses are in striking contrast to the second *sakoku* decree issued only two years later in 1635. In this incarnation, the first article reads simply, "The sending of ships to foreign countries is strictly forbidden."[124] Gone is the provision for the *hōshosen,* and by extension those privileged families allowed foreign trade. From this date all foreign trade in Japanese ships was suspended regardless of one's status or connections at court. Similarly, there was no longer a "grace period" for Japanese who had been living abroad for even a short time. In the 1635 version of the decree, all Japanese trying to enter the country were, without exception, subject to punishment by death. With the promulgation of the *sakoku* decree of 1635, therefore, all Japanese trade and travel abroad was categorically suspended. What were the reasons behind the bakufu's decision to ban its own people from engaging in a trade that was at times lucrative and, with the exception of a few minor incidents, relatively peaceful?

When the Dutch on Taiwan and the Spanish in Siam effectively ignored the shogunal guarantee of safe passage implicit in the *shuinjō* by either attacking or incarcerating Japanese ships, it might appear to have been a relatively minor incident in terms of international diplomacy. The Dutch were quick to offer their apologies and they fully compensated the Japanese for their losses, and even sent a special embassy to Edo to officially apologize and resolve any lingering complications. The Portuguese did much the same in an effort to convince the Japanese authorities that they were not responsible for the actions of the Spanish, sending an official embassy to Edo to apologize to the shogun and ask for a resumption of trade. From the viewpoint of the bakufu, however, these incidents were anything but minor affairs and required a response.

First of all, these international entanglements took place only a few decades after the Tokugawa definitively established their supremacy in Japan at the Battle of Sekigahara. More recent still were the Osaka campaigns in which Ieyasu and Hidetada finally eradicated the last vestiges of Toyotomi claims to legitimacy. The bakufu at this point still perceived that it was not entirely secure in its domination of Japanese politics. Western daimyo such as the Shimazu and Hosokawa were still quite powerful and were still very much a force to be reckoned with, not to mention the fact that many western domains had not forgotten the shame that Sekigahara entailed for them.[125] Furthermore, the bakufu's legitimacy rested on the assumption that it was a military government established to protect Japan and maintain stability after so many years of civil strife. The transition to a by and large civil, bureaucratic role for the samurai lay far in the future. Therefore, when a tangible threat to Tokugawa power and prestige presented itself, it demanded a swift response. Rather than risk everything on a campaign against the Spanish in Manila, the Dutch in Taiwan, or in Siam, however, the bakufu chose the relatively safe expedient of severing relations with those areas. Only when the Dutch and the Portuguese prostrated themselves fully at the feet of the shogun did he relent and allow a resumption of trade. In the case of the Dutch, it was the sending of a special envoy, and ultimately the extradition to Japan of Pieter Nuijts himself, that placated the shogun and offered him a way to "save diplomatic face." Sumptuous gifts (including the lantern that can still be seen at Nikkō, for example) also served to reinforce Tokugawa legitimacy, a point aptly made by scholars such as Ronald Toby and Tashirō Kazui.[126]

The bakufu likewise perceived Christianity as a threat to its authority because the religion divided the allegiance of its adherents between itself and an outside locus, be it the Pope in Rome, a European monarch, or even a foreign God.[127] It is doubtful that the Tokugawa authorities were overly concerned about the spiritual implications of Christianity, but certainly the worldly implications were very much in the minds of officials in Edo. This anxiety was only heightened by the fact that the main area of Christian influence lay in the domains of the very daimyo that had fought against the Tokugawa less than a generation earlier. Although the long Tokugawa peace obscures our view of the early Edo period, it certainly was not inconceivable to the bakufu that a coalition of western daimyo united, however genuinely, by the Christian faith could rise up against Tokugawa hegemony.[128] One need only consider that many of the *rōnin* (masterless samurai) who sided with Toyotomi Hideyori in Ieyasu's 1615 Osaka campaigns were in fact Christian.[129] This fact was certainly not lost on Ieyasu and his successors, and helps to explain why the persecution of Christianity began in earnest soon after Hideyori was vanquished.

Furthermore, the role of Christianity as an "advance guard" for the colonization of Japan, while naïve in hindsight, must have been at least a consideration in the mind of the shogun, even if the boast of Francisco Sanda is apocryphal.[130] The 1622 attempt by two Spanish priests to smuggle themselves into the country aboard a Japanese vessel from Manila was an alarming event that served to confirm the bakufu in their fears of a subversive religion.According to Iwao, the Dutch and English seized on this fear of Catholicism and took every opportunity to convince the Japanese that the Spanish had imperialist designs on Japan. This was an attempt to not only get the Spanish and Portuguese evicted from Japan, but also to prompt the bakufu to suppress the *shuinsen* trade, a major source of competition to the East India companies.[131]

In the end the shogun chose a policy that would not only remove the threat of attacks on Japanese ships, but would also eliminate the threat of Catholic subversion within Japan. This policy had the added benefit of allowing Japan to indirectly maintain its extensive trade throughout Asia. Externally, the Spanish and Portuguese were expelled from Japan while the Dutch and Chinese were allowed to stay, and internally, the bakufu banned all Japanese travel abroad. This brought to a close the *shuinsen* trade that helped make Japanese merchants such an integral part of East Asian trade.[132] It did not, however, bring an end to Japanese involvement with that trade. Rather, after banning the *shuinsen* trade, Japanese involvement with the economy of Asia continued to be considerable, although it was now carried out in ships that were not Japanese.

Endnotes

1. Arano Yasunori, ed., *Nihon no Jidai Shi 14: Edo Bakufu to Higashi Ajia* (Tokyo: Yoshikawa Kōbunkan, 2003), 32.
2. Emma Helen Blair and James Robertson, eds., *The Philippine Islands, 1493–1898, Vol. 10* (Cleveland; The Arthur H. Clark Co., 1904), 212.
3. Nicholas Couckebacker, president of the Dutch facory at Hirado, noted in his diary, "When many Japanese come to Taiwan, trade with the Chinese is difficult." Dutch efforts to persuade the bakufu to ban Japanese ships from sailing to Taiwan paid off in May of 1634. See NKKS, Vol. I, 38, 107.
4. Iwao, *Shuinsen to Nihonmachi*, 17.
5. Iwano Hisashi, "Filipin Bōeki to Sukezaemon/Kiemon," in *Nihon Rekishi 9: Shuinsen to Minami e ni Senkisha*, ed. Ōishi Shinzaburō (Tokyo: Gyōsei, 1986), 34.
6. *Purchas His Pilgrims, Part I*, 137. Purchas also states that the Japanese were not allowed to enter any port in the Indies while bearing arms. This seems to be an exaggeration since in the early seventeenth century there were many cases of Japanese mercenaries in the employ of the Portuguese, Dutch, and several Asian potentates. There does seem to be, however, several accounts of Japanese merchants resorting to violence and behaving in a generally riotous way, although this can perhaps be attributed to a lack of any real central control within Japan at the time.
7. Coolhaas, ed., *Pieter van den Broecke in Azië*, 142.
8. Alfonso d'Albequerque, *The Commentaries of the Great Alfonso D'Albuquerque, Second Viceroy of India*, Vol. III, trans. Walter Birch (London: The Hakluyt Society, 1880), 88–90. There is a degree of confusion here because d'Albuquerque refers to these people as *Gores* from the island of *Leuqueu*, which would seem to suggest that they were in fact merchants from the Ryūkyū Islands. From the descriptions provided of the people, their manners, and their mercantile activities, however, most scholars have concluded that they were in fact Japanese. On this controversy, see Richard Whiteway, *The Rise of Portuguese Power in India 1497–1550* (London: Santiago de Compostela, Susil Gupta, 1967).
9. Mary Elizabeth Berry has written the best political biography of Toyotomi Hideyoshi to date, and while she deals very selectively with the issue of overseas trade, the work does convey a sense of Hideyoshi's overall policy towards foreign countries, as well as his

effort to control piracy in the waters around Japan. See Mary Elizabeth Berry, *Hideyoshi* (Cambridge: The Council on East Asian Studies and Harvard University Press, 1989), 101, 130–138.

10. Quoted in Kota Kodama, ed., *Shiryō ni Yoru Nihon no Ayumi, Kinsei Hen* (Tokyo: Yoshikawa Kōbunkan, 1957–72), 55.
11. Ibid., 3.
12. Nakata argues that the *shuinjō* originated with Ieyasu, while Iwao states that historical documents from slightly later clearly demonstrate that Hideyoshi issued these documents to merchants of Sakai, Kyoto, and Nagasaki. Nagazumi arrives at a natural compromise by attributing to Hideyoshi the issuance of the permits (something that seems fairly concrete considering his issuance of red–seal documents for everything else), but reserving the establishment of the system itself to Ieyasu. See Nagazumi, *Shuinsen*, 2–5.
13. Robert Innes, "The Door Ajar: Japan's Foreign Trade in the Seventeenth Century" (doctoral dissertation, University of Michigan, 1980), 78–79.
14. For a general overview of piracy from a Chinese perspective, see James Geiss' article "The Chia-Ching reign, 1522–1566," in *The Cambridge History of China, Vol. 7: The Ming Dynasty, 1368–1644, Part I*, 490–505, ed. Frederick Mote and Denis Twitchet. See also Kwan-wai So, *Japanese Piracy in Ming China During the Sixteenth Century* (Lansing: 1975) and Jurgis Elisonas, "The Inseparable Trinity," 235–300.
15. Phillip Curtin, *Cross Cultural Trade in World History* (Cambridge: Cambridge University Press, 1984), 167.
16. Certainly early Japanese piracy was associated with coastal raids and a good deal of violence. Benjamin Hazard, in his study of the early *wakō* notes that in the thirteenth century, Japanese attacks on the Korean coast became somewhat endemic and coincided with a condition of semiautonomy in Kyushu and a general condition of famine in the region. The so-called "new men" in Kyushu were interested in trade with Korea, and when the Koreans did not respond favorably, they resorted to raids on coastal villages. Later piracy, however, while still retaining an element of violence, also included illicit trade activities as defined by the Ming maritime prohibitions. For early Japanese piracy see Benjamin Hazard, "The Formative Years of the Wako, 1223–63," *Monumenta Nipponica* 22: 3–4 (1967). For an exhaustive treatment of the subject, see Ishihara Michihiro, *Nihon Rekishi Sōsho 7: Wakō* (Tokyo: Yoshikawa Kōbunkan, 1964).

17. According to Nakamura Tadashi, after the Ming emperor renewed enforcement of the maritime bans, there were three such places at which Chinese and Japanese could meet: Taiwan, Luzon, and Cochin. See Nakamura Tadashi, "Taiwan wo Meguru Nichi-Ran Kankei," in *Shuinsen to Minami e no Senkisha*, ed. Ōishi Shinzaburō (Tokyo: Gyōsei, 1986), 78–79.
18. Jacques Gernet notes that the *wakō* were in fact a very mixed group of Japanese, Chinese, Koreans, and other Asian peoples. He also states that "piracy" was rife all along the coast of China because the potential profits were so high, and it was impossible to effectively patrol the more than 3,000 miles of Chinese coastline. See Jacques Gernet, *A History of Chinese Civilization* (Cambridge: Cambridge University Press, 1982), 417–422.
19. James Geiss, "The Chia-Ching Reign, 1522–1566," 490.
20. Emperor Jingtai (1450–56), in the mid-fifteenth century, issued trade permits (called *kangō*) to tributary states. Any ships trading without these official documents were treated as pirates. See Nagazumi, *Shuinsen*, 6.
21. For a good summary of Japanese piracy in the China Sea region, see Jurgis Elisonas, "The Inseparable Trinity," 235–300. For a brief discussion of Wang Chih, see pp. 249–250.
22. Michael Cooper, ed., *Joao Rodrigues's Account of Sixteenth-Century Japan* (London: The Hakluyt Society, 2001), 45.
23. Ibid., 2.
24. For a Ming official's account of the prevalence of *wakō* activity at this time, see Kōta, ed., *Shiryō ni yoru Nihon no Ayumi, Kinsei Hen, 20.*
25. Katō, "Bawansen, Shuinsen, Hōshosen," 125.
26. Iwano, "Filipin Bōeki to Tsukezaemon/Kiemon," 36.
27. Nagazumi Yōko states that for Hideyoshi, the issuance of *shuinjō* was a formal way to distinguish between legitimate trade and piracy. In the process, it also lent a degree of control to Hideyoshi over foreign affairs. See Nagazumi, "17 Seiki no Higashi Ajia Bōeki," in *Ajia Koekiken to Nihon Kōgyōka, 1500–1900,* ed. Kawakastu Heita and Hamashita Takeshi (Tokyo: Liburo, 1991), 103–128.
28. For an overview of this pre–Sekigahara activity, see Arano's *Edo Bakufu to Higashi Ajia*, 24–25. Interestingly, the author describes an order from Ieyasu to Uesugi Kagekatsu to make Korea send an official envoy to Japan. Failing this, Ieyasu indicated his intention to invade Korea yet again. This was apparently a rumor heard "directly from Kobayakawa Hideaki," but I can find no evidence of this threat in any official bakufu history.

29. Iwao, *Shuinsen Bōeki Shi no Kenkyū*, 52.
30. Nakamura Hidetaka also recognizes Ieyasu's efforts to establish peaceful relations with Korea in his use of the term "good neighbor policy." For a general overview of Japanese-Korean relations at this time, see his book entitled *Nissen Kankei Shi no Kenkyū, Volume II* (Tokyo: Yoshikawa Kōbunkan, 1969).
31. Fujii Jyōji, "Jyū Nana Seiki no Nihon-Buke no Kokka no Keisei," in *Iwanami Kōza Nihon Tsūshi 12: Kinsei 2*, ed. Asao Naohiro (Tokyo: Iwanami Shoten, 1993), 12.
32. There were in effect two types of *shuinjō.* One type was given to Japanese merchants who wanted to trade with a foreign country, which were ostensibly good for only a single voyage and were nontransferable. The second type, however, was broader in scope and was given to foreign merchants who wanted to come to Japan for trade. Examples of this type of permit include those given to the English and the Dutch, as well as those included in these letters to Southeast Asian countries.
33. Fujii Jōji, *Edo Kaifu* (Tokyo: Shūeisha, 1992), 128.
34. These attempts ultimately failed, and when in 1619 the Ming finally offered to restore relations, Hidetada refused! Toby ascribes this refusal to the fact that the bakufu was no longer as concerned with establishing its legitimacy (the Toyotomi were eradicated in 1615), but were rather more interested in moving the country from a Sino-centric worldview to a Japan-centered one. Furthermore, Chinese ships were calling in large numbers at Nagasaki, thereby obviating the need for commercial ties with the Ming. For a good overview of Tokugawa international politics and the question of legitimacy, see Toby, *The Early Tokugawa Bakufu*, and "Reopening the Question of Sakoku."
35. European trade with Japan was initially primarily in Chinese goods, so that it can plausibly be claimed that the majority of early foreign trade was "indirect trade" with China.
36. For a good overall survey of Japanese trade with the Ryukyu Islands, as well as two opposing views of its relations to the Japanese polity, see Sydney Crawcour, "Notes on Shipping and Trade in Japan and the Ryūkyūs," *The Journal of Asian Studies* 23: 3 (1964): 377–381, and Robert Sakai, "The Satsuma-Ryūkyū Trade and the Tokugawa Seclusion Policy," *The Journal of Asian Studies* 23: 3 (1964): 391–403.
37. Kawajima Genjirō, *Shuinsen Bōeki Shi* (Tokyo: Naigai Shuppan Kabushikigaisha, 1922), 167–169.
38. The Dutch maintained the fiction that Holland was a monarchy when, it fact, it was a republic in which the *Stadhouder* was essentially a first

among equals. Even though this position was unofficially hereditary (Maurice was the brother of the original *Stadhouder* William the Silent, later dubbed William I), a monarchy as such was not established until the early nineteenth century. For an original record of these and other letters, see Nakamura Tadashi's edited version of Sūden's *Ikoku Nikki.* This version is particularly helpful in that there is a detailed table of contents arranged by year with a brief description of each entry.

39. Murakami Naojirō has collected several letters, most of them between the Japanese and the Spanish in the Philippines, and published them in a volume entitled *Ikoku Ōfuku Skōkan Shū* (Tokyo: Omatsu-dō Shoten, 1966). For these two particular letters, see pp. 88–93.
40. In fact, Ieyasu was reluctant to allow any of the survivors of *De Liefde* to leave Japan. In December 1605, however, Melchior van Santvoort asked permission to leave the country, promising to bring the Dutch to Japan if he were allowed to travel to Patani. This petition was granted and serves to illustrate Ieyasu's interest in the Europeans as trading partners. See Dekker, *De Betrekkingen Tuschen de Oostindische Compagnie en Japan*, 8.
41. It must be remembered that the divide between Protestant and Catholic in Europe was an incredibly deep one. It is an irony of history that European powers were often more tolerant of Asian religions and customs than they were of each other's. For the Dutch and the Portuguese both, adherents to the wrong faith were criminals and heretics, often worthy of death (or worse). Therefore, Dutch participation in the Shimabara Rebellion (a rebellion that was widely perceived at the time as being Christian) was not entirely immoral in seventeenth century European terms because the Christians in question were "papists." Similarly, the English and Dutch felt no compunction about turning over captured priests to the bakufu, knowing full well that they would be tortured and executed.
42. For a comprehensive discussion of the origins of *shuinjō*, see Iwao Seiichi's *Shuinsen to Nihonmachi*, a treatment of Japanese activity overseas in the early Tokugawa period. Iwao notes that the permits issued by the Muromachi bakufu were called *inpan*, and thus the ships were known as *inpansen*, p. 26.
43. Innes, *The Door Ajar*, 116.
44. Nagazumi, *Shuinsen*, 6.
45. Om Prakash puts the matter very succinctly thus: "An extensive and sophisticated indigenous network of maritime trade considerably predated the arrival of the Europeans in Asia at the end of the 15th Century." See Om Prakash, "Trade in a Culturally Hostile Environment: Europeans

in the Japan Trade, 1550–1700," in *Clashes of Culture: Essays in Honor of Niels Steensgard*, ed. Christian Jens, et al., 50–79. (Odense, Odense University Press 1992).

46. Furber, *Rival Empires of Trade*, 26. "[The Portuguese] had determined that they could not exercise control over the Asian country trade without the use of *cartazes*—licenses or passes which country captains must carry to exempt their ships from seizure, and which nearly always obligated them to pay customs duties at a Portuguese port in the course of a voyage." One suspects that this was not only a system designed to make a profit on trade that would have occurred anyway, but also a way to justify Portuguese attacks on ships that did not carry such permits.
47. It was perhaps because the Dutch were able to exploit the "country trade" in a way that none of the other Europeans had done that this system of permits was less important and less extensive for them.
48. The primary source for the *shuinjō is* Sūden's *Ikoku Nikki*, but another accessible source is the *Tokugawa Jikki.* From Keichō 5 to Keichō 10 (1600–1605), the issuance of *shuinjō* to various countries and individuals occupied a prominent position in this official bakufu history. See KTTJ, Vol. 38, 369–402.
49. An example of an application for a *shuinjō* is found in the *Tokugawa Jikki* on Keichō 8/8/2. On this date, Matsuura Shigenobu received a *shuinjō* from the bakufu after having requested one from the *rōjū* previously. The issuance of these permits was painstakingly detailed in both the *Edo Bakufu Nikki* as well as the *Tokugawa Jikki*, a telling indication of their importance. See KTTJ, Vol. 38, 386.
50. Iwao, *Shuinsen Bōeki Shi no Kenkyū*, 127.
51. Iwao Seiichi, "Shuinsen Boeki-ke no Seikaku," in *Ronshū Bakuhan Taisei Shi 8: Taigai Kankei to Sakoku*, ed. Fujino Tamotsu (Tokyo: Yūzankaku, 1995), 15.
52. Kawajima, *Shuinsen Bōeki Shi*, 94. The author also provides a detailed list of who received *shuinjō*, the date of their issuance, and the destination for which they were issued. See pp. 75–92.
53. Coolhaas, ed., *Generalle Missiven, Deel I*, 314.
54. Leonard Blussé, M. E. van Opstall, and Ts'ao Yung-Ho, eds., De *Dagregisters van het Kasteel Zeelandia, Taiwan, Deel I, 1629–1641* ('s-Gravenhage: Martinus Nijhoff, 1986), 90. Hereafter DKZT.
55. Ibid., 173.
56. The Dutch issued an edict to the natives on Formosa in which the sale of deerskins to the Japanese, even if they possessed a legitimate *shuinjō*, was forbidden. See DKZT, Deel I, 194.

57. The *Ikoku Nikki*, along with the name of the person requesting the *shuinjō,* also records the name of the official issuing it as well as other information such as the proposed destination. Although the names of Honda and Hasegawa appear quite frequently in this capacity, other names such as Itakura Katsushige also appear with some regularity. The lowest rank official able to approve a request was that of Nagasaki *bugyō*, demonstrating the seriousness with which the bakufu regarded the *shuinjō*. See Nakamura Tadashi's edited version of the *Ikoku Nikki*, which reproduces the original text in photographed form.
58. Iwao, *Shuinsen to Nihonmachi*, 30.
59. Innes, *The Door Ajar*, 108.
60. Zoku Gunsho Ruijū Kansei-kai, *Tōdaiki/Sunpuki* (Tokyo: Zoku Gunsho Ruiju Kansei-kai, 1995), 238.
61. Nakamura, ed., *Ikoku Nikki*, 1.
62. Sūden was not the first priest to serve in this capacity; two relatively well-known priests that served before him were Bukōji Jōtai (1548–1607) and Enkoji Genkitsu (1544–1612).
63. Iwao, "Shuinsen Bōeki-ke no Seikaku," 16.
64. For the process of preparing for a *shuinsen* voyage, see Iwao's essay "Shuinsen Bōeki Ke no Seikaku," 16–17.
65. Fujii, *Edo Kaibuki*, 133.
66. The most complete treatment of this phenomenon is probably Iwao's aforementioned essay. See endnote 159 for full citation.
67. Kawajima, *Shuinsen Bōeki-shi*, 148.
68. Iwao, *Shuinsen to Nihonmachi*, 30.
69. Iwao, "Shuinsen Boeki Ke no Seikaku," 20.
70. This was, incidentally, similar to the practice of the English East India Company which, contrary to VOC practice, rented ships rather than build their own.
71. Iwao, *Shuinsen Bōeki Shi no Kenkyū*, 328–338.
72. For a solid biography of Adams, including a rather detailed account of his five voyages while in Japan, see William Corr, *Adams the Pilot: The Life and Times of Captain William Adams, 1564–1620* (London: Japan Library, 1995), chapter XIV.
73. Kawajima, *Shuinsen Bōeki-shi*, 102–03.
74. Meilink-Roelofsz. notes that "Portuguese roteiros or sailing directions were translated into Japanese for the use of native helmsmen." See her *Asian Trade and European Influence*, 124. This journal also deals with Western technological innovations quite apart from the nautical

world. For example, Ikeda provides a detailed account of the rationale behind the Western Gregorian calendar.

75. According to Meilink-Roelofsz. and Charles Boxer, the Japanese government ordered all Japanese junks to have a Portuguese pilot on board. See Boxer, "Fildalgos in the Far East," 19, 101 and Meilink-Roelofsz., *Asian Trade and European Influence*, 124. I have not been able to find this order in any of the Japanese sources I have looked at, but considering the sheer volume of Hideyoshi's edicts, to say nothing of early Tokugawa decrees, this is perhaps not entirely surprising.
76. Innes, *The Door Ajar*, 98–99.
77. According to Derek Masarella, Cocks allowed this to occur in the hopes of fostering goodwill between the English and the Japanese on the company's second voyage to Ayuthia. In other cases, however, Cocks complained bitterly about the practice. See Masarella, *A World Elsewhere*, 157.
78. For a discussion of these practices with regard to the English, see C. J. Purnell, "The Log-Book of William Adams, 1614–19," *Transactions and Proceedings of the Japan Society* 13: 2 (1915).
79. Cocks often accuses Adams of preferring the Japanese (and what is worse the Dutch) over the English. Masarella, in *A World Elsewhere*, has shown that on the contrary, Adams performed loyal service to the English, often putting his own interests behind those of the company.
80. Curtin, *Cross Cultural Trade in World History*, 167.
81. Watanabe Yōgoro, *Kinsei Nihon Bōeki Ron no Tenkai, 1600–1866* (Tokyo: Bunka Shobo Hakubun-sha, 1978), 54.
82. For the most complete treatment of the *Nihonmachi*, including brief overviews of each major settlement, see Iwao's *Shuinsen to Nihonmachi.* References to Japanese living overseas can also be gleaned from the huge number of Dutch sources found in the VOC archives in den Hague. Published *dagregisters* include those kept at Batavia, Taiwan, Hirado, and Deshima, and a published version of the *Generalle Missiven* also has many references to Japanese living in areas throughout Asia.
83. According to Iwao, a Japanese merchant from Kyoto was even living as far away as Surat in India. Iwao Seiichi, *Kinsei ni okeru Nihonjin no Nanyō Hatten* (Tokyo: Keimeikai/Hatsubaijō Hokuryōkan, 1941), 21.
84. Arano Yasunori notes that the head of the *nihonmachi* was called a *shahbandar,* from a Persian word meaning an official in charge of a port. See *Edo Bakufu to Higashi Ajia*, 83.
85. Ibid., 83.
86. In 1580, Governor Ronquillo de Penalos wrote from Manila that there were several Japanese "pirate ships" at Luzon, and several more were

expected to arrive. Another Spanish observer of the time also noted that the Japanese were much more war-like than the Chinese, and that this led the Spanish and Japanese into conflict on several occasions. See Katō, "Bawan, Shuinsen, Hōshosen," 127.

87. Iwano, "Filipin Bōeki to Sukezaemon/Kiemon," 36.
88. Iwao, *Shuinsen to Nihonmachi*, 111–12.
89. The Japanese community at Ayuthia was able to exploit tensions that had arisen between the Siamese and the Chinese during the 1620s. As a result, Siam became the most profitable commercial destination for Japanese *shuinsen* merchants. See Curtin, *Cross Cultural Trade in World History*, 167–68.
90. Nagazumi Yōko, "Yamada Nagamasa—Shijitsu to Densetsu," in *Nihon Rekishi 9: Shuinsen to Minami e no Senkisha*, ed. Ōishi Shinzaburō (Tokyo: Gyōsei, 1986), 48–49.
91. One major reason why trade between Siam and Japan flourished was that many of the most sought after luxury goods could be found in Siam. These included deerskins, sharkskins, elephant tusks, and a whole host of other luxury goods that found a ready market in Japan. For a more detailed analysis of the role of Asian goods in Japanese trade patterns, see chapter 5.
92. Nagazumi, *Shuinsen*, 106.
93. *Tōdaiki/Sunpuki*, 216: Keichō 16/8 (September, 1611).
94. Ibid., 226–239.
95. Hayashi Fukusai, *Tsūkō Ichiran, Vol. 7* (Tokyo: Kokusho Kankōkai 1967), 1–31. The letters that were exchanged between the shogun and the king of Siam are reproduced in this volume of Hayashi's nineteenth century compendium on foreign countries.
96. Iwano, "Filipin Bōeki to Sukezaemon/Kiemon," 51.
97. Ibid., 60.
98. Nagazumi, *Shuinsen*, 60.
99. For a discussion of the attempt to revive Siamese-Japanese relations, see Professor Iwao's still quite relevant "Taijin no Tai Nikkoku Bōeki Hukkatsu Undō," *Tō-A Ronsō* 4: 85 (1941).
100. Whether the Japanese government knew that these ships were coming from Siam cannot be determined with any certainty, although the Dutch were certainly aware of it and would most likely have made it known to the bakufu. For a more detailed account of the Siamese-Japanese "trade by proxy," see E. M. Satow, "Notes on the Intercourse Between Japan and Siam in the Seventeenth Century," *Transactions of the Asiatic Society of Japan* 13 (1885): 139–210.

101. Sarasin Viraphol, *Tribute and Profit: Sino-Siamese Trade, 1652–1853* (Cambridge: Council for East Asian Studies and Harvard University Press, 1977), 59.
102. Arano Yasunori states that one of the main reasons the bakufu adopted the *shuinsen* system was so that, if Japanese vessels without the shogunal permits were attacked, it would be able to absolve itself of all responsibility for those ships. Therefore, the shogun would be able to avoid embroiling himself in the many petty conflicts that inevitably arose in the course of foreign commerce. Put simply (and somewhat self-evidently), Arano states that the *shuinjō* "protected those that had them, and did not protect those who did not." See *Edo Bakufu to Higashi Ajia*, 28.
103. Quoted in Blair and Robertson, eds., *The Philippine Islands, Vol. 18*, 228–230.
104. Masarella, *A World Elsewhere*, 299.
105. Katō, "Bawansen, Shuinsen, Hoshosen," 132.
106. King Sebastian of Portugal died at the Battle of Alcazarquivir on August 4, 1578, leaving a vacant throne with no real heirs. After a short regency by the king's rather aged uncle (a cardinal in the Catholic Church), Phillip II of Spain was judged to have the strongest claim to the throne, since his mother was Empress Isabella of Portugal. In April of 1581, therefore, Phillip was proclaimed King of Portugal, although his rights as such were vastly curtailed. In the words of J. H. Elliot, "although the Iberian Peninsula was now at last formally united beneath a single monarch, Portugal remained, even more than Aragon or Catalonia, a semi-independent state, associated with, but not incorporated into, the Crown of Castile." See J. H. Elliot, *Europe Divided, 1559–1598* (Oxford: Blackwell Publishers, 1968), 186–189.
107. To be fair it was extremely difficult, if not impossible, for Europeans of the time to understand the complex governing structure of Japan. Europeans consistently regarded the shogun as the "emperor" and the emperor as the "pope." This is not even taking into account the added confusion of shoguns and emperors abdicating in favor of their sons, yet still exercising influence behind the scenes. In my experience, this system of governing dynamics far surpassed any complexities that arose in a contemporary European government!
108. Coincidentally, this occurred at the same time that Dutch shipping was suspended as a result of the Nuijts affair on Taiwan; see chapter 5.
109. This change in procedure did not mean that the shogun's permission was no longer necessary, but rather that the councilors now exercised a degree of control (and thus responsibility) that was lacking previously. Nicholas Couckebacker, the head of the Dutch factory at Hirado,

noted this change in procedure in 1631 in his diary; see Nagazumi Yoko, trans., *Hirado Oranda Shokan no Nikki, Vol. 2* (Tokyo: Iwanami Shoten, 1969), 551.

110. Katō, "Bawan, Shuinsen, Hoshosen," 132. For the shogunal edict regarding the new requirement of a *hōsho,* see KTTJ, Vol. 39, 516: Kan'ei 8/6/20 (July 19, 1631).
111. Innes, *The Door Ajar*, 137.
112. Iwao, *Shuinsen Bōeki Shi no Kenkyū*, 362–63.
113. Even though the events here were more than three decades removed from the Battle of Sekigahara, the memory of powerful western daimyo arrayed against the Tokugawa was still quite strong, and the fact that both foreign commerce and Christianity were most prevalent in these very western domains certainly heightened bakufu fears.
114. The "Hirayama incident," as this event came to be known, will be dealt with more fully in chapter 6.
115. Iwao, *Shuinsen Bōeki Shi no Kenkyū*, 378.
116. Nicholas Couckebacker noted this decree in his diary for May 7, 1634. See NKKS, Vol. I, 107.
117. For a detailed analysis of the Nuijts affair, see chapter 5.
118. Iwao, *Shuinsen Bōeki Shi no Kenkyū*, 382.
119. Although neither Dutch nor Japanese sources spell this last point out precisely, the bakufu consciously rejected Suetsugu's proposal to take over Taiwan. Nor was his demand that the Dutch hand over the island to the Japanese taken seriously by Edo. For a more detailed description of these proceedings, see chapter 5, concerning the role of Taiwan in Japanese-Asian trade.
120. NKKS, Vol. I, 107.
121. Ibid., 107.
122. Katō, "Bawan, Shuinsen, Hōshosen," 131.
123. The texts of all five versions of the *sakoku* edicts can be found in Ishii Ryosuke's edited set entitled *Tokugawa Kinrei-kō.* See especially the last chapter of volume six, chapter 67, dealing with regulations concerning commerce inside of and outside of Japan. Ishii Ryosuke, ed., *Tokugawa Kinrei Ko, Volume 6* (Tokyo: Kurobunsha, 1960), 365–439. All translations are the author's unless otherwise stated.
124. This edict can also be found in KTTJ, Vol. 39, 590: Kan'ei 10/2/28 (April 6, 1633).
125. According to Robert Innes, "The abolition of the *shuinsen* did not imply the Tokugawa had decided to reduce the volume of Japan's foreign trade with other countries. It was a decision to entrust the conduct of the nation's external commerce to merchants and shippers who

posed no challenge to the evolving social and political system rather than a decision to limit the quantity or value of the trade with the outside world." See *The Door Ajar*, 156.

126. Toby, The *Early Tokugawa Bakufu and Seventeenth Century Japanese Relations with East Asia.* See also his article, "Reopening the Question of Sakoku," and Kazui and Downing–Videen, "Foreign Relations During the Edo Period: Sakoku Re-examined."
127. Elisonas, "Christianity and the Daimyo," 301.
128. Elisonas notes that, "With the contiguous territories of Ōmura, Arima, and Amakusa converted, a Christian bloc seemed to be coming into existence in the 'Shimo' mission area." He continues, "under [Arima Harunobu's] patronage, Takaku developed into a solidly Christian region, one where the practice of the Christian faith continued, resisting extinction to the uttermost, even after being driven underground by the general persecution pursued in earnest by the Tokugawa regime after 1614." Ibid., 335.
129. Watanabe, *Kinsei Nihon Bōeki Ron*, 89.
130. Francisco Sanda was the pilot of a Spanish vessel named the *San Felipe* that was wrecked off the coast of Tosa, at a place called Urado. In a boast to local authorities, he claimed that Spanish policy was to use Christian missionaries to gain the trust of the local population before invading and colonizing. Although the story is generally regarded as true, there seem to be no extant contemporary records of this claim. For a fuller account of this event, as well as bakufu fears of the Spanish "colonization policy," see Iwao, "Sakoku," 113–158.
131. Iwao, *Shuinsen Bōeki Shi no Kenkyū*, 379.
132. A final consideration as to why the bakufu chose to suspend Japanese trade abroad is purely pragmatic. The Dutch had finally, after more than two decades of trying to break into the Chinese market, found a source of raw silk on Taiwan and in Tonkin. Therefore, with the Dutch, Portuguese, and Chinese all importing silk and luxury goods from Southeast Asia, Japan was well supplied. Furthermore, the scale of *shuinsen* trade on the eve of its abolition was quite small, with only seven families allowed (and probably able) to trade abroad. With the suspension of Japanese foreign trade, there was no shortage of foreign goods, nor were those families still trading with Southeast Asia hit particularly hard, although to be sure, they lobbied for the renewal of their former privileges until the 1650s. Therefore, along with theoretical considerations of power and legitimacy must be considered the purely practical as well.

Chapter 3

"Bones of the Earth": The Role of Silver in Japan's Foreign Trade, 1600–1668

John Locke wrote that gold and silver, "being little useful to the life of man, in proportion to food, raiment, and carriage has its value only from the consort of men."[1] Silver, however, was not merely *useful* for early European trade in Asia, but was rather of the highest necessity. As several scholars have pointed out, Europe suffered a severe and chronic deficit in the balance of trade with Asia that could only be remedied by the large-scale transfer of precious metals. Therefore, the sixteenth through the nineteenth centuries, beginning with the Spanish and Portuguese encroachment into the commercial world of maritime Asia, represents a period characterized by a steady flow of silver from Europe and the New World to Asia. This period was also witness to the profound impact that Japanese silver had on the international economy. Japan's role in the Asian economy, in particular, a role characterized by the large scale export of silver in return for a variety of exotic, value-laden goods from throughout Asia, has been largely overshadowed by the numerous studies concerning the European expansion into Asia. By overlooking the role of Japanese silver in the economy of Asia, however, we miss an extremely important aspect of the Asian economy in the seventeenth century.

Among the early European trading ventures in Asia, the Dutch East India Company enjoyed the greatest success insofar as it was remarkably adept at exploiting the "country trade." This meant that as far as possible, the company tried to become self-sufficient by using Asian resources to procure Asian goods. It was the dream of Governor-General Jan Pieterszoon Coen, for example, to eliminate shipments of precious metals from Europe altogether, and to use capital procured locally to finance the various factories scattered throughout Asia. This vision, while never fully realized, seemed to be within reach when the VOC established a factory in Japan in the early years of the seventeenth century. While initially not very successful, by the 1630s, company agents in Hirado were shipping silver out of Japan literally by the ton. This silver was in turn used to finance a large part of company operations throughout the Indian Ocean. In fact, for a few brief decades in the mid-seventeenth century, one can argue convincingly that the company's Asian enterprises were being maintained largely by exports of Japanese precious metals. Peter Rietbergen describes the function of the factory at Hirado succinctly: "In short, Japan offered a solution for many of the most structural problems that the company confronted in Asia."[2]

It is hard to overstate the role of Japan in the economy of Asia during the seventeenth century. Because the landed aristocracy was increasingly divorced from the means of production and became more or less an urban elite, the samurai, at least those in the upper stratum, had the time and the resources to devote to the purchase of luxury goods that were imported from throughout Asia. Furthermore, with the rise of a powerful merchant class that coincided with increasing urbanization and the large-scale need of converting rice into money, capital in large amounts became available for investment in overseas ventures. And finally, the very existence of huge quantities of liquid capital, mainly in the form of silver and copper extracted from Japan's rich mines, made it almost inevitable that Japan would play a leading role in the Asian economy, both through its own merchants and those of various foreign powers. Hayami Akira in fact has labelled the period 1570–1630 as a decisive transformation in Japan towards "modernity," stating that society became increasingly unified, urbanized, and commercialised, and that there was also established the beginnings of a capitalist system of nationwide markets.[3] Dennis Flynn likewise argues that with the establishment of Tokugawa hegemony, the shogun allied himself with the merchant class in an effort to invest heavily in areas such as "agricultural and urban infrastructure." The result, according to Flynn, was an "indigenous, market based economy" that would effect economic repercussions throughout the region.[4]

Undoubtedly the most pronounced effect that Japan had on the Asian economy was the sheer quantity of silver produced and exported in the sixteenth and seventeenth centuries. Joao Rodrigues tells us that:

> [t]he land of Japan yields every sort of metal and there are many mines producing, for example, a great deal of iron, copper (mixed with silver), lead, tin, and a little mercury. The principle mines are those of silver and may be found throughout the country. Such mines are situated in Kanayama in Chūgoku, in the kingdom of Iwai, on the island of Sado in the northern sea, and in many other places. They say that the method of extracting the silver from the mines is not very ancient and that they began this for the first time in the city of Hakata not many years ago. But now experience has made them very skilful and much silver is used throughout the kingdom…All the nobles now possess goodly treasures of gold and silver. In the year 1609, while we were at Daifu's court at Suruga, his principal treasurer made a count of all his hoard, and there were 83 million taels of silver alone, let alone the great store of gold…There are also gold mines. Some of them are in the mountains, where they extract gold mixed with silver and separate it by using mercury. Some if it is extracted from the mines as gold dust, and some is obtained as very thin

> dust from the mud of the riverbeds, and this is the best source of all. The biggest supply of gold is found in the kingdom of Ōshu in Kantō.[5]

The figures for silver production are staggering, and in fact, at its height rivalled the output of the great silver mines of the New World. In his celebrated journal *Itinerario*, Jan Huygen van Linschotten, a "Hollander" in the employ of the Portuguese, recorded that Japan exported nothing but silver, and that the Portuguese made a tremendous profit from the trade between Japan and Macao.[6] It is largely because of people such as Linschotten who worked with the Portuguese in Asia and witnessed their commercial success in Japan that the Dutch sought out Japan in the first place. The profits that the Dutch eventually came to enjoy upon tapping into this source of wealth led them to take every precaution in dealing with the Japanese authorities, so as not to disrupt their favorable position. The story of the VOC and its relationship with Japan, therefore, is one that can aptly be considered from the viewpoint of precious metals. This chapter will therefore attempt to outline the conditions within and outside of Japan that led that country to become the foremost silver-producing country in Asia, and indeed one of the foremost producers in the world. This chapter will also deal with the effects that Japanese silver had on Asian and world trade for the better part of the seventeenth century. And finally, we will address the special role of the Dutch East India Company in Japan with regard to precious metals and VOC distribution of those metals throughout Asia.

THE SILVER REVOLUTION IN JAPAN

The powerful Mōri daimyo, when giving instructions to his vassals concerning the operation of the silver mines in the Iwami province, had the following paternal advice to give: "When there is a disturbance at the silver mine, do not hesitate to use bows and arrows."[7] Regardless of the social conditions of Sengoku Japan that this quote may bring to light, it is an indication of how important silver was in Japanese society both during the Warring States period and in the subsequent Tokugawa peace.[8] That role cannot be overstated in examining these turbulent times in Japanese history, and indeed the development and use of precious metals contributed to profound changes that would affect literally all aspects of society.

During the late Warring States period, the production of silver was very much a concern of the various powerful daimyo. Most of the major contenders for supremacy within Japan had already opened several mines within their provinces and had carefully provided for their exploitation. The mines soon became a source of major contention between daimyo as they played out their military chess match for control over ever more territory. The famous Iwami silver mine, for example, was first in the possession of the Ōuchi family before being seized by the Mōri; the Ikuno mine was in the possession of the Yamana family before being taken by Nobunaga; and the mines on Sado Island were originally controlled by the Uesugi family before being ceded to the Tokugawa after the Battle of Sekigahara. In each of these cases, the daimyo involved placed great emphasis on the exploitation of the mines in order to strengthen the economies of their respective provinces. Sugimoto and Swain, in their treatise on scientific advances in pre-Meiji times, state that the technological innovation necessary for productive mining was a direct result of daimyo patronage of the merchant class, especially those merchants who had the opportunity to come into contact with the foreigners then in Japan.[9] The development of a mining industry, therefore, was not only a concern of the military leaders, but was also recognized as a source of influence and advancement by the powerful merchant families.

One of the most illustrative examples of daimyo emphasis on silver can be seen in the rivalry between two of the most powerful sengoku warriors, Takeda Shingen and Uesugi Kenshin. Both daimyo were involved in repeated, extended military campaigns, more often than not against each other. In order to support these campaigns, they sought to open and develop a number of mines that had recently been discovered within their provinces. The Ueda silver mine was discovered in 1551 (Tenmon 19) and was immediately exploited by the

Uesugi, while the Takeda likewise opened up a number of mines in the provinces of Kai, Shinano, and Suruga. In fact, upon Shingen's death, his *daikan* in Suruga presented his son-in-law and heir with 2,000 pieces of gold that were in the domainal treasury. Furthermore, Shingen used this newfound silver to purchase weapons and provisions necessary for the maintenance of his armies. He also presented rewards to his officers in the form of gold and silver, in lieu of the more traditional grants of land. An unintended side effect of an emphasis on precious metals was that a cash-based economy rapidly developed within the provinces of the daimyo who were able to effectively exploit silver and gold mines.[10]

Hideyoshi recognized very early on the value that gold and silver had in terms of military success. When attacking the powerful Shimazu family of Kyushu in 1587, his army used twelve horses to transport the precious metals needed for the purchase of supplies. Similarly, when attacking the Odawara in northern Japan, Nakatsu Masaie, *bugyō* of supplies for Hideyoshi's armies, took 10,000 bars of gold to cover the expenditures of military provisions. Furthermore, when attacking the Mōri, one of the foremost goals of the campaign was to capture the rich silver mines in Iwami province.[11] Silver and gold were also of great importance during Hideyoshi's attempted invasion of Korea in the 1590s; the Japanese armies carried with them a considerable amount of precious metal for use in acquiring supplies for the troops as well as for gifts to the opposing generals during negotiations.[12] Finally, Hideyoshi was not only a unifier in a territorial sense, but also in an economic sense. His extensive land surveys, of course, are well documented, but he also organized the mines of the various provinces by placing them under his own personal authority and by assigning *bugyō* for the supervision of each of them.[13]

No one was more precocious in recognizing the potential of silver mining, nor more assiduous in its control, however, than Tokugawa Ieyasu. As early as 1573, he laid out in striking detail his policy regarding the mining of precious metals in a tract entitled *Yama no Rei Gojyūsan Ka-jyō* (a fifty-three article directive concerning mountains).[14] This document is an exhaustive treatment of mining policy, including directives concerning the administration of individual mines, the employment of mine workers, and an especially heavy emphasis on the use of mining specialists. Article 48, for instance, states that in order to produce as much metal as possible, the operator of the mine must employ various artisans such as ore locators, trench diggers, and those with a detailed knowledge of smelting techniques. These directives illustrate the far-sightedness of Ieyasu's policies by devoting such detail to the issue of precious metal production, policies that would help to transform Japan's economy in the subsequent Edo period. Underlying Ieyasu's mining code is naturally the fundamental premise of Tokugawa control. From very early on, Ieyasu went to great lengths to create an orderly society in his provinces and to rationalize the economy within them. One can see in directives such as the one previously discussed that Ieyasu and his successors were obsessed with control; later codes regulating literally every aspect of life—the *Buke Shohatto*, *Kuge Shohatto*, and the *Ji'in Shohatto* (codes of conduct for the samurai, the courtiers, and the priesthood respectively)—are well known. This early document demonstrating Ieyasu's economic awareness and ambition is simply one more example of Tokugawa attention to detail and concern with the control of Japanese society in all its aspects: social, political, economic, and religious.

There were many conditions within and outside of Japan that allowed the production of silver to skyrocket in the second half of the sixteenth century. Advances in almost every aspect of mining occurred, from the accurate locating of rich veins to the smelting of the ores that were discovered. In the case of the latter, technical knowledge from China and Europe was of prime importance and was adapted to particular Japanese circumstances by a few enterprising individuals. With the help of these new mining techniques, nationwide production of silver increased, setting off one of the most spectacular periods of economic growth in premodern Japan. Iwao Seiichi maintains that by the beginning of Japan's early modern period, there were forty silver and sixty gold mines operating in

Japan, an economic reality that would have a significant impact on the ensuing Edo period.[15]

In 1533, a Hakata merchant by the name of Kamiya Jūtei returned from a trip to China and immediately set about using a new method of smelting silver that he had learned on the continent. Termed the *haibukihō*, or the "ash-blowing method," this process of separating silver from copper ore was to prove a great boon for increasing silver supplies within Japan.[16] Until the advent of this technique, the primary means of obtaining silver from ore was a method known as "density refining," in which the raw ore was placed in a type of sieve and washed thoroughly with water. Because silver is a rather heavy element, it would stay in the sieve (called a *zaruage*) while other extraneous particles were washed out of the compound. This device was later elaborated into a machine called the "shaking table," which consisted of a box, one end of which was left open. The compound was placed in the box and the whole machine was continuously shaken back and forth, whereupon the lighter particles exited at the open end while the heavier particles gathered at the opposite, closed end. The remaining substance was then removed and shaken through a straw mat called a *neko*. The silver and gold particles were caught in the "eyes" of the mat while the unwanted material simply passed through unhindered.[17]

With the new "ash-blowing" technique imported from China, however, a much more efficient and productive system for obtaining pure silver from copper ore came to be used. In order to extract the copper, the ore was heated to its molten state and lead added to the compound. The function of the lead was to absorb the copper, which cooled into a layer of ash, leaving only silver beneath when the compound was cooled. All that remained was to "blow" away the ashes on top to yield the desired metal.[18] This method was originally used to great effect at the Iwami silver mine, but within a few years it had spread to most of the other great mines and helped to make Japan one of the most productive silver producing regions in the world.

Another method of smelting ore that became popular in the mid-sixteenth century was the amalgam method in which mercury was used to separate gold and silver from an impure compound. Japanese craftsmen and merchants almost certainly learned this process from the Spanish and Portuguese, especially considering that the amalgam method was first developed and used extensively in the silver mines of Mexico and Peru and that the Japanese came into regular contact with the Iberians at this time.[19] When liquid mercury is added to a compound containing either gold or silver, the mercury binds with the impurities, leaving the precious metals free. The compound is then heated so that the mercury evaporates, leaving only the silver and gold.[20] A rather indirect measure of how widespread this method had become in the course of the late sixteenth and early seventeenth centuries is the amount of mercury imported on Dutch ships. In the daily records of commercial activity kept in the Dutch East India Company's office on Taiwan, a number of entries dealing with often-large shipments of mercury to Japan appear. On July 17, 1639, for example, the Dutch ship *De Roch* left Taiwan for Japan with forty-eight cases of mercury.[21] As mercury was of little use in such quantities for anything but the production of silver, we may surmise that the VOC was in fact supplying the means for the Japanese to produce the silver that was vital to their trade. The same is true for lead: huge shipments were often imported into Japan so that silver could be produced in a large enough quantity to support Japan's precious metal-driven trade.

With the increased emphasis on mining production of the new Tokugawa regime, a new class of specialist arose to facilitate the demand for precious metals. Generally lumped together into the category of *yamashi*, or "mountain masters," these artisans in fact spanned a wide range of specialties, each concerned with a particular technological aspect of mining.[22] Again, it was Ieyasu who first placed such an emphasis on these artisans in his fifty-three article injunction on mining. Article 48 exhorts the overseers of mines to pay special heed to the value of skilful workers, as doing so will lead to increased productivity.[23] Okubo Nagayasu, Ieyasu's choice as overseer of the famous Iwami mine, took this advice to heart and was rewarded lavishly for his efforts.

Nagayasu was originally in the employ of the Takeda family when, in 1601, he swore allegiance to Ieyasu, who appointed him to the post of *bugyō* of the Iwami silver mine. Upon receiving this commission, he appointed a *yamashi* by the name of Yasuwara Inkin to take charge of the technical aspects of mining operations. Because of Yasuwara's great expertise, Iwami's production of silver rose rapidly to 3,600 *kan* per year, a huge increase over previous years.[24] According to the *Tokugawa Jikki*, Nagayasu was rewarded handsomely by Ieyasu because of his success, and in 1603 (Keichō 8) was additionally granted the supervision of the gold and silver mines on Sado Island.[25] Because of Ieyasu's emphasis on entrusting the technological aspects of mining to specialists, the output at mines across the country skyrocketed at the beginning of the seventeenth century, leading to a huge increase in Tokugawa family fortunes. At Ieyasu's death, for example, there were 1,930,000 *ryō* of precious metals in the shogunal treasury and several active mines that were producing 160,000 *ryō* annually.[26]

The three major areas in which technological advances in mining were especially pronounced seem rather primitive today, but were in fact huge leaps that allowed for vastly increased production of precious metals. These were the digging of mineshafts, the controlling of the water that invariably flooded into a mine when it reached a certain depth, and the creation of enough light to work by without the production of noxious fumes from the torches that characterized earlier lighting techniques. The first innovation dealt with the method of digging mine shafts into a deposit of ore. The method of choice in former times was simply to dig horizontal trenches along more or less exposed veins near the surface, effectively ignoring the ore below. With the rise of the new specialists and an increased awareness of mine surveying in order to locate probable concentrations of ore, however, shafts were now drilled systematically into the vein so as to maximize the potential of the mine.[27] Because of this new innovation in digging shafts, an individual mine could be worked for much longer and far more systematically, thus driving up overall production.

The second problem was that when digging large tunnels, especially in a region with a relatively high water table such as Japan, there was a constant encroachment of water into the tunnels. To combat this nuisance, workers dug drainage tunnels, allowing the water to escape to a reservoir located at some distance from the mine. The digging of these tunnels often involved cutting through considerable distances of solid rock. In 1633, for example, a trench measuring 2,880 *shaku* in length was dug from the mine to a nearby reservoir.[28] As time went on, a type of Archimedean pump came into use that was more time- and labor-efficient and that allowed miners to mechanically pump water out of the shaft to the surface. This new type of pump was essentially a screw made of bamboo that was placed within a tube wider at the bottom than it was at the top. As the screw was rotated, pockets of water were lifted along the screw's length until eventually coming to the surface, where the water was channeled via a drainage trench into a reservoir.[29]

Along with improved methods of dealing with water, improvements in ventilation also contributed to increased productivity. In the days before electrical lighting, the only alternative was to use some sort of flame, an alternative that invariably produced both smoke and noxious fumes. In order to deal with this problem, the use of secondary shafts was employed. As in the case of drainage, miners would dig a number of secondary shafts along the depth of the main mine to draw off the smoke and fumes from the torches. Moreover, a new method of lighting was introduced in which oil was burned in lieu of the age-old bamboo torch, which gave off a tremendous amount of smoke. Miners would place a quantity of oil in an open container such as a shell and light it. The burning oil yielded a steady, long-lasting source of light that produced far less smoke than torches did.[30]

The new technologies associated with the cutting of drainage and ventilation shafts gradually came to be incorporated into other aspects of Tokugawa society. For example, during Ieyasu's summer campaign against the Toyotomi forces in Osaka castle, we read in the *Tokugawa Jikki* that he ordered miners from the Iwami silver mine to come to Osaka in order to dig tunnels under the castle walls.[31] In all, over three hundred miners arrived from Iwami, a figure that in and of itself demonstrates the huge scale of mining activity during the early Edo period. Similarly, three days later Ieyasu ordered the workers at the Iwashū silver mine to bore through the walls of the castle in an effort to breach the almost impregnable Toyotomi defenses.[32] Likewise, technologies originally developed for mining came to be used in other contexts as well; the Archimedean screw, for example, came to be incorporated into the world of agriculture for improved irrigation methods.

With this brief analysis of the workings of Japanese silver mining, we now turn to an analysis of the amounts of silver produced in Japan. Before dealing with this question, however, it must be recognized that it is almost impossible to say with any great degree of precision the total quantity of any precious metal produced, especially before the beginning of the seventeenth century. With the arrival of the Portuguese and the Dutch, reliable records of how much silver left the country in their ships exist, but even at the height of European export, this represented only a fraction of the amount produced. Silver was also exported in great quantities to Korea via the island of Tsushima and large amounts were loaded illegally onto Chinese ships in return for their valuable cargoes of silk. Because this trade was, for a time, illegal in the eyes of both the Ming and Japanese authorities, there is no reliable account of how much silver was being smuggled into China, although the amount was undoubtedly considerable. In addition to all of these complications, the illegal private trade between Japanese merchants and ships from various locations throughout Southeast Asia must also be taken into account. Because of these unrecorded sources of the outflow of silver, it is difficult to say with any degree of certainty the total amount of silver Japan extracted from its mines; the best we can do is arrive at an educated guess using the sources available to us.

Fumoto Saburō states that between 1602 and 1868, the Sado silver mines alone produced a total of 1,781,178 kilograms of silver.[33] Fumoto is, however, reluctant to put forward a figure for before this date; but because from 1602 to 1614 the output was nearly 100,000 kilograms, it can probably be assumed that, given that the last decade of the sixteenth century was similar in terms of Japan's technological capacity and relative political stability, this period also saw a considerable output of silver. Kobata Atsushi has placed the total output of the Iwami silver mine from 1581 to 1706 at 2,080,498 kilograms of silver. However, this figure only represents the official quantity collected by first Hideyoshi and later the Tokugawa bakufu. Kobata recognizes that it was not unusual for the government to receive only one-fourth, or at best one-third, of the total output of a mine, so that the aforementioned figure would effectively have to be at least tripled to arrive at the true output of the Iwami mine.[34] Moreover, according to Iwao Seiichi, silver exports to China continued to rise throughout the seventeenth century, reaching its acme in 1661 at the staggering figure of 2.6 million *taels*. Kishimoto-Nakayama's research indicates in fact that China depended so heavily on the export of Japanese silver that its drastic reduction in the 1660s must be seen as a primary factor in the Kangxi depression of the 1660s and 1670s.[35] For a pre-Tokugawa period estimate of Japanese silver production, Nagahara Keiji and Yamamura Kozo believe that in the latter half of the sixteenth century, Japanese mines produced about 200,000 kilograms of silver, that is to say about one-third of all the silver produced in the world at that time.[36] When one considers that the silver mines of both Mexico and Peru were operational at the same time, it becomes apparent how significant Japan's silver production was to the world economy.

The Flow of Silver from West to East

Chinese demand for silver was insatiable. Because of a number of historical conditions that converged at the end of the sixteenth and the beginning of the seventeenth centuries, silver flowed steadily into the Asian continent from Europe, the New World, and Japan for over a century. There were two major reasons why this "silver river" flowed so unceasingly into East Asia, and into China in particular. First, in the words of K. N. Chaudhuri, "the export of treasure, when associated with the external trade of two politically and geographically separated regions [results in] the disparity in the price of precious metals in these respective areas."[37] In other words, a merchant in Europe could buy much less than a merchant in Asia with the same amount of silver because of the high value of silver in Asia relative to Europe. Rudolph Blitz, in his study of mercantilism, states the matter more precisely when he notes that the ratio of silver to gold in Spain was 16 to 1, in England 15 to 1, but in China 9 to 1, and that this fact provided a strong incentive to send silver abroad. The East India Companies, which had been formed in England and The United Provinces in 1600 and 1602 respectively, represented the most visible channel through which European silver was used to its maximum value in Asia.[38]

The second reason why silver naturally flowed from the West to Asia was the fact that there was a severe trade deficit between Europe and the East. As a noted Dutch merchant of the seventeenth century remarked, when trade is carried out with lands in which there is little interest for European (in this case Dutch) goods, the result is that precious metals must be used as the sole medium of exchange.[39] In this "balance of payment" theory, Europeans suffered a trade deficit with Asia because, while there was an extremely high demand in the West for Asian goods, there was very little demand in Asia for European goods beyond the "knickknacks" and "curiosos" that seemed to be in such demand in the East. In Asia as a whole, however, it was often possible to obtain desired local goods from one location by importing goods from another location that were in demand. The Dutch, for example, were able to obtain much of the spices they needed by exchanging cloth goods from India in the Spice Islands. In this way, the VOC was able to lessen its dependence on large shipments of precious metals from Europe by tapping into the complex "country trade" that had characterized the Asian economic world for centuries. One area in which silver remained extremely important for the Dutch, however, was in trade with Chinese merchants; and it was this consideration that made a sustained trade with Japan, with its abundant supply of precious metals and craving for Chinese goods, so important.

Because the Chinese had a well-established tradition of overseas commercial relations, it was not uncommon to find Chinese junks in various Southeast Asian ports from very early on. These merchants also became frequent visitors at Batavia, Manila, and the various harbors in Kyushu. The considerable Chinese presence in ports across Southeast Asia meant that Chinese demand for goods from these areas were satisfied largely by their own merchants, effectively eliminating the need for the Portuguese and Dutch to import spices, cloth, and the like. Silver, however, was a different matter. Even though Chinese junks were continuously importing a tremendous quantity of the precious metal to the mainland, the demand never seemed to be exhausted. Therefore, the Iberian powers, and in time the Dutch and English as well, found a ready market for silver when they traded with Chinese merchants, a commodity they eagerly traded for valuable porcelain and silk products. In 1615, for example, of the total value of merchandise sent to Asia from Holland aboard VOC ships, silver accounted for 94 percent of the entire cargo.[40] This situation was to be drastically altered when the company was finally able to tap into the precious metal-driven markets of Japan.

The silver that was so essential for European commerce in the East and that supported the Spanish, Portuguese, and Dutch commercial empires found its way to Asia through three main routes. Silver flowed first and foremost from the Spanish mines of Mexico (Nova España) and Peru across the Atlantic to Seville before being shipped through the major commercial centers of Europe to European trading factories in Asia. Another channel was for silver to be carried in Spanish galleons directly from Acapulco in Mexico to the Philippines, and from Manila on to China. Finally, the third route by which silver found its way to the Asian continent was in Japanese, Portuguese, Chinese, or Dutch ships leaving Japan. This silver was obtained in exchange for a variety of Asian goods brought to Japan for the express purpose of procuring silver from the islands. A common feature of all three major routes was that they all led either directly or indirectly to the Asian mainland, and to China in particular.

Of these three silver routes, the most widely studied is that from the New World to Asia via Europe. Because of the union of the Portuguese and Spanish crowns in 1580, Portugal gained relatively free access to the rich supplies of Spanish silver imported from the New World into Seville. It is estimated, for example, that at the end of the sixteenth century Portugal was sending forty-two tons of silver each year to Goa, and from that city on to various ports in Asia.[41] This figure does not include the substantial quantities of American silver bought by the English and Dutch from Spanish mints in the form of *reals of eight* (the de facto official currency throughout the world in the late sixteenth century)[42] and shipped to Asia. By the time that the New World silver mines began to decline in the 1620s, it is clear that massive quantities of their output had reached Asia by way of the various European commercial powers.

The Zacatecas silver mine in what today is Mexico reached its peak production in 1606 and maintained that level for a little over a decade.[43] At roughly the same time the San Luis Potosí mine also reached its zenith of production so that in the early years of the seventeenth century, huge quantities of silver were being shipped to Europe by Spanish "silver fleets," and also to Manila from the city of Acapulco. In the early 1600s, if the testimony of the colonial government in Mexico is to be believed, Manila was receiving five million pesos a year, or just under 150,000 kilograms of silver from the colonial mines.[44] This is an almost unbelievable sum; rather than lower our estimate, however, we should probably place export figures much higher, since there were certainly substantial illegal dealings in silver in the Spanish colonial territories.[45]

Furthermore, the founding of the city of Manila in 1571 served to vastly increase the supply of silver in Asia as it served as a convenient "depot" for New World silver on its way to the Asian mainland. From 1616–1620, for example, Manila's trade reached a value of over 600,000 pesos per year, and did not dip below the 500,000 mark until after 1645.[46] J. H. Dales holds that the Spanish and Portuguese trade in silver and gold at this time served to transform entirely the previously "medieval" economy of Europe from an economy of bilateralism to one of multilateralism.[47] Whereas previously merchants traded with each other on a relatively simple commodity-to-commodity basis, with the rise of an abundance of American silver, merchants now expanded their trade to include items that were not of immediate importance to them, but that could be used to obtain desired goods in a secondary or even tertiary trade.

For our purposes here, the most important aspect of the silver trade is the Dutch acquisition from the Spanish port of Cadiz (amongst other secondary places of silver) and its subsequent shipment to VOC factories in the East. The main organ of the Dutch silver acquisition was the Amsterdam *Wisselbank*, an organization established in 1609 to fulfill a variety of commercial functions including the purchase of precious metals from depots such as Cadiz, and the subsequent redistribution of those metals to Dutch interests such at the VOC.[48] By the 1680s, the bank had received the authority from the States General to borrow money against precious metals, thereby helping to make Amsterdam the de facto center for trade in silver and gold. This gave rise to a somewhat ironic situation in which the Netherlands, a country with no indigenous mining resources of its own, became one of the most important links in the trade in precious metals.

A prominent feature of the economy of Europe throughout the seventeenth century was the flow of silver from the Mediterranean to the Low Countries, and to Amsterdam in particular. J. G. van Dillen, in his research into the monetary history of Amsterdam and the *Wisselbank*, asserts that more than any other factor, the "re-exporting" of the Spanish "silver fleet" to the Netherlands led to the tremendous growth not only in the East India trade, but in the Baltic and Levant trades as well.[49] Despite the fact that for almost a quarter of the century Spain had an embargo in place against the Netherlands as a result of the ongoing Eighty-Years War for Dutch independence, silver still managed to find its way north in great quantities.[50] The Italian city-states also provided the Netherlands with a considerable quantity of silver. One of the reasons that the northward flow of precious metals was inevitable was the tremendous Dutch success in transporting Baltic grain to the Mediterranean, and in return shipping Mediterranean goods such as wine and olives to the Baltic and Russia. In Sicily, for example, Dutch ships were used even in the inter-Italian trade (to the extent that an "Italy" existed): grain from Sicily was carried to several Italian city-states in the north, while goods such as grain and cloth were carried to coastal ports all along the peninsula from Sicily.[51] Moreover, because Antwerp, the commercial hub of Europe during most of the sixteenth century, was effectively closed by a continuous Dutch blockade from 1585, Amsterdam arose in its place as the center of the lucrative north-south European trade.[52] Therefore, the VOC was founded just when Amsterdam was rapidly becoming a central player in the European commercial world and an emerging central market for precious metals. This position undoubtedly helped to make the company an early success since it was well placed to send out massive shipments of capital to a region that demanded ever-greater shipments in order to compensate for a severe trade deficit.

The quantity of silver sent to Asia on company ships from the various VOC *kamers* (in particular the *kamers* of Amsterdam and Zeeland) is truly staggering. Pieter van Dam records that in 1642 alone, twenty-two tons of silver were sent to VOC factories in Asia.[53] In 1603, the first year of the company's existence, 650,000 Dutch *gulden* were sent to Asia, a similar quantity being shipped every year after that, mostly in the form of Spanish *reals of eight*. Around the middle of the century, Dutch coinage became generally accepted in Asian countries and hence eclipsed the *real of eight* as a de facto official currency in international trade.[54] The quantity of silver sent out from the Netherlands in any given year was a reflection of the orders of the various factories from Asia. In the end the *Hoge Regering*, or high council, in first Bantam, and then from 1619 in Batavia, sent out a yearly estimate of how much precious metal would be needed for all of the Asian factories in Asia. The *Herren Zeventien* would then try to fill that order as best they could, although rarely was the full quantity sent. This procedure was so detailed and complicated that a separate committee was set up called "the treasury," whose major function was to deal with the issue of capital procurement and shipments.[55] The treasury was empowered, among other things, to buy silver and gold from the *Wisselbank* according to the yearly demand.[56] Most of this metal was then used to finance the growing VOC trade empire in Asia in the form of large shipments of silver and gold.

Silver shipped from the Netherlands was sent in most cases to Batavia, where the *Hoge Regering* was then responsible for distributing it to other factories in Asia. The general tendency was for silver to go to various ports in the Indonesian archipelago, Ceylon, and Bengal. Gold, on the other hand, was almost always shipped to Persia, Surat, and again Bengal.[57] Because of the risk in sending such a huge quantity of capital to Asia, the company became extremely interested in locating indigenous Asian sources of precious metals so as to support the Asian trade network with a minimum of capital input from Europe. Jan Pieterszoon Coen realized very early that a self-supporting trade network could bring the company enormous profits since Asian trade would effectively be able to pay for itself. This meant that the *retourfloot* would represent pure profits rather than a "repayment" of the precious metals that were sent out the previous year. This ambitious goal came to be partially realized in the seventeenth century when the quantity of precious metals on Asian-bound company ships remained level from 1630 to 1680.[58]

In order to begin this cycle of self-sufficiency, however, it was first necessary to build a base of European silver in order to tap into the preexisting Asian trade networks (for example, the large-scale procurement of Chinese silk). To that end Coen repeatedly requested that the *Herren Zeventien* initially send as much silver as possible to Asia in order for the company to take steps towards becoming self-sufficient. For example, Indian textiles, bought with the European silver, could be traded in Indonesia for spices and pepper, which would in turn be sold to the Chinese merchants for items such as silk and porcelain. These Chinese goods could then be sold in Japan for silver, which could be used to finance further purchases of Indian goods, and so forth in a self-perpetuating cycle. In such a way the company would become self-sufficient; but as a precondition, a great quantity of precious metals was initially needed to start the process.[59]

JAPANESE SILVER AND FOREIGN TRADE

While silver was undoubtedly important in and of itself in premodern Japanese culture and society, even more important were the benefits that it could literally "buy" in the form of Chinese goods, and later, goods brought from all over the world. Japanese silver came to be valued in Asia not only because of its sheer quantity, but also because of its high quality. According to Nicolas Puyck, a Dutch merchant who was a part of the first journey to the shogunal court in 1609, Japanese silver was "of better quality than *reals of eight*."[60] The silver coins issued by the shogunate were of a consistent purity of 80 percent silver, which made them a convenient unit of export and medium of trade in Asia. By the 1640s, Dutch officials could write to the directors in Europe that Japanese silver was "much sought after" throughout all of Asia.[61] The main beneficiaries in this trade were the Chinese, the Portuguese, and later the Dutch, all of whom played a substantial role in the import of Asian commodities into Japan. These three groups, in the course of about a century from the 1560s to the 1660s, took away a huge quantity of Japanese silver and carried it to several ports throughout Asia, thereby making the role of Japanese precious metals a truly international one.

The Portuguese

The history of Portuguese contact with Japan has been well documented and need not be discussed in any great detail here. What is important is that from very early on, the Portuguese learned that they could use their base at Macao on the Chinese mainland to provide Japan with silk in all of its various forms. This trade in silk goods was a complicated process involving three stages and several countries. First, the Portuguese crown appointed a *Capitão-mór* (the "High Captain" was a title given by the Portuguese crown to a nobleman that denoted his right to rule over a part of the Portuguese empire, in this case Macau) to outfit a ship and provide the expenses for its voyage. This was done at first by the captain himself, but as the voyages become ever more lucrative, a system of investment was established whereby almost all segments of Macao society had a stake in the trade. By the time the Portuguese were expelled from Japan in 1639, the great ship from Macao was in essence a joint venture between a great number of investors. After the initial capital was raised, the ship sailed to various ports in Southeast Asia where spices were bought to be traded on the Chinese market for silk, both raw and woven. The Chinese silk was then taken to Japan where an insatiable demand enabled the Portuguese merchants to take away vast quantities of silver and use it for the maintenance of their trade network throughout the Indian Ocean.[62] It is estimated that each year the Portuguese took away from 15,000 to 30,000 kilograms of silver in return for the silk goods brought from China.[63] Ralph Fitch, the English traveler and noted observer of early modern Asian societies, recorded in 1580 that the Portuguese obtained 600,000 *cruzados* every year from their trade with Japan and that 200,000 of these were put back into the Chinese silk market for the next year's venture.[64] The trade with Macao was so lucrative, in fact, that the Jesuits in Japan, who played a large role in facilitating the trade, were constantly petitioned by Japanese courtiers and daimyo to invest silver for them in Macao.[65]

The Dutch were well aware that the trade between Macao and Nagasaki was a principal source of Portuguese profits in Asia. In a 1639 letter from Governor-General van Diemen to the *Herren Zeventien*, van Diemen asserts once again that if the Portuguese trade between Macao and Japan could somehow be disrupted, the entire Portuguese commercial empire in Asia would "dry up" and they would be forced to abandon Macao (the idea being that the Dutch would then take their place).[66] To this end, Admiral Cornelis Reyerszoon, with a fleet of thirteen heavily armed warships, attacked Macao in 1622. The expedition, far from achieving the Dutch dream of a Portugal-free China, failed miserably, after which the fleet was forced to retire first to the Pescadores, and then (with tacit Chinese approval) to Taiwan. It was this failure in fact that led to the founding of a Dutch presence on the island and their indirect access to the Chinese silk market.[67] The Dutch would have to wait almost two decades before the Portuguese presence in Japan was eliminated. Once that happened, however, Dutch profits soared to unprecedented heights as predicted, partly because of the absence of the Portuguese and partly because of the VOC's newfound ability to obtain Chinese silk on Taiwan.

The Chinese

Unlike the Portuguese, the Chinese did not have to "discover" Japan; diplomatic relations between the neighbors existed, rather, from the very emergence of a centralized state in the Japanese archipelago in the early centuries C.E. From the very beginning precious metals played an important role in the commerce across the China Sea and through Korea. In Japan's medieval period, for example, the ratio of the value of silver against that of gold was 1:5 (1:6 at most) in Japan, but from 1:12 to 1:13 on the Chinese mainland.[68] This led, therefore, to a steady flow of Chinese silver into Japan in exchange for Japanese gold. This situation was reversed, however, with the onset of the huge increase in the production of Japanese silver from the mid-sixteenth century. At this time the value ratio was essentially reversed, and the Japanese demand for Chinese gold was satisfied by a huge increase in the export of silver. Around the year 1610, for example, it was possible for Chinese merchants to realize a profit of 60 percent simply by exchanging Chinese gold for Japanese silver.[69]

Ostensibly, the Ming Empire strictly prohibited trade between China and Japan in the mid-sixteenth century. Japanese *wakō,* or pirate bands, had been ravaging the coast of China, especially in the southern provinces such as Fujian, for centuries. In the 1540s, however, the destructive activity of the *wakō* had once again increased considerably, prompting the Ming authorities to prohibit foreign trade altogether. Despite the prohibition, however, Chinese ships were frequent visitors to ports in Kyushu and continued to take away vast quantities of silver in return for primarily Chinese products such as silk.[70]

In 1567 the Ming relaxed its general ban on maritime trade, although contact with the Japanese was still strictly prohibited. The ban continued to have little effect, however, as Chinese ships continued to visit Japanese ports in ever increasing numbers. The Chinese demand for silver coupled with an insatiable Japanese demand for Chinese goods made it almost inevitable that the Ming decrees would be all but ignored. Furthermore, in 1610 (Keichō 15), the Tokugawa authorities for the first time issued a *shuinjō* to a Chinese captain who had arrived from Canton. After this tacit approval by the shogunate, Chinese trade at Nagasaki was in practice (if not in name) legitimate, and the floodgates were open: in 1614, sixty ships visited Nagasaki followed by a peak in 1626 of ninety ships.[71]

The export of Japanese silver by Chinese merchants reached its highest point in the mid- to late-seventeenth century, despite bakufu attempts to limit its outflow. From 1648 to 1673, for example, an estimated total of 193,950 *kan* of silver in the form of both cash and silver utensils (a convenient way to get around the limits placed on silver cash export: utensils were not included in the quotas) was taken away from Japan.[72] As with the Portuguese, the Dutch tried repeatedly to limit Chinese competition in the Japanese market. The most extreme methods involved outright piracy: taking Chinese ships at sea and confiscating their cargoes of silk goods bound for Japan. Richard Cocks noted several occasions in which the Dutch towed a Chinese "prize" into Hirado. On June 6, 1618, to cite just a single example, Cocks recorded that the Dutch had taken six Chinese junks and burned a Spanish Galleon in the course of one of their "hunting expeditions."[73]

For a long time, the Japanese authorities were willing to turn a blind eye to the ravages visited upon the shipping of other nations by the VOC, but they eventually became increasingly irritated by the incessant attacks on both Iberian and Chinese junks alike. In Cocks' diary, we are told that the "emperor" was growing increasingly angry over Dutch provocations, especially because many of them were carried out in Japanese waters.[74] Jacques Specx, the *opperhoofd* (chief merchant) at Hirado, sensing that the authorities were displeased, wrote in a letter to the Governor-General that the Japanese think of the Dutch as pirates and that this lawless activity should be curtailed around Japan to placate the authorities.[75] Heeding this advice, Governor-General Coen ordered that Chinese ships between Japan and the coast of China be allowed free passage.[76] The Dutch, however, remained obsessed with the Chinese "threat" to their prosperity and dwelled at length in their letters and diaries on how best to deal with them. Pieter van Dam, for instance, noted that the Dutch expended an enormous amount of energy trying to divert Chinese junks from Nagasaki to either Batavia or Taiwan, from where the Dutch could serve in the lucrative capacity of middlemen in the Japan trade.[77]

With the decline of the Ming and the prolonged civil war that resulted in the establishment of the Qing Empire in the mid 1640s, the Dutch were finally able to pursue trade in Japan without a substantial Chinese presence. It is no accident that it was precisely at this time that company profits were most pronounced. This did not mean that Chinese competition was totally lacking, however, for the powerful Zheng family with their commercial base on the Southeast coast of China were routinely circumventing the Dutch on Taiwan and sending ships directly to Nagasaki. Furthermore, when the Qing finally defeated the remnants of the Zheng forces on Taiwan in the early 1680s and once again allowed commercial activity to resume, the Dutch faced a renewed onslaught of Chinese ships coming to Japan to trade. This competition, combined with trade restrictions on the quantity of goods imported into Japan, served to severely limit Dutch profits at Nagasaki.

The Japanese Shuinsen Merchants

Until the shogunate banned its own people from traveling outside of Japan, the Dutch faced considerable competition from Japanese merchants who had been trading in most major ports of Southeast Asia for years. In fact, until the Japanese merchants were no longer able to participate directly in international commerce, the Dutch were prevented from reaping the huge profits in silver that they did in the 1630s and after. In the *Generale Missiven* and the *Dagregisters* kept at both Batavia and Taiwan, the Japanese *shuinsen* merchants make a number of appearances, invariably accompanied by Dutch lamentations about lost profits at the hands of these ubiquitous merchants. In a 1626 letter to the *Herren Zeventien*, Governor-General Specx wrote that in the previous year the Japanese came to Taiwan in their own ships with the aim of buying silk from Chinese merchants who came to the island expressly for this purpose. They brought with them 70,000 *taels* of silver and received in return silk that Specx claimed was not particularly high in quality.[78] The company could do little, however, as long as Japanese merchants continued to ply the seas with the silver that Chinese merchants and others so desired. The VOC officials in Asia rightly believed that if they could somehow limit the Japanese in this trade, their own profits would soar. This contention proved remarkably accurate when indeed the shogunate eventually banned Japanese merchants from participating in overseas trade.

Perhaps because of a fixation on *sakoku*, it is often overlooked that in the fifteenth and sixteenth centuries, Japan had a rather well-developed seafaring tradition, and that Japanese merchants frequently traded with Southeast Asia.[79] Date Masamune, the powerful Christian daimyo who sent an embassy to Europe, used one of his own ships of 500 tons to make the journey. The Dutch in fact often commented on the good quality of Japanese ships, and this from a nation renowned for its shipbuilding capacity.[80] Several innovations in ship construction occurred in the mid-1500s. Most notable was the change in the ship design itself: instead of the older *ryūkotsusen*, or dug-out ships, a new type was developed called the *tana'ita* ship which consisted of a series of wooden planks fitted together with iron nails and cut into the shape of a ship. These ships had the advantage of being much bigger than previous vessels and thus were able to carry a more substantial cargo.[81] Japanese merchants used these well-constructed ships to sail to several ports in Southeast Asia in search of such luxury items as spices, sandalwood, deerskins, and, naturally, silk. By the beginning of the seventeenth century, the system of Japanese overseas trade was a well-developed one that came to be regulated, if not controlled, by first Hideyoshi and then the Tokugawa shogunate.

In 1589 Toyotomi Hideyoshi furthered his political control over Japan by placing the foreign trade of the powerful Kyushu daimyo under his control. Along with his policy of monopolizing the purchase of Chinese silk and other foreign goods, Hideyoshi placed officials directly in Nagasaki and began issuing passes to Japanese merchants who wanted to trade in various ports in Asia. This system was not particularly new since as early as the Muromachi period the Ashikaga shogun had issued *shuinjō* to merchants wishing to conduct business overseas. Under Hideyoshi, however, the system reached new levels of control. From 1592, trading passes were issued from Hideyoshi's castle at Nagoya to merchants in Kyoto, Nagasaki, and Sakai, and were generally valid for a single journey.[82] There were two main reasons for the establishment of these commercial regulations. The first was of course to extend Hideyoshi's control over a rather important aspect of the western daimyo's power, and the other was to control piracy. The Spanish governor of the Philippines, for example, requested that Hideyoshi supply all Japanese ships with an official seal so that legitimate vessels could be distinguished from those of pirates who, at the time, constituted a large and disruptive presence on the island of Luzon.[83]

Although Hideyoshi revived the formal *shuinjō* system, it came to full fruition under the auspices of Tokugawa Ieyasu, who adopted the system for his own government, officially established in 1603 when the emperor "bestowed" the title of shogun on Ieyasu. Under the Tokugawa, the number of ships traveling from Japan increased drastically, as did the amount of capital in silver. In the roughly three decades between 1601 and the *sakoku* decrees of 1635, a total of 355 *shuinjō* were issued to nineteen places in Southeast Asia including Taiwan, Java, Annam, Luzon, Siam, Cambodia, Patani, Malacca, and the Moluccas.[84] One finds in the entries of the *Tokugawa Jikki* for these years a number of references to the issuance of *shuinjō*; for the middle Keichō era (roughly 1603–1610) in fact, there is a great emphasis on the shogun's role in issuing these commercial privileges as they are noted rather prominently in the text. On the eleventh day of the first month of Keichō 15 (1610), for example, *shuinjō* to Annam, Luzon, Siam, and Cochin were all issued in the course of a single day.[85]

The great western daimyo initially dominated the *shuinsen* trade, although there were a number of passes issued to influential merchants, Tokugawa officials, and Buddhist temples. The ships used in this trade ranged in size from two to three hundred tons to seventy to eighty tons each, a figure that should serve to give some idea as to the high volume of foreign trade during this period.[86] For example, in 1633 and 1634, at the end of the period of Japanese overseas trade, Japanese *shuinsen* imported 250,000 *catties* of raw silk, a figure that is at least as high as the amount of silk imported on Chinese ships and several times higher than both Dutch and Portuguese imports.[87]

In his exhaustive research on the *shuinsen* trade, Iwao Seiichi estimates that the average quantity of silver on outbound Japanese ships was 530 *kan*. From 1604 to 1616, an average of 15 ships per year departed Japan, yielding a total average silver export per year of 7,500 *kan*. For the years 1617 to 1635, an average of eight ships per year were dispatched, yielding an average silver export of 4,000 *kan* per year.[88] Needless to say, this is a significant quantity of silver and represented a sizeable factor in the Asian trade patterns of the early seventeenth century. Without Japanese trade and the quantities of silver that it represented, the economy of the region as a whole would not have been nearly as complex and lucrative.

As noted previously, Japanese merchants were frequent visitors to ports throughout Southeast Asia, from the Indonesian archipelago to Taiwan, and distributed their silver over this entire region, providing the area with a sizeable influx of capital. The list of articles imported in return for Japanese silver is extensive; and since the quantities were certainly not insignificant, Japanese merchants certainly had a sizeable impact on overall trade in several of the ports in Asia. Therefore it was with more than a little consternation that VOC officials recorded the extensive activity of the *shuinsen* merchants in their diaries and reports. According to Katō Eiichi, "The red seal ships had constituted the Dutch's most serious competition, and Dutch trading activity flourished following [their] disappearance."[89] When in 1635 the shogunate decided to ban Japanese merchants from overseas trade altogether, the Dutch, using Taiwan as a base, served as middlemen between China, Southeast Asia, and Japan, thereby taking over the large profits that were previously controlled by *shuinsen* merchants. It was only after Japanese trade was curtailed that Dutch silver exports from Japan became truly significant, thereby helping to drive the overall profits of the VOC to unprecedented heights.[90]

Although Japanese *shuinsen* merchants were banned from traveling and trading abroad, one group was exempt from this prohibition. The Sō house, daimyo of the island of Tsushima, had for centuries carried on a prosperous trade with Korea and had served as intermediaries between successive Japanese and Korean governments. When in 1635 the bakufu decided to restrict overseas trade by its own merchants, the Sō were conspicuously absent from these prohibitions insofar as they played a vital function for the Tokugawa authorities. Through Tsushima, the Tokugawa were able to establish and maintain diplomatic relations with Korea on terms that, to the Japanese, were constructed to appear tributary.[91] This was only achieved with a great deal of difficulty and a bit of diplomatic subterfuge on the part of the Sō house, but nevertheless the lavish Korean embassies that paid their respects at Edo, Kyoto, and Nikkō came to play an important role in legitimating Tokugawa rule. The Korean court sent embassies to Edo on auspicious occasions, such as the ascension of a new shogun and, more importantly for our purposes, it allowed Japan to send an annual trading mission to the port of Pusan. In 1609, commercial relations between the Sō and the Korean court were formalized with a treaty allowing twenty ships per year to visit Korea, although very soon thereafter this limit was effectively ignored.[92] As part of the treaty arrangements, the Sō were allowed a territorial concession in the city of Pusan (reminiscent of the bakufu's constriction of foreign trade to enclaves in Nagasaki) in which Japanese merchants could live and where Japanese and Korean goods could be stored. As with so many other aspects of Japanese foreign trade of the time, silver played a significant role as one of the primary exports to Korea.

At the peak of trade relations between Tsushima and Korea, silver accounted for half of all Japanese exports. For example, in 1686 over ten tons of silver was exported to Korea in Sō ships in return for mostly raw, white silk.[93] This is in stark contrast to the situation at Nagasaki, where the bakufu had severely limited Chinese exports of silver and banned that of the Dutch entirely. Even with the government's prohibition on silver export of the 1660s, however, the Sō were entirely exempt. In fact, a dual policy existed for much of the first half of the bakufu's existence with respect to Korean trade. When in 1697, for example, the bakufu debased its silver coinage from 80 percent fine to 64 percent fine, the Sō house was allowed sole use of the old standard of coinage so as not to upset trade relations with Korea.[94] With the rising demand in Japan for Korean ginseng, and of course the steady demand for silk, the Sō house enjoyed a lucrative trade position far superior to that of the Chinese or the Dutch. It is easy to forget that through Tsushima, Japan continued to export several tons of silver per year even after the bakufu severely limited its export from Nagasaki.

The Dutch East India Company

Governor-General Coen could dream of a self-sufficient commercial empire in Asia because of the company's position in Japan and its ability to procure from that country a tremendous quantity of silver. For the first century of the VOC's existence, the company relied heavily on Japanese silver, followed by gold and copper. Furthermore, the important role that Japanese precious metals played in the history of the VOC was facilitated by the use of Taiwan as a link between the "bank" that was Japan and the company's major trading areas of South and Southeast Asia. The Dutch factory on Taiwan and its strategic location astride one of the most lucrative trade routes in Asia gave the VOC a decided advantage over all of its commercial rivals. It is quite telling that after the bakufu banned silver exports in 1668 and the Dutch lost Taiwan to the Zheng family in 1662, the company suffered a severe blow that was only alleviated by the shogun's approval of gold and copper exports. When restrictions were also placed on the export of these precious metals, however, the VOC went into a decline that was to characterize it for the rest of its existence.

Pieter van Dam, the well-known chronicler of the first century of the VOC's history, dwells in some detail on company affairs in the Japanese islands. He emphasizes that with the rise in silver exports from Hirado, the *Herren Zeventien* were no longer obliged to send as much precious metals from the Netherlands and that indeed, the company was sometimes even able to ship Japanese silver home aboard the *retourfloot.*[95] He also states that in times past the Portuguese used Japan for much the same purposes; rather than send out richly laden ships from Lisbon, they were able to use Japanese precious metals "as ballast" in ships sailing between Nagasaki and Macao.[96] Femme Gaastra claims that by 1650, Japan was by far the most important supplier of silver for the company—more important even than the Netherlands itself with over one million *gulden* per year taken away from the archipelago.[97] Therefore, because the VOC was able to supply the Japanese with the commodities that were in such high demand in the islands, it was able in return to obtain a great quantity of silver in Asia, thereby obviating the need for such large shipments of European silver while at the same time establishing the foundation upon which its entire Asian operation was supported. The insatiable Japanese demand for Chinese and Southeast Asian luxury goods allowed the Dutch to use their base in Taiwan, along with their unique position in Hirado and later at Nagasaki, to reap enormous benefits for the company. Furthermore, the VOC's success in Japan had repercussions throughout Asia and the larger world because such a large quantity of silver came to be redistributed to several areas aboard Dutch ships.

It is in the context of competition with the Chinese, Japanese, and Portuguese merchants that Dutch trade with Japan has been viewed thus far, and it is in this same context that the export of silver from Japan should be examined. As long as Japanese merchants were allowed to trade relatively freely by the shogunate, the Dutch faced stiff competition in providing Asian commodities demanded by the Japanese, such as sandalwood, deerskins, sugar, spices, and silk. Furthermore, until the Portuguese could be effectively barred from trade with Japan, the Dutch would continue to have problems making significant profits in that country since the Portuguese were able to capitalize on their valuable base at Macao from which they procured Chinese silk for the Japanese market. The VOC, on the other hand, was all but excluded from the Chinese trade, at least until its factory on Taiwan began to reap greater rewards in the 1630s. And finally, as long as stable and regular Chinese trade flourished in Japan, Dutch profits would suffer because of an abundant supply of silk that the relative ease of the trip from the Asian continent to Japan engendered.

As fate would have it, all three of the aforementioned conditions turned in favor of the VOC in the 1630s and 1640s, allowing company profits to reach unprecedented heights. Japanese merchants were forbidden from trading abroad by a government that felt increasingly threatened by foreign contact; the Portuguese were banished from Japan because of their Roman Catholicism and an increased fear of a Christian revolt along the lines of Shimabara; and the Chinese were effectively limited in international commerce by the disruptions of the civil war that toppled the Ming and brought the Qing to power. It is against this backdrop that we will examine the silver that the Dutch exported from Japan during the seventeenth century.

The most important factor in the VOC's ability to procure large quantities of silver in Japan was initially the trade with Chinese merchants. There was a huge demand for Chinese silk among the upper classes of Japan, and as long as the Dutch were excluded from this market, silver acquisitions would always be unremarkable. Jan Pieterszoon Coen stated the matter succinctly in a September 1622 letter to the *Herren Zeventien* in which he informed them that if the Dutch wanted to have access to Japanese "money," they would have to find some way to emulate the Spanish and Portuguese in importing Chinese silk.[98] With the establishment of Dutch power on the island of Taiwan, the VOC was finally able to indirectly tap into this source of silk. Because trade between Japan and the Chinese was officially banned by the Ming authorities (although to be sure Chinese ships still regularly came to Japan), the Dutch were able to act as middlemen between Chinese merchants and the Japanese until the eventual rise of the Qing restored unofficial commercial relations between Japan and the mainland. Until this time, however, the Dutch were able to exploit their intermediary position and as a result drastically increase their export of silver from the archipelago.

A brief perusal of Dutch trade records kept by the merchants on Taiwan immediately shows the preeminent role of Japanese silver in Asian trade. Because Taiwan acted as a relay station for goods going to and coming from Japan, these records are particularly invaluable for obtaining an overall picture of the vicissitudes of the Japan trade.[99] In 1625, for example, the ship *'t Wapen van Zeelandt* was sent to Japan via Taiwan with 725,995 *gulden* of merchandise with instructions to obtain for Batavia 500 or 600 *lasten* of rice, and as much silver as could be purchased with the remaining goods.[100] In the 1630s and 1640s, moreover, the pages of the Taiwanese *dagregisters* are filled with references to ships arriving laden with Japanese silver. In 1637, for example, the ship *Petten* arrived in Taiwan on the fourteenth of January with 150,000 *taels* of silver and 350 *picols* of copper. About a month later (on the thirteenth of February) the *Grol* brought to Taiwan 50,000 *taels* of silver and 300 *picols* of copper, followed one week later by the *Rarop* with 140,000 *taels* of silver and 508 *picols* of copper. Just four days later, a ship from Japan brought 60,000 more *taels* of silver and a large quantity of rice for Batavia. One of the reasons for this huge increase in the quantity of silver from Japan was the shogunal edict prohibiting Japanese citizens from traveling abroad, to which the head of the Taiwanese factory gratefully prayed, "God grant the continuation of the Japanese edict!"[101]

In terms of the quantity of silver exported in VOC ships for 1637 alone, the president of the Taiwanese factory gives us the startling figure of 2,142,364 *taels*. He then goes on to note that the profits from Japan were not as good this year as in previous years![102] As seen from these Taiwan records, silver exports from Japan in the 1630s and 1640s moved at an unprecedented scale and continued to be so for the next few decades. Clearly, this silver was used to finance Dutch factories in other parts of Asia. In 1638, for example, the ships *Groote Bredam* and the *Sandtvoort* were sent to Surat in India with 200,000 *taels* of Japanese silver.[103] In December of 1639, ships were sent to Tonkin with 150,000 *taels* of silver and to Siam with 25,*000 taels*.[104] Again, in 1645, ships from Nagasaki arrived in Taiwan with a cargo of 1,838,250 *gulden* in silver, of which almost its entirety was sent on to the Coromandel Coast and Batavia. In the same year, the ships *Schiedam* and *Haen* were dispatched from Taiwan with 1,187,825 *gulden* in Japanese silver and Chinese gold destined for Surat, Persia, and Coromandel.[105] Thus, for much of the seventeenth century, the VOC was able to support a good deal of their entire Asian trade network with Japanese precious metals.[106]

By the end of the 1630s, Dutch exports from Japan were 80 to 90 percent silver. From 1635 to 1650, exports of silver from Hirado and Nagasaki dipped below 400,000 *taels* in only three years, while the high point was reached in the five years from 1637 to 1641. In 1639, exports reached the unprecedented height of slightly more than 2.5 million *taels* of silver.[107] Before the mid 1630s, exports were much more modest with a total silver export of 1,216,000 *taels* between 1622 and 1635.[108] The silver that was previously exported in such great quantity by Japanese *shuinsen* merchants for the purchase of Asian goods was now used by the VOC to import these same goods for them. Japan was of such value to the company that when friction arose between the Japanese authorities at Nagasaki, the Dutch spared no expense in resolving the situation, even to the extent of sending a special ambassador from Batavia to pay the company's respects to the shogun and to present him with lavish gifts. As the Governor-General at Batavia wrote to the *Herren Zeventien*, "If Japan were as miserly as the Moors of Persia, Surat, and Coromandel…we would not fear to lose it so much."[109]

The Dutch had a decided advantage over their East India Company rivals in that they were able from the beginning to exploit the "country trade." This meant that rather than simply sending ships to a particular destination and returning to Europe with the goods from that one area, the Dutch established a trade network that criss-crossed the region in a web of highly complex commercial routes in order to maximize profits and to make their trade as self-sufficient as possible. Nowhere is this policy more apparent than in the Dutch acquisition of Japanese silver. Many of the Southeast Asian factories seem to have been maintained simply to provide Japan with the luxury goods that it craved so that the VOC might continue this profitable export of Japanese precious metals. Siam, for example, was used primarily to provide the Japanese with sandalwood and deerskins, while Tonkin later became a primary source of silk for the Japan market since it was not subject to the *pancado.*[110] The silver that the VOC obtained in Japan in exchange for Southeast Asian goods was used in part to purchase Chinese gold on Taiwan, whence it was shipped to India where it fetched great profits.[111] Silver was also shipped to India in massive quantities as recounted by the Dutch captain Johan Saar who, in his account of his travels, called the fleet that traveled from Japan to India the "Dutch Silver Fleet."[112] Because Japanese silver was used to purchase Asian commodities that were brought to Japan, several of the smaller factories were supported by this "silver cycle." In the end, the most important commodity for the "country trade" in Asia was silver, and to ensure its acquisition, no expense was spared to provide the Japanese with the luxury goods they desired and to guarantee that friendly relations with the shogun and his officials were maintained.

The Damming of the "Silver River"

The company's favorable position with regard to the tremendous silver resource that Japan represented did not last through the seventeenth century. With the decline in the productivity of Japanese silver mines beginning as early as the 1630s, the bakufu began to worry about keeping enough silver in the country to adequately supply its own needs for minting coins.[113] Japan, in contrast to European governments who sought to raise bullion reserves by stimulating foreign trade, sought instead to raise reserves by strictly limiting the outflow of silver by drastically curtailing trade.[114] Already by the death of the third shogun Iemitsu in the mid 1650s, the bakufu was forced to use the last of the silver reserves set aside by Ieyasu (for military emergencies) to produce sufficient coinage for the country.[115] In 1669, for example, the *bugyō* of Nagasaki related to the shogun that the volume of silver exported from the country was four times the quantity used in the production of coins.[116] The Japanese authorities, alarmed at the vast quantity of silver flowing out of the country in foreign ships, decided to ban its export outright in 1668.[117] According to the *Nagasaki-ki*, silver exports for the years 1648–1667 dipped below 6,000 *kan* only four times, with exports for several years approaching or surpassing the 10,000 *kan* mark.[118] This is a truly astonishing figure, the more so since these numbers almost certainly represent a substantial under-reporting.

While the Chinese managed to persuade the authorities to lift the ban on silver soon thereafter, the Dutch had no such similar success, and the ban remained in place down to the "opening" of Japan in 1854. The Dutch, in lieu of silver, began to export the Japanese gold *koban* in earnest, made possible by the lifting of the ban on gold exports in 1664. In 1667 a total of 40,481 of these gold coins were exported for a net profit of 1,060,573 *gulden*. This sum represents about three times as much gold as was sent to Asia from the three largest VOC *kamers* in the Netherlands.[119] So many gold pieces were shipped out of Japan at this time that they were considered the standard currency at Batavia, where company servants often used them to remit their earnings back to Europe. Much of this gold was also sent to the Coromandel Coast, thereby making up for the gold that was formerly obtained on Taiwan. This was a fortuitous development since the loss of Taiwan to the Zheng family had been a severe blow to the VOC insofar as the island provided the company with a considerable supply of Chinese gold.

It is a historical coincidence that Japanese gold became readily available at the very moment that gold increased in value relative to silver throughout much of India, particularly in Bengal. To take advantage of this, the *Herren Zeventien*, in the early 1670s, began to order as much silk from Bengal as possible in order to exchange it in Japan for the valuable *koban*.[120] By doing so the company was able to reduce the shock of the shogunal ban on silver exports by turning to Japanese gold instead. Very soon, however, the bakufu also restricted the outflow of gold, after again becoming alarmed by the increasing quantity of this metal leaving the country. Arai Hakuseki, a shogunal advisor of some influence at the turn of the seventeenth century, summed up what the official position of the government should be towards the export of precious metals by likening them to the "bones of the earth:" once exhausted, silver, gold, and copper would never be replaceable.[121] Rather than ban the export of gold outright, however, the bakufu decided to raise the price of the *koban* from 56 to 58 *maas* per piece in 1670, and in 1672 the price was raised again to 68 *maas*.[122] The final blow to the company came in 1696 when the authorities decided to debase the *koban*. The new coins contained much less gold while the weight was kept the same, and most damaging to the company, the price was artificially maintained at 68 *maas*.[123] This effectively meant that the Dutch could no longer make a profit simply by selling Japanese gold in India, and although they continued for various reasons to export small quantities of Japanese gold at a net loss, they increasingly turned their attention to the export of copper.

The Dutch had exported Japanese copper almost from the beginning of their trade with the islands, but it was not until the 1650s that they began exporting it in any appreciable amount. It was at this time that European demand for copper grew to a point where it became highly profitable for the company to load the metal as ballast on the *retourfloot* and to sell it on the European market.[124] After a brief period in which the bakufu prohibited the export of copper, shipments once again recommenced in the 1670s on a scale that exceeded the relatively limited trade of previous years. According to Kristof Glamann, the total exports from Japan in 1680 amounted to 1,300,000 *gulden*, of which slightly over 80 percent was copper.[125] The copper trade was of such value to the company that the *Herren Zeventien* declared its acquisition essential to providing VOC factories all over Asia with the necessary capital to support their operations.[126] Here again, however, this situation was not to last, for Japanese authorities in 1698 limited Dutch exports to 25,000 *picols* of copper per year. These limits continued to become more restrictive throughout the first half of the eighteenth century until the 1730s and 1740s when the VOC began for the first time to show a net commercial loss in Japan. Although company trade in Japan as a whole was still turning a modest profit because of the company's policy of exporting debased Japanese gold at an exceptionally high price, the net result was a loss on the part for the Nagasaki factory (the loss being deducted from Japanese profits in Nagasaki).[127]

Throughout almost the entirety of the seventeenth century, the VOC was able to reap tremendous profits from its trade in Japanese precious metals. This trade was facilitated by a number of factors, mostly having to do with the company's elaborate system of inter-Asian trade patterns. In this regard, Taiwan was of paramount importance since it gave the Dutch a base from which to procure the all-important supply of Chinese silk that was subsequently traded in Japan for silver and other metals. Japanese precious metals in turn made it possible for the Dutch to sustain their far-reaching commercial empire in Asia, a region that generally represented no appreciable demand for European goods. Japanese metals also helped to sustain the company through a number of crises that otherwise might have led to a drastically reduced capacity for trade. In the 1670s, for example, war was raging in Europe, making it impossible for the *Herren Zeventien* to ship precious metals to Asia. It was precisely at this time, however, that the Japanese *koban* was in such demand in India, thereby providing an alternative source of gold and offsetting the shortage from Europe. Likewise, when the Japanese authorities curtailed the export of silver and gold, copper arose to take their place, thereby allowing the Dutch a few more years of prosperity in Asia before a general decline set in. In the end, the VOC's acquisition of Japanese precious metals and the tremendous prosperity that the company experienced in the seventeenth century cannot be fully separated.

Endnotes

1. As quoted in Charles Wilson, "Treasure and Trade Balances: Further Evidence," *The Economic History Review, New Series* 4: 2 (1951): 233.
2. *Pieter Rietbergen, Japan Verwoord: Nihon door Nederlandse Ogen, 1600-1799* (Amsterdam: Hotei Publishing, 2003), 44–45.
3. Hayami Akira, "A Great Transformation: Social and Economic Change in Sixteenth and Seventeenth Century Japan," *Bonner Zeitschrift für Japonologie* 8 (1986): 5.
4. Denis Flynn, "Comparing the Tokugawa Shogunate with Hapsburg Spain: Two Silver Based Empires in a Global Setting," in *The Political Economies of Merchant Empires*, ed. James D. Tracy (Cambridge: Cambridge University Press, 1991).
5. Cooper, ed., *Joao Rodrigues's Account of Sixteenth-Century Japan*, 104–05.
6. Jan Huygen van Linschotten's journal was published first in 1596 under the title *Itinerario, Voyage ofte Schipvaert van Jan Huygen van Linschotten naer Oost ofte Portugaels Indiën.* It was subsequently translated into Latin, English, and French around 1600 and came to play a large role in the first Dutch voyages to the "East Indies." The English captain John Saris, who set up the English factory in Japan in 1613, claims that he found Japan using nothing but the instructions in the *Itinerario*. For a modern annotated edition, see A. van der Moer, *Een Zestiende Eeuwse Hollander in het Verre Oosten en het Hoge Noorden: Leven en Werken, Reizen en Avonturen van Jan Huygen van Linschoten* ('s-Gravenhage: Martinus Nijhoff, 1979).
7. Sugiyama Hiroshi, *Nihon no Rekishi 11: Sengoku daimyō* (Tokyo: Chūo Kōronsha, 1974), 341.
8. It is commonly held that slave labor and criminals worked the gold and silver mines at this time.
9. Sugimoto Masayoshi and David Swain, *Science and Culture in Traditional Japan, AD 600–1854* (Cambridge: The MIT Press, 1978), 169.
10. Inoue Toshio, *Kenshin to Shingen* (Tokyo: Nihon Rekishi Shinsho, 1968), 202.
11. These figures are taken from Sugiyama, *Sengoku Daimyō*, 246; 340–341.
12. Kobata Atsushi, *Nihon Kahei Ryūtsūshi* (Tokyo: Tōkō Shoin, 1969), 437–444.
13. *Nihon Kagaku Gijitsushi Taikei (in 25 volumes), Vol. 20* (Tokyo: Nihon Kagaku-shi Gakkai, 1965), 14. Hereafter NKGT.

14. The entire text of this directive can be found in *Meiji-Zen Nihon Gijitsu Hattatsu-shi* (Tokyo: Nihon Gakushi-In), 106–110.
15. Iwao Seiichi, *Nihin no Rekishi 14: Sakoku* (Tokyo: Chūo Koronsha, 1966), 114.
16. Yokoi Tokifuyu, *Nihon Kōgyō Shiyō* (Tokyo: Yoshikawa Hanshichi, 1900), preface.
17. Okamura Shōji, *Hinawajū kara Kurofune made. Edo Jidai Gijitsu Shi* (Tokyo: Iwanami Shoten, 1970), 135.
18. Yamaguchi Keiji, "Kinginzan no Gijitsu to Shakai," in *Kōza no Nihon Gijitsu Shakai Shi.*
19. D. A. Brading and Harry Cross, "Colonial Silver Mining: Mexico and Peru," *Hispanic American Historical Review* 52 (1972): 545–579.
20. Sugimoto and Swain, *Science and Culture in Traditional Japan*, 181.
21. Leonard Blussé, M. E. van Opstall, and Ts'ao Yung-Ho, eds., *De Dagregisters van het Kasteel Zeelandia, Taiwan, 1629–1662, Vol. II* (Den Hague: Instituut voor Nederlandse Geschiedenis, 1995), 469.
22. The *Kokushi Daijiten* notes that the *yamashi* were also commonly called *kōzangyōsha* (mine workers). They attained a rather high level of influence in the Tokugawa era, often governing their own towns at the site of the mine and being paid out of the metal that they extracted. At the Inai silver mine in Akita *han*, for example, an elaborate system of supply was established so that the *yamashi* could go about their business as efficiently as possible. See Tsūji Tastuya, *Nihon no Rekishi 13: Edo Kaifu* (Tokyo: Chūo Kōronsha, 1966), 160–166.
23. *Meiji-Zen Nihon Gijitsu Hattatsu-shi*, item 48.
24. Tsūji, *Edo Kaifu*, 160.
25. KTTJ, Vol. I, 86.
26. Kitajima Masamoto, *Edo Bakufu no Kenryoku Kōzō* (Tokyo: Iwanami Shoten, 1964), 307.
27. Sasaki, "Kōgyō ni okeru Gijitsu no Hatten," 190.
28. NKGT, Vol. 20, 19.
29. The *Sado Nendaiki* (Chronicle of the Sado Years) contains a detailed description of the water screw and notes the rapid proliferation of this technology to all of the mineshafts on Sado Island. See Sado-gun *Kyōikukai, Sado Nendai Ki* (Kanazawa: Sado-gun Kyōikukan, 1938).
30. NKGT, Vol. 20, 18.
31. KTTJ, Vol. I, 748: Keichō 19/12 (January, 1615).
32. Ibid.
33. Fumoto Saburō, *Sado Kinginzan Shiwa* (Tokyo: Mitsubishi Kinzoku Kōgyō, 1973), 529.

34. Kobata, *Nihon Kōzan-shi no Kenkyū*, 122–137.
35. Mio Kishimoto-Nakayama, "The Kangxi Depression and Early Qing Local Markets," *Modern China* 10: 2 (1984): 233.
36. Nagahara Keiji and Yamamura Kozo, "Shaping the Process of Unification: Technological Progress in Sixteenth and Seventeenth Century Japan," *Journal of Japanese Studies* 14: 1 (1988): 82.
37. K. N. Chaudhuri, "The East India Company and the Export of Treasure in the Early Seventeenth Century," *The Economic History Review* 16: 1 (1963): 23.
38. Rudolph Blitz, "Mercantilist Policies and the Pattern of World Trade, 1500–1750," *The Journal of Economic History* 27: 1 (1967): 53.
39. Pieter de La Court de Jonge, *Interest van Holland, ofte Gronden van Hollandse Welvaren* ('t Amsterdam: Joan Cyprianus van der Gracht, 1662).
40. Om Prakash, "The Dutch East India Company in the Trade of the Indian Ocean," in *India and the Indian Ocean, 1500–1800*, ed. Ashin Das Gupta and M. N. Pearson (Oxford: Oxford University Press, 1977), 186.
41. Magalhaes-Godinho, *L'economie de L'empire Portugais aux XVe et XVIe Siecles*, 335.
42. Suzuki, *Kinsei Nichi-Ran Bōekishi no Kenkyū*, 41.
43. P. J. Blakewell, *Silver Mining and Society in Colonial Mexico, Zacatecas, 1546–1700* (Cambridge: Cambridge University Press, 1971), 242–246.
44. Woodrow Borah, *Early Colonial Trade Between Mexico and Peru* (Berkeley: University of California Press, 1954), 123.
45. William Atwell, "International Bullion Flows and the Chinese Economy circa 1530–1650," *Past and Present* 95 (1982): 74.
46. Anthony Reid, "An 'Age of Commerce' in Southeast Asian History," *Modern Asian Studies* 24: 1 (1990): 9.
47. J. H. Dales, "The Discoveries and Mercantilism: An Essay in History and Theory," *The Canadian Journal of Economic and Political Science* 21: 2 (1955): 145.
48. P. W. Klein, "De Zeventiende Eeuw (1585–1700)," in *De Economische Geshiedenis van Nederland*, ed. J. H. Stuijvenberg (Groningen: Wolters-Noordhoff, 1979), 107.
49. J. G. van Dillon, "Geld en Bank Wezen," in *Zeven Eeuwen Amsterdam, Vol. II: De Zeventiende Eeuw*, ed. A. E. d' Ailley (Amsterdam: Joost van den Vondel, 1947).
50. Israel, "A Conflict of Empires," 37.
51. Wätjen outlines in great detail the intricate trade patterns that developed between the Dutch and the various lands of the Mediterranean, especially

Spain and the Italian states. See his *Die Niederländer im Mittelmeergebiet zur Zeit ihrer Höchsten Machstellung* (Berlin: Curtius, 1909).
52. S. Hart, "Amsterdam Shipping and Trade to Northern Russia in the Seventeenth Century," *Mededelingen van de Nederlandse Vereningen voor Zeegeschiedenis* 26 (1973): 26–29.
53. Van Dam, *Beschryvingen, Deel I*, 633.
54. Ibid., 632.
55. Femme Gaastra, "The Exports of Precious Metal from Europe to Asia by the Dutch East India Company," in *Precious Metals in the Later Medieval and Early Modern Worlds*, ed. J.F. Richards (Durham: Carolina Academic Press, 1983), 448.
56. J. G. van Dillon has edited a massive work dealing with the *Wisselbanken* entitled *Bronnen tot de Geschiedenis der Wisselbanken* ('s-Gravenhage: Martinus Nijhoff, 1925). For the role of the bank in selling silver to the VOC, see Volume I, Chapter I.
57. Femme Gaastra, "De VOC in de 17e en 18e Eeuw: De Groei van een Bedrijf. Geld Tegen Goeden. Een Strukturele Verandering in het Nederlands-Aziatische Handelsverkeer," *Bijdragen en Mededelingen Betreffende Geschiedenis der Nederlanden* 91 (1976): 261.
58. Gaastra, "The Dutch East India Company and its Intra-Asiatic trade in Precious metals," 100.
59. Colenbrander, ed., *Jan Pietersz. Coen, Vol. I*, 485–486.
60. The entire text of Puyck 's description of his journey to the shogunal court can be found in M.E. van Opstall, ed., *De Reis van de Vloot van Pieter Willemsz. Verhoef naar Azië*, 1607–1612 ('s-Gravenhage: Martinus Nijhoff, 1972), 345–363.
61. W. Ph. Coolhaas, ed., *Generaal Missiven van Goveneurs Generaal en Raden aan de Herren XVII der Vereenigde Oostindische Compagnie, Deel II: 1639–1655* ('s-Gravenhage: Martinus Nijhoff, 1964), 412.
62. Bailey W. Diffe and George D. Winius outline this trading pattern, as well as the Portuguese presence in Asia as a whole, in their work, *Foundations of the Portuguese Empire 1415–1580* (Minneapolis: University of Minnesota Press, 1977), 392–399.
63. Yanai Kenji and Numata Jirō, *Kaigai Kōshōshi no Shiten, Vol. 2*, ed. Iwao Seiichi (Tokyo: Nihon Shoseki, 1975–76), 95.
64. Ralph Fitch, *Aanmerklyke Reys van Ralph Fitch, Koopman te Londen, Gedaan van Anno 1583 tot 1591: Na Ormus, Goa, Cambaya, Bacola, Chonderi, Pegu, Jamahay in Siam, en Weer na Pegu: van Daar na Malacca, Ceylon, Cochin, en de Geheel Kust can Oost-Indien nu Aldereerst uyt*

het Engelsch Vertaald; met Schoone Figueren, en een Volkomen Register (Leyden: Pieter van der Aa, 1706).
65. Cooper, "The Mechanics of the Macao-Nagasaki Silk Trade," 426.
66. Coolhaas, ed., *Generalle Missiven, Deel II*, 84.
67. Coolhaas, "De Vereenigde Oostindische Compagnie," 170.
68. *Kokushi Daijiten, Vol. 14* (entry for "gin") (Tokyo: Yoshikawa Kobunkan, 1984), 510.
69. Kobata, "The Production and Uses of Gold and Silver," 254.
70. Sakuma Shigeo, "Mindai Kaigai Shi Bōeki no Rekishiteki Haikai," *Shigaku Zasshi* 63: 1 (1953): 19–21.
71. Iwao, *Sakoku*, 148.
72. Figures for the export of silver by Chinese ships can be found in Kawaji Toshiakira, *Toyo Bunkō 124: Nagasaki Nikki, Shimoda Nikki* (Tokyo: Heibonsha, 1968).
73. Thompson, ed., *Diary of Richard Cocks*, Vol. II, 40.
74. Ibid., 295.
75. Nagazumi Yoko and Takeda Mariko, eds., *Hirado Oranda Shōkan Igirisu Shōkan Nikki: Nihon to no Sakoku e no Michi* (Tokyo: Soshiete, 1981), 27.
76. Ibid., 21.
77. Van Dam, *Beschryvinge, Deel II, part I*, 370.
78. Coolhaas, ed., *Generaal Missiven, Deel I*, 184–202.
79. Ikeda Kōun published a work in 1618 entitled *Genna Kōkaisho*, which is a manual for navigation that the author claimed to have learned from a Spanish naval captain by the name of Manuel Gonzalez. Included in the manual are instructions for sailing to various ports in Asia as well as basic Western techniques for navigating on the open ocean. This work can be found in a 1944 edition of the *Ikeda Kōun Henshū.*
80. Sugimoto and Swain, *Science and Culture in Traditional Japan*, 177–178.
81. For advances in shipbuilding technologies, see Ishii Kenji, *Nihon no Fune* (Tokyo: Sōgensha, 1957) and *Zusetsu Wasen Shiwa* (Tokyo: Shinseidō, 1983), as quoted in Nagahara and Yamamura, "Shaping the Process of Unification."
82. Watnabe, *Kinsei Nihon Bōeki-ron no Tenkai*, 20. For a discussion of the *shuinjō*, including Hideyoshi's role in their development, see chapter 2.
83. Ibid., 24.
84. Iwao, *Shuinsen to Nihonmachi*, 33.
85. KTTJ, Vol. 38, 507: Keichō 15/1/11 (February 4, 1610).

86. Nakata, "17 Seiki Shōtō no Taigai no Kosho," in *Nihon to Seiyō*, ed. Numata Jirō (Tokyo: Heibonsha, 1971), 153.
87. Eiichi Katō, "The Japanese-Dutch Trade in the Formative Period of the Seclusion Policy, Particularly in the Raw Silk Trade by the Dutch Factory at Hirado 1620–1640," *Acta Asiatica* 30 (1976): 66.
88. Iwao, *Shuinsen Bōekishi no Kenkyū*, 145–146, and *Shuinsen to Nihonmachi*, 75.
89. Katō, "Unification and Adaptation, The Early Shogunate and Dutch Trade Policies," 228.
90. The VOC president at Hirado reported the shogunal restrictions on Japanese trade on March 12, 1635. He stated that the bakufu was entirely deaf to the pleas of the great merchant families who claimed that their livelihoods would be destroyed. According to the president, the main reason for these restrictions was an increasing fear of Christianity. *Daghregister des Compoir Firando, Maert 12, 1635.*
91. Ronald Toby deals at great length with the Tokugawa's use of the Korean embassies as a symbol of legitimacy in *State and Diplomacy in Early Modern Japan: Asia in the Development of the Tokugawa Bakufu.*
92. Kazui Tashirō, *Kinsei Nitchō Tsūkō Bōekishi no Kenkyū* (Tokyo: Sōbunsha, 1981), 202–218.
93. Kazui Tashirō, "Exports of Japan's Silver to China via Korea and Changes in the Tokugawa Monetary System During the Seventeenth and Eighteenth Centuries," in *Metals and Monies in an Emerging Global Economy*, ed. Dennis Flynn and Arturo Giraldez (Aldershot: Variorum, 1997), 101.
94. Ibid., 103.
95. Van Dam, *Beschryvinge, Deel I, part. II*, 61.
96. Ibid., *Deel II, part. I*, 377.
97. Gaastra, "The Exports of Precious Metal," 464.
98. J. P. Coen, P. de Carpentier, W. van Antzen, Jacques Specx, Batavia, 6 September, 1622. VOC 1076, folios 3–26.
99. The following figures relating to the Japan trade through Taiwan can be found in the Taiwan Dagregisters edited by Blussé, Opstall, and Ts'ao under the title *De Dagregisters van het Kasteel Zeelandia, Taiwan.*
100. Ibid., 44.
101. Ibid., 357.
102. Ibid., 381.
103. Ibid., 441.
104. Ibid., 493.

105. Coolhaas, ed., *Generaal Missiven, Deel II*, 278–282.
106. Blussé, "No Boats to China," 53.
107. *Negotie Journalen 1636–1666. Het Archief van de Nederlandse Factorij in Japan, 1609–1860. Folios 836-860, Algemene Rijksarchief.*
108. Suzuki, *Kinsei Nichi-Ran Bōekishi no Kenkyū*, 47.
109. Coolhaas, ed., *Generaal Missiven, Deel I*, 244–246.
110. The *Pancado* was the Portuguese term for the Japanese term *Itowappu Nakama*, which can be translated as the "silk cartel." This was a group of merchants specifically designated by the bakufu to deal with raw, white Chinese silk and to set the prices at which the silk would be sold. The *Pancado* could refer to this cartel, or could also refer to the fixed price at which the silk would be sold. For a more complete description of this "cartel," see chapter 8.
111. Coolhaas, ed., *Generaal Missiven, Deel II*, 268
112. Johann Jacob Saar, *Verhaal van Drie Voorname Reizen naar Oostindiën; te Weten van Johan Jacobsz. Saar, Volkert Evertsz, en Albrecht Herport: Daarin, Beneffens de bezondere Voorvallen, hen Overkomen, de Historie en de Voornamste Dingen, die Sedert Vijventwintig Jaren Herwaarts, tot het Jaar Achtenzestig toe, in de Gewesten Geschied Zijn, Voorgestelt Worden* (Amsterdam: Jan Rieuwertsz. en Pieter Arentsz., 1671), 69–70.
113. Numata Jirō, "Edo Jidai no Bōeki to Taigai Kankei," in *Iwanami Kōza Nihon Rekishi, Vol. XIII*, ed. Ienaga Saburō (Tokyo: Iwanami Shoten, 1962–64), 41–76.
114. John Lee, "Trade and Economy in Pre-industrial East Asia, c.1500–c.1800: East Asia in the Age of Global Integration," *The Journal of Asian Studies* 58: 1 (1999): 9.
115. Kate Wildman Nakai, *Shogunal Politics: Arai Hakuseki and the Premises of Tokugawa Rule* (Cambridge: Harvard University Press, 1988), 98.
116. Hayashi Fukusai, "Koshūki" in *Tsūkō Ichiran (8 Volumes), Vol. 4* (Tokyo: 1967), 304.
117. Van Dam, *Beschryvinge, Deel II, part I* (Den Hague: Rijks Geschiedenis Publicatiën, 1977), 436.
118. Hayashi, "Nagasaki Ki," in *Tsūkō Ichiran (8 Volumes), Vol. 4* (Tokyo: Kokusho Kankokai, 1967), 332–335.
119. Yamawaki Teijirō, *Nagasaki no Oranda Shōkan: Seikai no naka no Sakoku Nihon* (Tokyo: Chuo Shinsho, 1980), 16.
120. "Herren Zeventien aan Governeur-Generaal en Raden," VOC 320, 1673.

121. Arai Hakuseki, "Honchō Hōka Tsūyō Jiryaku," in *Arai Hakuseki Zenshū, Vol. III*, ed. Imaizumi Teisuke (Tokyo: Yoshikawa Hanshichi, 1905–07), 673–674.
122. Van Dam, *Beschryvinge*, 446–469.
123. J. Fenstra Kuiper, *Japan en de Buitenwereld in de Achtiende Eeuw* ('s-Gravenhage: Martinus Nijhoff, 1921), 155.
124. Nachod, *Die Beziehungen der Niederlaendischen Oostindischen Kompagnie zu Japan.* The main reason why copper was in such demand in Europe was the state of almost continuous warfare that prevailed on the continent, giving rise to a huge demand for ammunition and artillery, both of which were produced from copper. This was especially true when the Dutch were at war with Sweden, which had a monopoly in the European copper trade.
125. Glamann, "The Dutch East India Company's Trade in Japanese Copper," 46.
126. Blussé, "No Boats to China," 72.
127. Glamann, "The Dutch East India Company's Trade in Japanese Copper," 73–74.

Chapter 4

A Beautiful Island: Dutch Taiwan as a Strategic Link Between Japan and Asia

For many non-specialists of East Asia, Taiwanese history begins in the 1870s with the Japanese "expedition" to the island that led to its eventual colonization and incorporation into the Japanese Empire. Perhaps some will have heard the romanized name of the romanticized "pirate" Coxinga and relate him somehow to the island, but beyond that, few people realize the role that the *Ihla Formosa*[1] played in the economic history of Asia in the seventeenth century.[2] For a brief period of time, the island was of the greatest importance to the economy of several countries, including Japan, China, Siam, Cambodia, and indirectly in places as far away as the Coromandel Coast, Bengal, and Persia. Because of its strategic position astride the trade routes between Japan and Southeast Asia, and because of a number of historical circumstances relating to Chinese-Japanese relations, Taiwan was a major factor in the development and prosperity of the Dutch East India Company in the first half of the seventeenth century. The island's role as a "redistribution center" for Japanese precious metals as well as its role as a "staging area" for Asian goods destined for the Japanese market ensured that Taiwan would occupy an important position in the Asian economy as a whole and more immediately in the fortunes of the VOC. Furthermore, the Dutch occupation of the island marks the real beginning of that country's serious trade with Japan in so far as the VOC, now able to tap into the Chinese silk market, was able for the first time to render trade with Japan truly profitable. This had widespread repercussions for Dutch trade in general because a steady supply of silk for the Japanese market meant that the VOC was able to tap into the vast supply of Japanese precious metals and thereby help to finance its other factories in Asia without the huge outlay of capital from Europe that plagued other companies, most notably the English East India Company.[3]

Not only was the Dutch occupation of Taiwan a boon for the VOC, but it also played a large role in the economic and political history of seventeenth-century Japan. Because the Dutch were finally able to supply Japan with more than a trifling quantity of silk, the bakufu felt little compunction in expelling the Portuguese when the latter's Catholicism became a pressing political issue (i.e. after the Shimabara Rebellion). The Japanese, eager to maintain a high level of imports from the continent, were previously reluctant to expel the Portuguese because the trade between Macao and Nagasaki satisfied a huge demand for luxury products, namely raw, Chinese silk. The Dutch, with their newfound capacity to import raw silk and other Asian goods, were able to convince the bakufu that the Portuguese were no longer necessary to support the patterns of consumption to which the Japanese elite had grown accustomed. By examining the trade patterns that connected Japan and Asia, in the middle of which was Taiwan, it becomes readily apparent that the Japanese economy had a tremendous impact on the continent in the seventeenth century.

This chapter, therefore, will examine the role of Taiwan in Japan's seventeenth-century foreign trade as it was conducted first in Japanese ships, and later vicariously through the ships of the Dutch East India Company.

Taiwan and Early Modern Japan

Taiwan became a prominent destination for Asian merchants from the late sixteenth century. Because of the continuing Ming ban on trade with Japan, the island served as a convenient meeting place for merchants from China and Japan, especially when the emperor in Beijing allowed commercial relations with many other areas in Asia (including Taiwan) to be reestablished in the late sixteenth century.[4] As John Wills notes in his study of Chinese maritime trade, not only were Chinese ships traveling to Taiwan, but they were in all probability also illegally traveling to Japan, under the guise of official trade with Taiwan.[5] The trade with Japan continued to be banned because of the persistence of *wakō* activity along the Chinese coastline; and although by this time many of the pirates were in fact Chinese, the popular perception of the Japanese as pirates remained. As Richard Cocks tells us quite succinctly, "…the hatred against the Japons was worse than against any other nation."[6] Similarly, Joao Rodrigues, in his account of sixteenth-century Japan, states, "many pirate fleets sailed from Japan to rob and devastate various coastal places of China and even inland areas along the rivers. All this made the Chinese greatly hate and fear the Japanese, regarding them as their worst enemies."[7]

English merchants note that from early in the seventeenth century, Chinese ships were making frequent voyages to the many safe harbors of Taiwan to carry out trade that would have otherwise been banned.[8] It is clear that as early as the 1570s Japanese merchants were coming to Taiwan to deal with their counterparts from the Southeastern Chinese province of Fujian in order to procure the raw Chinese silk that was in such demand in the archipelago.[9] Moreover, the Chinese were very interested in the camphor tree that was indigenous to Taiwan, and which was used as a medicine as well as an insect repellent.[10] For Japanese merchants, however, Taiwan was used primarily as a base for trade with the Chinese and for procurement of deerskins from the natives. John Wills describes the major role of Taiwan before the arrival of the Dutch as a "nexus where all parties could meet with a minimum of political complication."[11] Therefore, apart from an abundance of deerskins, the main importance of Taiwan for the Japanese lay in the strategic position of the island itself, the same consideration that would draw the Dutch to Taiwan in the 1620s.

As Oda Nobunaga and Toyotomi Hideyoshi gradually consolidated power within Japan, Taiwan (along with other Southeast Asian ports) began to play a role in the consciousness of the new rulers. Hideyoshi, it is clear, was sending letters to such countries as the Philippines and Korea, demanding that they pay tribute to him. At about the same time he also sent a letter to a kingdom known to the Japanese as "Takasago," in which he threatened to attack if the kingdom did not pay him tribute: "The Philippines and Ryukyu have sent tribute-bearing envoys to our country...Your country, however, has not yet sent any envoy to our military headquarters. This lack of loyalty will certainly bring the curse of Heaven upon you."[12] Takasago is generally recognized to have been an indigenous kingdom located on the island of Taiwan, although that seems to represent the extent of our knowledge.[13] After setting up a colony at the site of the future Spanish fort at Keelung (on the north coast of the island), Hideyoshi began to issue *shuinjō* to merchants of the three great mercantile cities of Nagasaki, Kyoto, and Sakai, recognizing their right to trade with the island.[14] This practice would be continued as the Tokugawa family consolidated their control in Japan from 1600. From this time until the Japanese government banned direct overseas trade by its own merchants in the mid 1630s, a total of thirty-six ships were authorized to trade with Taiwan.[15]

Japanese subjects were not the only merchants to be given *shuinjō* to trade at Taiwan; Chinese merchants resident in Japan also successfully petitioned the bakufu for this privilege. The most prolific of these Chinese was a merchant by the name of Li Tan, the "Andreas Dittis" of Richard Cocks' diary, often referred to simply as the "China Captain."[16] Li Tan, by the time of his death in 1625, had established a trading network that connected Japan, Taiwan, the Chinese coastal provinces, and Southeast Asia in a complex commercial web entirely independent of Ming jurisdiction. Upon Li's death, his extensive trading network was taken over by his able lieutenant Zheng Zhilong, who transferred his base of operations from Hirado to Amoy. Zheng was known to the Dutch as "Iquan" and was, in fact, treated by the VOC as an independent sovereign, although he was still ostensibly subject to the Ming emperor in Beijing. Ming control of the outlying provinces had eroded so drastically, however, that areas such as the southeast coastal provinces were essentially semiautonomous, as evidenced by the flourishing commercial empire operated by the Li and Zheng families that routinely flouted Ming prohibitions and only nominally recognized Ming authority. Zheng Zhilong was also the father of Zheng Chenggong, better known by the name "Coxinga," a figure who would have a profound impact on the island of Taiwan.[17]

In the midst of steadily increasing Japanese mercantile activity on Taiwan, Tokugawa Ieyasu in 1616 ordered the *daikan* of Nagasaki, Murayama Tōan, to "invade" the island and claim it for the bakufu. On May fourth of the following year, Maruyama left for the island with a force of two or three thousand troops. This venture proved in the end to be a military fiasco, and Murayama was later executed for his failure.[18] Although there is no motive included in the order to invade, there was a rumor circulating at the time that the last Toyotomi heir had somehow escaped from Osaka Castle during its destruction a few months earlier and fled to somewhere in Southeast Asia with a number of his Christian vassals. While in retrospect these rumors seem to have been unfounded, they were taken very seriously at the time, and may have been behind the aborted invasion of Taiwan, however unlikely this may seem to modern historians in retrospect.[19] Much more probable, however, is the simple fact that Ieyasu was extremely interested in foreign trade and felt that control of Taiwan would further his goals in this respect. We have already noted that the position of the island was extremely favorable for trade with Asia and that there was already an established tradition of Sino-Japanese trade on Taiwan, all considerations of which Ieyasu was surely aware.

What is absolutely clear is that the Japanese were highly interested in trade on Taiwan and were sailing there for that purpose quite regularly throughout the early years of the seventeenth century. In fact, until the third shogun Iemitsu forbad Japanese ships from journeying overseas in 1634, the Dutch often complained of heavy Japanese competition on Taiwan; the Governor-General of the VOC at Batavia, for example, in 1624 wrote to his superiors in the Netherlands that in order to maintain Dutch profits on the island, "it is to be hoped that no Japanese vessels will be licensed this year."[20] Only a few days later, however, it was recorded in the *Generalle Missiven* that in fact three Japanese junks arrived on Taiwan with 35,000 *taels* of silver with which to buy raw silk, silk piece goods, and deerskins, thus entirely circumventing the Dutch.[21] The Japanese ships that made the trip to Taiwan offered such keen competition because the goods that they bought on the island were precisely the goods that the Dutch were bringing to Japan. Consequently, a great deal of friction arose between the Japanese merchants and the VOC over the issue of the Taiwan trade. It is not altogether surprising, then, that the most severe disruption in the entire history of Japanese-Dutch relations was the result of Dutch efforts to tax Japanese ships that came to the island, an incident to which we shall return later.

THE VOC ON TAIWAN

Successive Governors-General of the VOC had advocated the establishment of a factory on Taiwan from quite early on. Because of a number of factors however, including hopes for direct trade with the Chinese mainland, this plan was never given serious attention. The Dutch arrival on Taiwan in 1624, therefore, was an historical accident that was the result of a compromise with local Ming officials rather than the result of a coherent company policy. After Admiral

Cornelis Ryerszoon's attack on the Portuguese commercial center at Macao was repulsed, the Dutch fleet retreated to the Pescadores and began preparations for building a fort. After repeated Chinese protests were ignored, the Ming sent a sizeable military force to clear the islands of the Dutch usurpers. Hostilities were avoided, however, when an agreement was reached whereby the Dutch would establish a factory on the more distant island of Taiwan where Chinese merchants would be allowed to visit and trade with them.[22]

This agreement seems to have been a completely local, ad hoc arrangement as the Ming government still rigidly maintained its unwillingness to trade with the Dutch.[23] Considering the relative weakness of Ming control in the maritime provinces such as Fujian, such an agreement would hardly be surprising. Furthermore, trade between the Dutch and the Chinese coastal merchants would be beneficial to both parties, a further incentive to avoid hostilities and to use a relatively distant place such as Taiwan as a place of rendezvous. The negotiations were led on the Chinese side by the governor of Fujian, Nan Chu-i, along with the ubiquitous Li Tan, whose extensive mercantile and political connections made him a natural intermediary between the Dutch and the Chinese.[24] It was apparently Li's idea that the Dutch remove to Taiwan, with the understanding that Chinese vessels could trade with the VOC on "neutral ground" (the Ming maritime prohibitions on trade did not apply to Taiwan, a diplomatic technicality no doubt, but a seemingly successful one).[25]

With the successful conclusion of this agreement, Taiwan again played the role of an intermediary meeting place for merchants who would otherwise not be able to trade. Upon the completion of Fort Zeelandia on a sandbar on the southern part of Taiwan, the Dutch finally gained a foothold, however tenuous, in the Chinese silk trade that would allow them to finally make their Japan venture profitable.[26] Katō Eiichi notes that with the Dutch position on Taiwan secure, and with a relatively steady supply of Chinese silk that the new factory was able to procure, Dutch profits rose markedly in the first ten years after the founding of Fort Zeelandia.[27] These profits were due almost entirely to the fact that the Dutch were able to utilize the strategic position of Taiwan astride the interconnected trade patterns between Japan and the Asian mainland, particularly the all-important silver-silk route between southeastern China and Kyushu.

Profits were also derived from an increase in Chinese emigration to Taiwan during the disorder of the Manchu invasion from the 1640s onward. The Dutch welcomed these settlers as a tax base, instituting a "protection tax," to pay for Dutch military support against the aborigines, a "poll tax" on every adult male from seven years of age, and taxes on deer hunting and fishing. Governor Coen very early on ordered Hans Putnam, the Governor-General on Taiwan, to encourage settlement by Chinese. This was accomplished in part by mounting expeditions to the interior of the island in an effort to "pacify" the aborigines, thereby protecting the new settlers from attack.[28] Chinese settlers eventually became a considerable source of revenue since there came to be as many as 25,000 Chinese families living on Taiwan.

The Dutch, finally able to obtain a supply of silk by means other than outright piracy, faced a major obstacle on Taiwan in the ever-present competition with Japanese merchants. Although the number of *shuinjō* that the bakufu issued to merchants was never very large, Dutch records reveal that several ships either fully or partly owned by Japanese regularly arrived on the island to trade with the Chinese and the natives. Martin Sonck, in a letter addressed to the Governor-General in Batavia, for example, complains about Chinese merchants smuggling silk onto Taiwan, carrying it across the island, and selling it secretly to the Japanese.[29] Similarly, Governor-General Coen writes in February 1624 that in the past year two Japanese ships brought 70,000 *taels* in silver with which to buy silk from the Chinese, therefore entirely bypassing the Dutch factory.[30] Governor-General Pieter Carpentier, echoing this lament, stated that every year, two or three Japanese ships arrived with the sole purpose of buying silk from the Chinese and deerskins from the natives, while three to four Chinese ships arrived yearly to supply this demand.[31] And finally, Nicholas Couckebacker, in a diary entry for the year 1633, states succinctly that, "When many Japanese junks come to

Taiwan, it is difficult to carry on trade with the Chinese."[32] The Dutch solution to this problem was to try to obtain a monopoly on goods such as sugar and deerskins and at the same time to somehow prevent Japanese ships from calling at the island.

The Dutch often complained to the bakufu of what they considered unfair commercial advantages on the part of the Japanese merchants, going so far as to send an ambassador to the shogun's court to request a stop to Japanese trade on Taiwan.[33] This embassy proved successful, for in May of 1634 the bakufu decreed that henceforth no Japanese merchants were allowed to trade on Taiwan.[34] Although the dispatch of an embassy and frequent Dutch petitions were certainly not the only, or perhaps even the major, considerations in the shogun's decision, there can be no doubt that the Dutch benefited greatly from this development. It was a clear victory for the company because it was now in a position to monopolize the purchase of Taiwanese goods and to take over the substantial trade previously carried on by Japanese merchants. This victory, however, came on the heels of an event that almost cost the Dutch their trade in Japan, and by extension on Taiwan as well. The affair has come to be known alternatively as the "Taiwan incident" or the "Nuijts affair," and is indicative of just how volatile Dutch trade in Japan could be.

The Taiwan Incident

Although the Dutch were certainly keen to dissuade Japanese merchants from coming to Taiwan for trade, there was also a practical reason for levying a 10 percent tax on all ships arriving at Castle Zeelandia. The Dutch factory was not located on the mainland of the island; rather it was built on a permanent sandbar just off of the Southern tip of the island (it was that sandbar that was called Taiwan; the name was later adopted to refer to the whole island, while the area on which Zeelandia was built came to be known as Tainan). Because of this precarious site (a position that would later prove disastrous to the Dutch who were forced to defend it), the harbor, while being a good one for incoming ships, had to be continuously maintained. It was for this reason that Martin Sonck, the president of the Taiwan factory, decided to levy the 10 percent "harbor tax" in 1625.[35] Also contributing to this decision was the fact that the Dutch suffered a number of restrictions and expenses in Japan (such as the endless gift-giving) that made them resentful of the relatively unencumbered Japanese trade on Taiwan.[36] Naturally the Japanese merchants protested this tax, and in fact several times simply refused to pay, complaining that they had been trading on the island for years before the arrival of the Dutch. The Japanese also argued that because the Dutch paid no harbor tax in Hirado, they should not be unfairly burdened with one either.[37] This, then, is the immediate background for the "Taiwan incident" that almost put an end to Dutch trade in Japan.

Although much of the blame for the "Taiwan incident" has fallen on the shoulders of the unfortunate Pieter Nuijts, it is not at all clear that this is justified. What is clear, however, is that the head of the Taiwan factory had a knack for making the captains of Japanese ships angry. For example, shortly after taking office in 1627, Nuijts received a tip from a Chinese merchant that a number of Japanese had arrived on the island heavily armed. When the Japanese ship in question was searched, the Dutch indeed found a great number of weapons; and when the Dutch relieved them of their arms, the Japanese sailors acted extremely haughty and riotous. This is, of course, Nuijts' own version of events; he wrote of this incident, "our suspicions were confirmed that the Japanese are not to be trusted any longer."[38] Nuijts vowed that he would continue to search Japanese junks until captains of a more reasonable temperament were employed. The president of the factory in Japan at the time, however, wrote somewhat prophetically in a letter to Nuijts that the Japanese were to be treated with discretion, or else great troubles would ensue in Japan.[39] Nuijts apparently did not take this advice to heart, and as a result, the VOC experienced a great number of difficulties in Japan over perceived slights to Japanese commercial interests on Taiwan.

In 1626 two ships received permission from the bakufu to trade at Taiwan, the captain of one being a sailor by the name of

Yamada Yahyōe. Not finding any Chinese silk merchants on the island, Yamada petitioned Nuijts for the rental of two Dutch vessels in which to sail to the coast of China in an effort to procure silk. Nuijts, for whatever reason, refused, and the two Japanese ships had to return to Japan empty-handed, a rather serious loss considering the substantial expense of outfitting an overseas expedition. The following year the same captain was in charge of a ship owned by Suetsugu Heizō, the *daikan* of Nagasaki, which again sailed to Taiwan in search of Chinese silk. This time Nuijts would not allow them to unload their ships, and because of the delays involved, the Japanese vessels missed the southern monsoons by which they were to return to Japan. The already disgruntled Yamada was furthermore required to pay the contentious harbor tax; and when he refused, Nuijts moved to have him arrested. This action was the final straw for the Japanese sailors who proceeded to take matters very literally into their own hands.

Pieter Nuijts began his diary entry for the fifth of July 1628 with the ominous words, "An extraordinary and serious event has occurred."[40] On this day, Captain Yamada demanded that his ships be set free, the confiscated goods returned, and that he be able to leave Taiwan immediately. When this demand was refused, he, along with his crew, broke into the Governor-General's quarters, and after a great deal of heavy fighting, took Nuijts, his young son, and Francois Caron prisoner.[41] Yamada bound his prisoners and threatened to kill the Governor-General if the Dutch troops surrounding the house did not lay down their arms, a demand they reluctantly complied with at the urging of Nuijts himself. The numbers involved were not particularly small; there were as many as 150 Japanese sailors (apparently fully armed, although how they armed themselves is a mystery), and of course an entire squadron of several hundred Dutch soldiers. These numbers, to say nothing of the tension enveloping the factory, could easily have led to a pitched battle and a great loss of life. Overt hostilities were avoided, however, and as Nuijts notes in his diary, the ensuing negotiations proved to be relatively cordial considering the circumstances.

The Japanese, represented by Yamada, demanded that there be a "hostage exchange" until both parties could reach Japan, where the situation would be officially resolved. In exchange for Pieter Nuijts, his son Lawrence, and three other important members of the Dutch factory, Yamada was willing to turn over his own son along with four other Japanese as hostages to the Dutch. These hostages would then make the voyage to Japan aboard their opposites' ships in order to ensure good faith. Once in Japan, they would be returned and formal negotiations between the two sides would take place.

In addition to this exchange, the Japanese sailors drew up a contract in which they demanded three concessions of the Dutch before departing. First of all, they wanted two hundred picols of raw silk from the Dutch storehouse to cover losses incurred when their ship was impounded. Secondly, the Dutch were to free eleven native Taiwanese who had been imprisoned by the Dutch and who were associated with the Japanese from a town called "Shinkō."[42] Finally, the Japanese demanded the return in full of the goods that were confiscated from their ships.[43] The governing council at Zeelandia was initially reluctant to accept these demands, especially the item concerning the 200 *picols* of silk; at this stage in Dutch-Japanese trade, the Dutch were still struggling to procure even modest amounts of raw Chinese silk, and 200 picols represented almost an entire year's shipment to Japan. In the end, however, Nuijts reassured the council that it was a small price to pay to keep relations with Japan running smoothly (and one would imagine his safety played a certain role in his acceptance of these terms).[44]

With the signing of the contract on July 3, 1628, both parties prepared to depart for Japan with their respective hostages. Contrary to what Nuijts believed, however, there was to be no speedy resolution to this incident once they reached Japan. This was partly the result of Nuijts' haughty behavior when he was later appointed an emissary to the shogun's court. More importantly, however (and probably unbeknownst to the Dutch), powerful Japanese officials had invested in the ships that were confiscated. Foremost among these was the Governor of Nagasaki, Suetsugu Heizō, known in the Dutch sources as

"Phesedonne." The Dutch were already out of favor at Nagasaki because of their continuous attacks on Portuguese and Chinese shipping, ships that often contained a great deal of Japanese silver, invested by wealthy Japanese such as Suetsugu. The Taiwan incident further enraged the governor, who used every weapon at his disposal to make sure that the Dutch paid for their actions on Taiwan. Within months after Nuijts' arrival in Japan, therefore, the bakufu "arrested" the Dutch at Hirado, allowing none of their ships in the harbor to leave. All trade between the Dutch and Japan was effectively suspended, and Neijenroode's earlier prediction about the imprudence of dealing harshly with the Japanese on Taiwan was realized.

It is indicative of the importance of the Japan trade to the VOC that Jan Pieterszoon Coen, Governor-General at Batavia, appointed Willem Jansen as a special ambassador to Japan in an effort to resolve the situation.[45] Upon reaching Edo, however, Jansen realized that his task would be an extremely difficult one; it is evident from his diaries that he thought that the Japanese, led by Suetsugu Heizō, were intentionally dragging out the proceedings in order to allow more time for Japanese junks to trade in Southeast Asia without Dutch competition. This perception may not be totally unfounded as a great number of Japanese junks were in fact sent to both Tonkin and Cochin during the lull in VOC trade.[46] Jansen was to spend two years at Edo without any result, and when the shogun finally did respond to the embassy, he presented the Dutch with a set of twelve demands, one of which was the immediate cession of Fort Zeelandia to the Japanese.[47] This demand the Dutch naturally refused, and after several more months at court, the bakufu ordered Jansen to return to Batavia in order to acquaint the authorities there with the situation, another move that the VOC suspected of being a delaying tactic. The Dutch had no choice, however, and in 1630 Jansen arrived back in Batavia empty handed.

Although many VOC officials were fully aware of the value of the factory at Hirado, the new Governor-General Jacques Specx was unique at Batavia because of his extensive dealings with the Japanese on a diplomatic level. He had served as a merchant in Japan and later as president of the factory, and therefore knew first-hand the patience and persistence needed in dealing with the shogun and his councilors. Specx was probably aware that when Jansen returned to Batavia empty-handed, it was simply a diplomatic ploy on the part of the shogun. He therefore refused to accept failure, sending Jansen back to Japan for another round of diplomacy.

As it turned out, nature was on the side of the Dutch; in 1630 Suetsugu died, followed shortly thereafter by the shogun Hidetada. The Japanese authorities now had far weightier issues to deal with than a minor commercial dispute, and so on Jansen's second trip to Edo the climate was more favorable for a resolution. While we should not ascribe too much importance to the deaths of Suetsugu and Hidetada, they should not be entirely overlooked; the succession of a new shogun early in the Tokugawa period was a precarious time for the nation politically, and the feud with the Dutch was after all largely personal (involving Suetsugu Heizo) a feud the former official's son had no desire to perpetuate.[48]

As noted previously, Jacques Specx had a great deal of experience in dealing with the Japanese authorities. While it can never be known for sure, Specx must have considered that the Japanese, especially after the death of Suetsugu, were looking for a way to end this stalemate while still "saving face." This may very well be the reason behind the Governor-General's decision to send Pieter Nuijts to Hirado.[49] In 1632, the *Warmont* left Batavia for Japan with Nuijts aboard. Upon his arrival he was immediately put under house arrest, in the custody of the Matsuura family of Hirado. When the Dutch turned Nuijts over to the bakufu, the authorities were presented with a relatively peaceful solution to the dilemma while still being able to claim victory in the negotiations. More to the point, they were able to maintain commercial relations with the Dutch on their own terms, a situation that benefited both parties insofar as the Dutch helped to fill an insatiable Japanese demand for Asian luxury goods, and of course made a handsome profit in the process. Furthermore, as Nagazumi Yōko points out, the relatively amicable resolution of the Nuijts affair proved to be a defining point in Japanese-Dutch relations because it established the good faith of the Dutch. By sending a special emissary and by showing a good deal of patience without resorting to violence, the Dutch clearly demonstrated that they were willing to play by Japanese rules.[50]

On December 15, 1631, a Chinese junk arrived in Taiwan from Japan and related the news that the VOC ship *De Parel* had arrived in Nagasaki and was allowed to trade.[51] This was probably the first notice outside of Japan that the Taiwan incident had been resolved and that the Dutch were again permitted to trade. This must have come as a tremendous relief particularly to the factory on Taiwan, since it was almost wholly dependant on the Japan trade for its existence. Official confirmation arrived later as Jansen stopped briefly at Taiwan on his way back to Batavia. The ordeal that threatened to jeopardize VOC trade with Japan (and as a result Taiwan) was over, at which the president of the Taiwan factory wrote in true seventeenth-century fashion, "God be praised."[52]

In an epilogue to the Taiwan incident (in reality much more than an "incident," as it lasted for three years), the Dutch, when they handed Nuijts over to the Japanese, did not leave him to languish in prison. Rather, as evidenced by several entries in the diary of the president of the Hirado factory, freeing their compatriot was one of the top priorities of the VOC in Japan.[53] Nuijts seems to have had the sympathy of company officials both in Japan and at Batavia and was never stigmatized as a failure in the way that Frederick Coyett would be upon surrendering Fort Zeelandia to the Zheng in 1662. The persistence with which the company petitioned the Japanese rulers for Nuijts' release was finally rewarded in the summer of 1634 when the shogun Iemitsu unexpectedly freed him and allowed him to leave Japan. Characteristically, this act of clemency was prompted by a sumptuous gift, the details of which warrant mentioning, as they shed some light on the importance of giving gifts as a means of diplomacy in early modern Japan.

Iemitsu, the third Tokugawa to hold the title of shogun, owed his ascendancy entirely to his grandfather Ieyasu, who insisted on the eldest son succeeding to the shogunate as a matter of course in order to regularize the succession. This went against the wishes of Hidetada, however, who believed another son to be much more capable than his firstborn. Ever the filial son, however, he put aside his own wishes and accepted Ieyasu's ruling that Iemitsu become the next shogun. This precedent initiated the practice of primogeniture that lasted the entirety of the Edo period.[54] Whether this was the reason why Iemitsu held his grandfather is such high esteem will probably forever remain unclear; he was, however, primarily responsible for the systematic adoration of Ieyasu's memory that had such a strong impact on the country for the next two hundred years.

Iemitsu's first act of homage was to remove the body of Ieyasu from his former grave to a shrine built especially for his grandfather at Nikkō. The various daimyo were all prevailed upon to support the construction of the shrine, ensuring that it would be an incredibly lavish undertaking. Similarly, daimyo were "strongly encouraged" to establish branch shrines in their respective provinces in order to more effectively honor the spirit of Ieyasu. Furthermore, in exchange for a small remuneration, the imperial court was pleased to raise Ieyasu to the status of both a Shinto deity as well as an incarnation of a Buddha. It was at this time that the Dutch decided to send Iemitsu an especially lavish present: a massive copper lantern made in Holland that was both intrinsically valuable and a beautiful work of craftsmanship. Iemitsu immediately had this treasure placed at the new shrine at Nikkō, and was so pleased with this gesture that he finally granted Pieter Nuijts his unconditional release.[55]

Although the lantern was undoubtedly a valuable gift in and of itself, the real value behind the offering lay in the legitimacy that such a gift lent to the new shogun. Questions of inferiority must certainly have weighed heavily on Iemitsu, and grandiose displays such as this surely bolstered his position as the rightful shogun. Incidentally, the lantern can still be seen today at Nikkō and serves to illustrate the workings of "gift diplomacy" that the Dutch used to such effect.

Although Nuijts was freed and company trade in Japan soon returned to normal, he paid a high personal price for his involvement in this affair. Although he was relatively well treated by the daimyo of Hirado during his four years of imprisonment, Nuijts' son Lawrence died during the initial crossing from Taiwan to Japan.[56]

Taiwan and VOC Prosperity

With the conclusion of the Taiwan incident, profits from the factories on Taiwan and in Hirado began to soar as the Dutch used the island as a base to procure Chinese goods that were in demand in Japan. In return, the VOC used Taiwan as a "redistribution center" in which Japanese silver and copper would be collected and sent to factories throughout Asia. For several years, beginning in the mid 1630s, Japan was consistently the most profitable factory in all of Asia, and it can be argued persuasively that this was partly because of the unique role of Taiwan as an intermediary in the trade between Asia and Japan.[57] This is evidenced by the fact that the drastic increase in company profits began immediately after the resumption of trade with Japan after the Taiwan incident. In 1635, for example, Hendrick Brouwer wrote from Batavia that the trade with Japan yielded no less than five tons of gold.[58] Because of the huge yield of Japanese precious metals, the VOC was effectively able in part to finance the rest of its Asian factories without resorting to large-scale precious metal exports from the west, a decided advantage over other Europeans companies.

One of the reasons why the factories in Japan and Taiwan were so productive was because of the confused state of affairs on the Chinese mainland. Although the Ming authorities had officially banned trade with Japan and had also refused several commercial overtures by the Dutch, the southeastern maritime provinces were largely politically autonomous and thus routinely flouted commercial prohibitions from Beijing. The Ming court was overwhelmed with its efforts to stave off a Manchu advance in the northeast, and consequently had little time or resources with which to enforce its economic policies in provinces such as Fujian. It was because of this state of affairs that merchants such as Li Tan and the Zheng were able to trade with the Dutch and the Japanese in direct contradiction to the Ming trade restrictions.

Zheng Zhihlong, known in Dutch sources as "Iquan," was born in 1604 and was baptized early in his life at Macao with the Christian name of Nicholas Iquan. At the age of twenty he traveled to Hirado where he became a merchant, entering the service of the powerful Li Tan. Upon the latter's death in 1625, Zheng inherited Li's organization and soonafter moved his base of operation from Hirado to Amoy (Xiamen) where he continued to build up his power base, in the process demonstrating the thin line between legitimate trade and piracy.[59] Here Ming politics become exceedingly complicated because the empire was steadily losing ground to the Manchu invaders from the northeast, and cities as far south as Amoy (Xiamen) fell prey to the invaders. These dire circumstances prompted the Ming to overlook Zheng's former illegal activities and to co-opt him into government service as a commodore of Fujian province.[60] In an act of supreme irony, Zheng was promoted in 1630 to the title of "admiral for the suppression of piracy."[61] Incidentally, it was the fall of Amoy (Xiamen) that prompted thousands of Chinese, on Zheng's advice, to flee the mainland to Taiwan, where they were accepted by the Dutch as a tax and agricultural base (and as subjects for conversion to Christianity, Taiwan being one of the few places in Asia that the Dutch made a concerted effort at proselytizing).[62] By the close of the 1620s, Zheng was firmly in control of most of the trade of Fujian, and from his base in that province he sent ships regularly to both Taiwan and Japan. In 1628, however, the VOC reached an understanding with Zhilong in which he would trade with the Dutch on Taiwan, who would then act as middlemen between the Chinese and the Japanese.[63] It was this role as middleman that initially made the Dutch trade with Japan so lucrative, even though Zheng routinely flouted this agreement.[64]

There are two more circumstances which converged within a five-year period that also served to make the Taiwan-Japan trade extremely lucrative for the VOC. The first concerned the Japanese themselves, and the second concerned the long-standing trade between the Japanese and the Portuguese at Macao. As mentioned previously, the Dutch were extremely eager to prohibit Japanese merchants from trading with the Chinese and natives on Taiwan and therefore petitioned the bakufu almost every year to ban this trade. If Japanese merchants came to Taiwan in any great number, the Dutch would be unable to obtain enough silk—the most important driving force behind the entire East Asian trade—for the Japanese market. They would also be unable to maintain their near monopoly on deerskins, another highly profitable trade in Japan. Therefore, it was with great relief that Nicholas Couckebacker noted in his diary in May of 1634 that the third shogun Iemitsu had prohibited Japanese merchants from traveling to Taiwan.[65] In accordance with this new edict, the Dutch issued strict regulations to the Chinese residents on the island that explicitly forbad them to sell deerskins to the Japanese, even if the Japanese possessed a *shuinjō*.[66]

The shogunal decree forbidding Japanese merchants to trade at Taiwan was followed shortly thereafter by an edict prohibiting Japanese from going abroad at all; this was the beginning of a general clampdown that would later come to be known as the *sakoku* decrees, and will be dealt with more fully hereafter.[67] In the meantime, the second circumstance that served to render VOC trade between Taiwan and Japan increasingly profitable involved the expulsion of the Portuguese from Japan in 1639 and the huge commercial gap that the Dutch were then able to fill.

In the diaries of the VOC officials, there is a persistent theme in the first third of the seventeenth century lamenting the entrenched Portuguese commercial position in Asia (this is quite aside from the recurrent theme of the Portuguese as "Papist" enemies with whom the Dutch were persistently at war). The Dutch averred time and again that if Portuguese trade between Macao and Nagasaki in particular could somehow be disrupted, it would translate into greater profits for the Dutch, especially now that the company had a foothold, however tenuous, in the Chinese silk market.[68] The Dutch sources therefore became optimistic as the Japanese authorities grew more and more disillusioned with the Portuguese over the issue of Christian missionaries.

Christianity had been officially proscribed for decades by the late 1630s, yet missionaries (especially Jesuit priests) continued to try to enter the country secretly, even in the face of mass executions and grueling torture. Matters quickly came to a head after the Shimabara Rebellion (often referred to by the Japanese as the "Arima Rebellion" after the domain in which it occurred) that the bakufu perceived, accurately or not, to be a Christian rebellion.[69] While the true cause of the uprising was almost certainly the severe taxation levied on the populace by the local daimyo, it is true that the number of Christians involved was significant. The bakufu moved quickly and brutally to suppress the rebellion, but because this took an embarrassingly long time, the Tokugawa began to seriously reevaluate relations with the Portuguese. Therefore, the Portuguese, who were of course Catholic, came to be perceived as an even greater threat than they had been previously, in light of the serious challenge to authority that the Shimabara uprising represented. This led the authorities to first restrict the Portuguese to the artificial island of Deshima in Nagasaki Bay, and then to ban them outright in 1639. Therefore, with the Portuguese banned from trading with Japan and Japanese merchants prohibited from traveling overseas, the connection between Dutch-controlled Taiwan and Japan took on added significance and helped usher in a period of prosperity unparalleled in VOC history.

The hatred that the Japanese felt towards the Portuguese extended to the Spanish as well, although Spanish merchants and missionaries had been exiled from Japan for almost two decades by the time the Portuguese were expelled. Recording a shogunal decree against the Spanish in his diary, Richard Cocks writes, "on pain of death no Japon shall go into New Spaine."[70] In 1624 Spanish merchants were ordered to leave Japan altogether, leaving only the Portuguese and Dutch as the sole Europeans allowed to trade in the country (the English had left voluntarily a year previous). Japanese hatred of the Spanish subsequently grew to such an extent that the authorities repeatedly asked the Dutch about the feasibility of a military strike against Manila, going so far as to propose on at least one occasion a joint Japanese-Dutch endeavor.[71]

It goes without saying that the Japanese were not happy to learn that the Spanish had erected a fort on the northern edge of Taiwan at a spot called Keelung.[72] The daimyo of Hirado as well as other shogunal officials had, on several occasions, expressed a desire that the Dutch take the Spanish fort, thereby removing the Spaniards from a strategically important area.[73] The Dutch, of course, were also eager to rid themselves of the Spanish and accordingly sent out a fleet of seven ships in August 1642 to attack Keelung under the command of Captain van Harousee. After a three-week siege of the castle, the Spanish surrendered with relatively little loss of life—a testament to how poorly defended the castle was, and an indication that the Spanish were not terribly interested in a fort on Taiwan (a fact borne out in Manila's refusal to send supplies of reinforcements to the fort).[74] Although the settlement was never profitable and only nominally defended, there was considerable joy in both Batavia and Japan upon learning of its destruction.[75] One reason for this was because the Dutch had consistently heard (and believed) rumors of rich gold mines in the interior of the island, and with the Spanish ousted there was no longer any chance of them beating the Dutch to this supposed "Taiwanese El Dorado."[76] Furthermore, and more realistically, there was no longer the possibility that the Spanish could use Taiwan as a base from which to enter the lucrative Chinese-Japanese trade as the Dutch had done.[77] Nor could they have used the island as a base from which to attack Dutch ships arriving from Japan and richly laden with precious metals. After all, the capture of an enemy's "silver fleet" was one of the most time-honored and devastating tactics of naval warfare, a fact demonstrated nicely by Piet Hein's celebrated capture of the Spanish treasure ship in the West Indies.

The importance of Taiwan as a link between Japan and Asia was certainly not lost on VOC officials at Hirado and Batavia. This is evidenced by their willingness to devote the resources necessary to make Casteel Zeelandia as profitable as possible; for example, in October of 1637 it was decided that a loan should be arranged between the VOC and various merchants in the big commercial cities of Japan to be used towards "jump-starting" the factory on Taiwan.

The Japanese authorities had regularly been asking the Dutch if they would be able to supply Japan with the same quantity of silk as the Portuguese had in years past, and Couckebacker consistently averred that the Dutch could easily undertake such a task using their factories in India, Tonkin, Quinam, and of course Taiwan.[78]

With the expectation that the VOC might soon find itself having to import a much greater quantity of goods than previously, two Dutch merchants, Cornelis van Saenen and Daniel Reijniersen, traveled to Osaka to arrange a loan of 400,000 *taels* to be put towards the development of the factory on Taiwan.[79] On October 11, the VOC borrowed 200,000 *taels* from an Osaka merchant at 1.5 percent interest over six months, followed by another 100,000 *taels* on November 7 from a Kyoto merchant. The final 100,000 *taels* were procured on the fifteenth of November to make the full 400,000. With this staggering quantity of silver, it is evident that the VOC fully recognized the potential of Taiwan in the Asian trade, and it should come as no surprise that from this time on the Taiwan-Japan connection became the most profitable in all of Asia.

Japanese Precious Metals and Taiwan

As an indication of how profitable the Japanese trade in Chinese goods could be, the Governor-General at Batavia wrote to his superiors that for every 500,000 *gulden* of Chinese goods imported into Japan, the VOC could make a profit of eighty tons of silver.[80] Likewise, Nicholas Couckebacker noted in a 1637 journal entry that "the rich Chinese trade is more and more realized in Taiwan."[81] According to Suzuki Yasuko, because of the increased trade with Japan that the factory on Taiwan made possible, the role of silver sent out from the Netherlands became less important to the VOC. She notes that after the establishment of the factory on Taiwan fostered a regular and profitable trade with Japan, the company turned away from its reliance on the *real of eight*, basing its inter-Asian trade instead on Japanese silver. Because the Dutch were able to obtain such a large quantity of Japanese precious metal, not only did VOC profits soar, but also this new source of bullion came to function as an engine that drove the inter-Asian trade.[82]

One of the factors that made Taiwan such a profitable link in the Japan trade was the role it played as a site of exchange between Japanese silver and Chinese gold. One of the easiest ways to make a profit in early modern Asia was simply to exchange precious metals in areas in which the exchange rate between gold and silver fluctuated. Gold was very often of differing values relative to silver in different localities, so that being able to buy it in an area in which the gold-to-silver ratio was low and sell it in another location where the ratio was high was one of the strengths of the VOC, especially since it had such a pervasive network of factories throughout Asia. For example, Japanese silver was exchanged for Chinese gold on Taiwan at a 1.5 percent profit. This may not seem to be extraordinarily high, but when the sheer quantity of silver involved is taken into account it becomes quite a profit, and this was helped by the fact that there was almost always an insatiable demand for silver in China. Furthermore, in the 1640s gold was extremely valuable relative to silver on the Indian coast; therefore the Dutch sent the gold that they obtained on Taiwan to the Coromandel Coast and Surat where they could again make huge profits on the purchase of Indian goods since gold had a far greater purchasing power than silver. To round out the cycle, these Indian goods were then resold in markets such as Japan or the Indonesian archipelago where they were in great demand.[83] This extremely profitable network of precious metal exchange, with Taiwan at the center, led Governor-General van Diemen to write, "God will that gold come from China, and if not, then more silver!"[84]

While it is undoubtedly inappropriate to refer to Japan as a capitalist society in the early seventeenth century, it is true that at least the upper stratum of Japanese society was highly commercialized.[85] Furthermore, recent research into the economic history of Tokugawa Japan has tended to recognize that as the period progressed, even remote villages were turning to the market to supplement their often-meager incomes that came only from the cultivation of rice.[86] Because of the emergence of large markets that specialized in the exchange of rice for cash (with the largest being at Osaka) there was a great deal of money circulating throughout the country, money that was often used in the early seventeenth century to invest in overseas trade. Dutch sources suggest that it was not at all uncommon for Kyushu daimyo to invest considerable quantities of silver in trade with places such as Siam, Cambodia, and Taiwan. Even when the *shuinsen* system was brought to an end by the so-called *sakoku* decrees, wealthy daimyo were investing in Dutch ships, especially ships involved in trade with Taiwan.[87] A good example of this can be seen in December of 1634 when the chief "accountant" of the daimyo of Hirado sent 5,000 *taels* of silver to Taiwan (via the VOC) in order to procure "various goods" that were expected to yield a profit in Japan.[88] Similarly, the daimyo of Owari borrowed 10,000 *taels* from the Dutch at 1 percent interest per month to invest in VOC trade on Taiwan.[89]

Japanese foreign investment was not limited to Dutch ships, of course, but also involved the Portuguese ships that came yearly from Macao. Because of the large quantity of cash that wealthy Japanese invested in these ships, the bakufu, while taking a rather indifferent stance on Dutch attacks on Portuguese shipping in general, sternly warned the Dutch against the taking of the galleons plying the waters between Japan and Macao. Nicholas Couckebacker wrote in no uncertain terms that the shogun was moved to prohibit the Dutch from attacking the great *nao* in response to a four-article petition presented by the Portuguese merchants.[90] It should be noted, however, that the shogun's concern was not prompted by a great love of the Portuguese, but rather by the fact that so much of the silver on the ship to Macao was in fact Japanese silver invested by daimyo, high-ranking bakufu officials, and wealthy merchants.[91]

The primary reason why the factory on Taiwan was so important to the VOC was that it served as a commercial link between Japan and the rest of Asia. Most Dutch ships en route to Japan from other factories in Asia stopped at the island, and conversely the Japanese "silver ships" routinely delivered their precious metals to Zeelandia in order to be redistributed across Asia. A careful examination of the records kept by the Dutch in Asia clearly reveals how central Taiwan was to the fortunes of the company at this time. For example, the president of the Dutch factory in Japan faithfully recorded the destination of the ships that left his factory, and more often than not, he noted that these ships stopped on Taiwan en route to other factories such as Siam, Cambodia, or the Indian coast. In the same way, the president of the Dutch factory on Taiwan recorded in great detail incoming ships and their cargoes. According to these records, most of the cargo was destined for Japan where it would be sold for mainly precious metals: silver until 1668, followed thereafter by gold and copper. A third set of documents allows us to see more generally the flow of goods and precious metals through Taiwan; the *Generale Missiven* were general reports on the affairs of the VOC in Asia that were written by the Governor-General in Batavia in order to give the *Herren XVII* in the Netherlands a general overview of company activities. By examining these reports, it becomes immediately apparent that Taiwan was a vital link in the trade between the treasure house that was Japan and the Dutch factories in the rest of Asia.[92]

The initial function of the factory at Taiwan was as a place for procurement of Chinese silk. It is indicative of how valuable silk was to the VOC trade in Asia that before Taiwan came under Dutch control, company profits were relatively modest and were gained at the expense of huge shipments of silver and gold from the Netherlands. After the silk trade began in earnest, however, the Japanese factory was consistently the most profitable in all of Asia and remained so until the Japanese authorities began to restrict this trade by volume late in the seventeenth century.

Along with a steady supply of Chinese silk, Taiwan was extremely valuable to the VOC in its capacity to provide a huge number of deerskins every year. As we shall see in chapter 6, this commodity was consistently one of the most profitable in the trade with Japan. In fact, much of the friction that arose between Japanese merchants and the Dutch on Taiwan in the 1620s and 30s revolved around the contentious issue of the harvesting of deerskins. The Dutch not only realized a tremendous profit by carrying the skins to Japan themselves, but they also charged the native and Chinese hunters a tax of one *real of eight* per hunting license, a practice they could not enforce if the skins were being sold to Japanese merchants directly.[93] Both of these commodities translated into huge profits for the VOC as they were sold in Japan for mainly precious metals; these metals could then be used to support VOC operation throughout Asia.

Not all of the Japanese silver and copper sent to Taiwan was redistributed to other factories; some remained on the island as a means of purchasing Chinese goods from mainland merchants as well as deerskins from the Chinese and native hunters, and of course for upkeep of the factory itself. The bulk of Japanese precious metals, however, remained on the island for only a short time before being sent on to other factories. In 1644, for example, Governor-General Antonio van Diemen wrote to the *Herren Zeventien* that silver obtained in Japan was bound especially for Surat, Persia, Malacca, and Coromandel after having been collected on Taiwan.[94] By examining the Dutch diaries kept in the factories of both Taiwan and Japan, we can gain an appreciation of how much precious metal was being channeled through the island. Furthermore, because the diaries contain the final destination of each ship as well as the cargoes of these ships, a general idea of the importance of Taiwan as a link between Japan and Asia in terms of both goods and precious metals quickly emerges.

Nicholas Couckebacker spelled out the unique relationship that existed between Japan and Taiwan in a diary entry for January 16, 1635: every year a great quantity of Japanese silver was sent to Taiwan along with a list of goods that were expected to sell well in Japan during the following season. A portion of the silver was then used to purchase those goods as well as a number of presents for the shogun and with the sundry lesser officials with whom the company had dealings.[95] The remaining silver (the amount used for the following year's trade in Japan was generally quite small) was redirected to factories such as those in Siam, Cambodia, Tonkin, Cochin, and on the Indian Coast, depending on where it was needed. A good example of this redistribution can be seen at the end of the trading season in Japan in the year 1636. After all of the Dutch ships had arrived at Hirado, the goods were put into storage and, in accordance with the laws of Japan, were sold all at once. After the sale, the ships were reloaded with Japanese precious metals as well as the various other goods bought in Japan, and were sent on their way. In November of 1636, eight ships departed Japan for various ports in Asia, every one of them stopping first at Taiwan.[96] A total of 150,000 cases of silver (one case contained 1,000 *taels*) went to Taiwan aboard these ships and were redistributed from there, according to "the demand of Southeast Asia and The Netherlands."[97] The *Noortwijk*, for example, carried a cargo of thirty cases of silver and stopped only briefly at Taiwan before proceeding on to Batavia. In the same way the *Groll* departed Hirado with 60,000 *taels* of silver, part of which was to be offloaded at Taiwan, the rest being sent to Tonkin in order to buy silk for next year's trading season in Japan.

The very next year, the president of the factory at Taiwan recorded that not only was the silver of four ships from Japan to be redistributed to other factories, but likewise 400 bales of white rice were to be sent to factories that were in need of foodstuffs.[98] Two years later, in 1639, five ships arrived at Taiwan with 900 cases of Japanese silver. This was a staggering amount, and again most of it found its way to other Dutch factories in Asia.[99] To cite one last example, in 1645, at the height of the Japan factory's profitability, Governor-General van der Lijn reported to the *Herren Zeventien* that 1,838,250 *gulden* in Japanese silver was sent in six ships to Taiwan, whence it was sent on to other factories in Asia, mainly to Coromandel and Batavia.[100] These six ships carried not only silver, but also other commodities important to Taiwan: copper, wood, and rice. Although copper, like silver, was redistributed to areas in which it was in great demand such as India, the other commodities were also important for the upkeep of the company's factories at Taiwan and Batavia.

Wood was often bought in Japan and sent to Taiwan for the maintenance of and additions to the company's storehouses and defenses on the island. We read, for example, that on the first of December

1635, the *Oudewater* departed for Taiwan with the usual cargo of silver, but it also carried a substantial quantity of lumber. Towards the end of the same month, shortly after the departure of the *Oudewater*, the daimyo of Hirado paid 2,000 *taels* of his debt to the company in lumber and rice.[101] This was a boon to the company since it came at precisely the time when Castle Zeelandia was becoming a serious venture. It is only logical to assume, therefore, that the wood obtained from Japan was used in the construction of the settlement on the island, especially since there is no mention of it being redistributed to other areas in Asia. The lumber obtained from Japan must also have been used to repair VOC ships as they arrived at Taiwan. This is not spelled out specifically in the sources, but given the difficulty of sailing in the waters between Japan and Southeast Asia, as well as the fact that Taiwan served as a sort of rendezvous point for all the ships going to and coming from Japan, it is logical to assume that at least some of the wood must have been used for the upkeep of Dutch ships.

Rice was also an increasingly important Japanese export to Taiwan, as well as to the VOC headquarters at Batavia. Yao Keisuke, in an important study on the VOC export of Japanese rice, illustrated nicely how several factories in Asia, and in particular Taiwan and Batavia, were dependent in part on Japanese rice to maintain their stores of foodstuffs. One of the most interesting aspects of this study is that, in lieu of silver, both the Matsuura and Hosokawa families paid their considerable debts to the VOC in rice. This practice was initiated in 1626 when the daimyo of Hirado, in order to pay off a debt of 288 *kan* of silver, authorized the sale of rice to the company. In the period 1626–1628, the company received 3,720 bales of rice (worth 14,251.5 *gulden*) from the Matsuura. The fact that this figure represents the lowest export total of any year until the Dutch were moved to Nagasaki in 1640 reveals just how much rice was being exported on VOC ships. The high point came in 1639 when the company received a total of 12,000 bales of rice (worth 62,668 *gulden*).[102] By 1637, in fact, 93 percent of all goods given to the Dutch by the Matsuura family was rice.

After the move to Nagasaki in 1640, however, the Dutch stopped their dealings with the Matsuura and began to obtain their rice instead from the Hosokawa family. Here again rice exports were very large so that by the end of the 1640s the company was exporting over 5,000 bales of Hosokawa rice.[103] As noted earlier, most of this rice was sent to Taiwan and Batavia, thus alleviating the chronic food shortages faced by the company in those areas. The effect of the VOC on the rice market of Japan can be seen in Taiwan's surrender to the Zheng in 1662 when the market was greatly affected by the sudden drop in exports. Before 1662, rice from western domains such as those of the Hosokawa and the Matsuura was often sold overseas, but after the loss of Taiwan, the sale of rice became an entirely domestic affair in which Nagasaki became simply a regional rice market rather than an international one.[104]

Not only was Taiwan an area in which Japanese silver was collected before being redistributed to other Dutch factories, it was also a staging area for goods destined for the Japanese market from other markets in Asia. There was a truly amazing diversity of goods being brought to Japan in the seventeenth century, from luxury goods produced in the Netherlands, to Indian cotton goods, to a variety of exotic goods from Southeast Asia such as sandalwood, elephant tusks, deerskins, ray skins, and sugar, to name but a few. While it is true that there were ships that sailed directly to Japan from other factories in Asia, it was usually the case that ships first stopped at Taiwan before continuing on to Japan. In the diaries of the presidents of the Japan factory, for example, it is usually noted that a particular ship came to Japan *via* Taiwan; and if that was not the case, it is almost always stated explicitly that that ship was sent *directly* from another factory. Couckebacker noted on July 10, 1638, for example, that there were many ships in Japan in that year form Batavia, Siam, Cambodia, and Tonkin, all of which came through Taiwan.[105]

A good example of this pattern is a fleet of ships that was anchored at Taiwan in August 1634, each of the ships in various stages of preparing for the Japan voyage. The *Bredamme*, *Oudewater*, *Wancan*, and the *Vliegende Boode* all departed for Japan at roughly the same time and were all laden with goods such as Chinese silk, sandalwood, porcelain, sugar, and deerskins.[106] Three years later (1637), Couckebacker recorded in his journal that seven ships with over two million *gulden* in Chinese goods arrived at Hirado, at least four of them either originating from Taiwan, or (like the *Oudewater*) coming via Taiwan from another factory in Asia, in this case Batavia.[107] Similarly, in August of 1640, eight ships arrived in Japan from Taiwan, this time with a total cargo of over five million *gulden*.[108] Through these isolated examples, one can easily see that Taiwan played a role as a "staging area" from which to deliver a great variety and quantity of goods to the Japanese market, a market that in return provided the VOC with an almost unbelievable quantity of precious metals.

For a variety of reasons it was extremely convenient for the company to be able to gather its ships at Taiwan before sending them off in quick succession to Japan. This was in part because the Japanese authorities only allowed the Dutch a very brief period of time in which to conduct their trade. By shogunal decree, all foreign ships were required to leave Japan no later than the twentieth day of the ninth month each year. In addition, in order to prevent attacks on Portuguese shipping in Japanese waters, the Dutch were obliged to wait twenty days after the departure of the Portuguese to leave, a slight exception being allowed for ships that arrived excessively late in the season. This meant that because of the necessity of catching prevailing monsoon winds, the Dutch were left with only a very limited window of trade. Therefore, being able to coordinate the sending of VOC ships beforehand must have been a tremendous advantage for the Dutch.[109] Conversely, Taiwan was convenient for the VOC because the factory in Japan was not allowed to store any unsold merchandise in its warehouses; rather, the ships were required to take any remaining goods with them upon their departure.[110] Because outbound ships almost always stopped at Taiwan regardless, it was an added convenience to be able to store these unsold goods so close to Japan. Furthermore, because Taiwan was relatively close to Japan, and because most of the goods bound for Japan first arrived in Taiwan, the VOC was able to more effectively control the supply of goods. This is evidenced especially in the case of sandalwood, a commodity in abundant supply in Southeast Asia and particularly valuable in Japan. In order to keep the price high, the VOC often stored a great quantity of the wood at Taiwan, sending only modest supplies to Japan in any given season.

The Loss of Taiwan

When the Dutch originally erected Fort Zeelandia on Taiwan, it was not built on the mainland, but rather on a permanent sandbar just off of the southern tip of the main island. This location was perhaps ideal for the loading and unloading of ships because of the relatively good harbor created by the sandbar, but in terms of defense, it was anything but ideal. This was to become very much a problem in the early 1660s when the Dutch were faced with the prospect of an invasion by the forces of Zheng Chenggong (Coxinga).

Zheng Chenggong is an enigmatic figure; although many accounts of his deeds having been recorded, the line between truth and fiction is often blurred. Donald Keene wrote of Coxinga, "The lives of few men in history are richer in dramatic possibilities...[and] even those who have professed to be writing biographical accounts have been led into colorful tales which have every merit save that of truth."[111] Zheng was born in Japan to a mother with the surname Tagawa, but very soon thereafter moved with his father to China. Although Zheng is almost invariably remembered as a swashbuckling pirate and adventurer, he, in fact, held a first degree by the age of fifteen, having received a classical education at Shanghai at the insistence of his father.[112] Perhaps it is this thorough indoctrination in the Confucian classics that explains Zheng's commitment to the Ming cause. It is from Zheng's relationship with the Ming emperor Tang Wang in Fuzhou that he received the imperial surname, Kuo Hsing-yeh, which through Western perversion becomes the name "Coxinga."

Zheng, taking over his father's maritime operations after the latter's submission to the Qing, was defeated on the mainland by the armies of the newly established empire. After Zheng's initially successful campaign to take Nanjing by sailing up the Yangtze River, the Qing rallied their forces and effectively crushed what little hope remained for a Ming revival.[113] The ban on maritime commerce was subsequently reinforced in an effort to starve the Zheng and other rebellious coastal communities into submission.[114] As a result of his defeat, Zheng was forced to find a new base for his commercial operations and related Ming loyalist activities. Unfortunately for the Dutch, Zheng turned his attention toward Taiwan, probably because a large population of Fujianese who were sympathetic to his cause had previously immigrated to the island. Accordingly the order to attack came in 1661. As a diplomatic pretext for the invasion, Zheng claimed that the island belonged to him as an inheritance from his father, who had been wont to trade with the Japanese in the various harbors of the island before the Dutch founded Castle Zeelandia.[115] The Dutch of course were not swayed by this argument and therefore prepared to defend themselves the best they could, despite overwhelming odds.

Frederick Coyett, the president of the factory on Taiwan at the time of the Dutch defeat, was blamed for the loss of the island, and was banished to an island in the Indonesian archipelago as punishment. There he was left to languish for several years until finally freed by the *Stadhouder* of the Netherlands, a release brought about by the more influential members of Coyett's friends and family. While in exile, Coyett wrote a treatise called *Verwaarloosde Formosa.* This work is, not surprisingly, a protestation vis-à-vis the author's innocence regarding the loss of Taiwan; he instead places the blame squarely on the shoulders of the highest company officials. According to Coyett, the VOC was fully aware of the precarious situation created by Zheng's string of defeats at the hands of the Qing armies and knew that he was at least considering Taiwan as a new base for his displaced forces. It may be that the officials at Batavia were not aware of the overwhelming force that Zheng would bring to bear against the Dutch, but nonetheless, the attack should not have come as a great surprise. This is all the more so since the Dutch factory in Japan had warned Batavia as early as 1646 of possible Zheng designs on the island. Coyett furthermore asserts that in order to forestall such an eventuality he requested on several occasions reinforcements for Taiwan's defense, as well as material to strengthen Fort Zeelandia against an attack. These requests were repeatedly turned down, however, and Coyett therefore accused the company of actively choosing not to believe the reports of a Zheng mobilization and instead preoccupying itself with other trivial matters.

In February 1662, the Dutch at Taiwan, after having held out against impossible odds, signed an eighteen-clause treaty of surrender that allowed them to leave the island peacefully, but which required the cession of all of the wealth of the factory, amounting to 471,000 *gulden*.[116] Item two in the treaty of surrender reads, "Castle Zeelandia, with its outworks, artillery, remaining war materials, merchandise, money, and other properties belonging to the Honorable Company, [is] to be surrendered to Lord Coxinga."[117] These losses, which were not overly significant in terms of overall company profits, were held against Coyett personally, as was the failure to defend the island against the invaders. In fact, the full wrath of the VOC was brought to bear on the unfortunate Coyett regardless of the fact that he held out on Taiwan as long as possible against an impossibly superior enemy, given the meager provisions and defenses at his disposal. For this perceived failure, he was recalled to Batavia in disgrace and, after a swift trial, sentenced to death for his crimes. In an act of leniency, however, the council at Batavia commuted his sentence in 1666 to banishment to the island of Puyo-Ay in the Banda group.[118] According to Coyett, the role of petty intrigue in the highest echelons of the VOC administration played a major role in the company's failure to heed his warnings about the danger of Zheng Chenggong. In *Neglected Formosa,* he blames above all the very company officials who condemned his actions, writing, "[i]t is very sad that, by reason of mutual disputes and disturbances among their servants, the company lost such a precious treasure as Formosa..."[119]

On the surface it seems that the loss of Taiwan was in many respects a bitter blow to the VOC. Upon further analysis, however, the loss was not as severe as it might otherwise have been. As it happened, a number of historical circumstances converged that would have rendered the island less important than it had been in the previous decades. While it is certainly true that company officials were alarmed at the loss of the island and that Governor-General Maetsuyker vowed swift retaliation for the loss, by his own admission this was because any show of weakness on the part of the Dutch only served to damage the company's reputation in Asia.[120] In terms of being able to procure a steady supply of silk, however, the company had turned away from the large-scale procurement of Chinese silk that characterized the Japan trade in the early years and that made Taiwan such a vital link in the VOC trade with Japan.

Beginning in the 1640s, the VOC began to purchase large quantities of silk from Tonkin, and after the middle of the century increasingly from Bengal and Persia.[121] These new sources of supply served the company's interests extremely well insofar as silk was relatively plentiful in these areas, the Dutch had ready access to it through factories established in those locations, and silk other than the Chinese variety had the added advantage of not being subject to the *itowappu* ("silk cartel"). Furthermore, after the fall of the Ming dynasty, the Qing allowed Chinese ships from the coastal provinces to travel to Japan even though there was no resumption of formal diplomatic ties. This meant that with the large-scale participation of Chinese merchants in the silk trade at Nagasaki, there was no longer any incentive for them to use the Dutch on Taiwan as middlemen. Suzuki Yasuko notes that with increased contact between Chinese and Japanese merchants, the Dutch turned away from Chinese silk and concentrated instead on Tonkin. She notes also that this shift is indicated in the Dutch sources by an increasing quantity of silver sent to Tonkin for the procurement of local silk.[122] In fact, VOC officials recorded with some consternation that because there were so many more Chinese trading at Nagasaki than previously, and that this resulted in a large quantity of silk, prices were driven down on all silk imports regardless of whether the product came from Taiwan, Tonkin, Bengal, or anywhere else.[123]

Another factor that made Taiwan less important than it had been was the shogunate's prohibition in 1688 which banned the export of silver. With this development, the company lost the advantage of being able to exchange Japanese silver for Chinese gold on Taiwan, thus nullifying one of the major commercial advantages of the island. Furthermore, with the shogun's decision to allow the export of copper and gold in lieu of silver, it became much more profitable to ship copper directly to areas such as Bengal, Persia, and the Coromandel Coast where it was in great demand and brought a handsome profit.[124]

In terms of the commodities obtained on Taiwan, the large-scale shipment of deerskins from the island had begun to decline as early as the 1640s. In 1640, for example, the company was obliged to ban hunting for one year in response to a drastic drop in the population of deer.[125] Although hunting resumed the next year, the levels of export never returned to what they had been prior to 1640. From 1636, traditional forms of hunting gave way to the use of pitfalls to trap deer, a method that allowed hunters to harvest deer at a greatly expanded rate. The Dutch in response instituted a hunting season in an effort to relieve the wholesale slaughter of deer, but to almost no avail.[126] It was this failure that led the Dutch to ban hunting for a year in 1640. It was also at this time that the factories in Siam and Cambodia began to offer stiff competition in the export of deerskins, so that Taiwan became less crucial in this respect. Of greater significance to the company than the loss of Taiwanese deerskins was the loss of a rich sugar-producing region. By the time the Dutch were forced out of Taiwan, a sizeable Chinese agrarian community existed on the island and was engaged in intensive sugar cane cultivation. These Chinese farmers had immigrated to Taiwan mainly from coastal provinces such as Fujian and Guangzhou. In fact, the island came to serve as an outlet for excess population in these provinces when the population skyrocketed in the mid-seventeenth century. In 1683 there were approximately 200,000 people living on the island, and by the middle of the next century, that figure rose fivefold to about one million people.[127] Chinese settlers also flocked to the island in order to avoid the disturbances that plagued the mainland during the Qing conquest. Because Ming forces were diverted to the Northeast to fight the Manchu invaders, the coastal provinces deteriorated into a state of near anarchy, with organized gangs of pirates wreaking havoc all along the coastline.[128]

Sugar production on the island skyrocketed in the seventeenth century with the influx of so many Chinese farmers. In 1658, for example, 600,000 *catties* of Taiwanese sugar were exported to Japan, a consideration that, along with the export of Chinese silk and deerskins, made Taiwan a consistently profitable factory.[129] Again, however, after a peak in production in the late 1650s, Taiwanese sugar became less important because the large-scale production of sugar in both Brazil and the West Indies drove down prices all over the world.[130] Furthermore, with the new trade restrictions placed on the Dutch in Japan, it is doubtful whether the VOC would have continued importing such large amounts of Taiwanese goods when other more profitable goods would surely have been sent.

In 1684 the bakufu placed the most rigorous trade restrictions yet on Dutch and Chinese merchants in Nagasaki. While the Chinese were allowed to sell goods worth 6,000 *kan* of silver a year, the Dutch were only allowed to sell the equivalent of 3,400 *kan*. This so-called "fixed ceiling" system was the final stage in an effort to control the amount of trade with foreigners, and more specifically the outflow of precious metals from the country. It is important to note, however, that these restrictions did not mean that the Japanese were no longer interested in foreign goods. Rather, the strict control of imports was an effort to control the rapidly depleting supplies of metal within Japan. Towards the end of the seventeenth century, Confucian advisors to the shogun, most notably Arai Hakuseki, were concerned that Japan was losing all of its wealth in a trade that was facilitated primarily by the outflow of Japanese silver, gold, and copper.[131] When it became apparent that precious metal supplies in Japan were becoming dangerously low, the bakufu, having tried a number of measures previously, had to find some way to staunch this depletion. The fact that the measure ultimately adopted was so strict is less a testament to bakufu reaction against foreign trade and more a result of the seriousness of the internal situation with regard to precious metal supplies.

This was the final restriction placed on foreign trade and it lasted until the "opening" of the county in the 1850s.[132] Because of these restrictions, which were indeed quite severe considering the previous magnitude of VOC trade, it is improbable that the Dutch would have continued to send Taiwanese sugar to Japan in any appreciable amount. The VOC instead would have certainly chosen to concentrate on more valuable goods such as silk, sandalwood, elephant tusks, and other luxury goods from Southeast Asia. Therefore, in the end, the loss of Taiwan was not the bitter blow to the company that it appears at first glance. Indicative of this is the fact that in 1683, after the Qing army defeated the last of the Zheng forces on the island, the Chinese naval commander Shih-Lang offered to sell Taiwan back to the Dutch. The VOC, however, was not interested and declined the offer without much serious discussion.[133] Therefore, rather than regard the loss of Taiwan as a severe blow to company trade in East Asia, we should identify the increased trade restrictions as well as the increased Chinese competition that occurred at roughly the same time as the real culprits in the decline of VOC fortunes in East Asia.

ENDNOTES

1. The Dutchman Jan Huygen van Linschotten supposedly gave this name to the island upon visiting it in 1592 while serving on a Portuguese vessel. This story is doubtful at best since Linschotten, according to his own writings, never seems to have journeyed as far east as Taiwan. He certainly mentions the island in his celebrated *Itinerario*, but whether or not he was responsible for naming it is another matter. At any rate, the name means "beautiful island" in Portuguese, and came to be used widely until the adoption of Taiwan in the twentieth century. The name Taiwan referred to the small island on which the Dutch erected Fort Zeelandia, now known as Tainan on modern maps. The island was officially called Formosa by the VOC, but they often used the term Taiwan (with various bizarre spellings!) to refer to the island as a whole. Because Formosa carries a particularly heavy colonial connotation, I have chosen to call the island Taiwan, even though this is in many respects an anachronism.
2. There are a handful of good works dealing with pre-modern Taiwan and its role in the Asian economy: John Wills' "The Seventeenth-Century Transformation" and John Shepherd's *Statecraft and Political Economy on the Taiwan Frontier, 1600–1800* (Stanford: Stanford University Press, 1993) are two excellent examples that I have found extremely useful and insightful. Tonio Andrade and Leonard Blussé have also written a number of articles concerning the Dutch relationship with the Chinese on Taiwan during this period. Blussé, in particular, has been of enormous help to me as he and his colleagues have edited and published the *dagregisters* kept on Taiwan. Finally, Iwao Seiichi's work on the Japanese relationship with Taiwan in this period, though dated, is still very much relevant. There, is, of course, a good deal of literature on this subject in Chinese: Tu Cheng-sheng, for example, has published a beautiful book entitled *Ilha Formosa: The Emergence of Taiwan on the World Scene in the Seventeenth Century* that contains a great deal of illustrations of artifacts related to the Dutch trade on Taiwan.
3. For the role of precious metals in Dutch-Asian trade, see the following chapter. The relatively abundant supply of metal in Japan did not mean that the Dutch did not send out large shipments of bullion from the Netherlands. Rather, they were simply less dependant than other companies on Europe as the sole provider of capital to finance the Asian

trade, and hence were more able to establish the "country trade" that made their venture so profitable.

4. The Ming lifted the maritime ban on trade with Southeast Asia because it effectively ruined the economy of Fujian Province. The ban on trade with the Japanese, however, was kept firmly in place. See Ts'ao Yung-ho, "Chinese Overseas Trade in the Late Ming Period," *Proceedings, International Association of Historians of Asia, Second Biennial Conference* (Taipei: Chinese Historical Association 1962), 429–457. While the Ming initially licensed fifty ships to trade with Southeast Asia, this number rapidly increased until in 1,597, no fewer than 117 of which went abroad. See Reid, "An 'Age of Commerce,'" 9.
5. John Wills, "Maritime China from Wang Chih to Shih Lang: Themes in Peripheral History," in *From Ming to Ch'ing: Conquest, Region, and Continuity in Seventeenth Century China*, ed. Jonathon Spence and John Wills (New Haven: Yale University Press, 1979), 213.
6. *Diary of Richard Cocks, Book I*, 20. Watanabe Yōgoro states that after the initial violent attacks of the *wakō,* Chinese as well as Japanese resorted to piracy in an effort to flout Ming bans on maritime trade. He estimates that by the sixteenth and early seventeenth centuries, 70 percent of the pirates were ethnically Chinese. See his *Kinsei Nihon Bōeki Ron*, 19.
7. Cooper, ed., *Joao Rodrigues's Account of Sixteenth-Century Japan,* 60–61.
8. *East India Company's Records, China, Vol. X*, 25.
9. Nagazumi, *Shuinsen*, 170.
10. Denny Roy, *Taiwan: A Political History* (Ithaca: Cornell University Press, 2003), 14. Robert Swinhoe describes the process of distilling camphor from the trees to make a resin that was put in bags of one *picol* each. The camphor was then sold in places such as China, where it was used as a medicine, and India, where the people used it as a lubricant for their bodies. "Notes on the Island of Formosa," *Journal of the Royal Geographical Society of London* 34 (1864): 6–18.
11. Wills, "The Seventeenth-Century Transformation," 88.
12. Kuno Yoshio, *Japanese Expansion on the Asiatic Continent, Vol. 1* (Berkeley: University of California Press, 1937), 311–312.
13. Hung Chien-Chao, *A History of Taiwan* (Rimini: Il Cerchio, 2000), 15.
14. Massarella, *A World Elsewhere*, 132.
15. Iwao, *Shuinsen*, 220.
16. Iwao Seiichi, "Li Tan, Chief of the Chinese Residents at Hirado, Japan, in the last days of the Ming Dynasty," *Memoirs of the Research*

Department of the Tōyō Bunkō, Volume 17 (Tokyo: Toyo Bunko, 1958), 27–83.

17. John Wills gives a brief but concise history of this period and its actors in his excellent essay "Maritime China from Wang Chih to Shih Lang."
18. Tōan was not executed simply for failing to take the island, but was rather implicated in a bribery scandal involving Arima Harunobu, both of whom were Christians. In the eyes of the bakufu however, military defeat was a great personal shame for the losing general; Tōan, therefore, was presumably already out of favor with the authorities when he was implicated in this scandal. Incidentally, Tōan, who helped to found a Jesuit church in Nagasaki, is considered a martyr by the Jesuits, and although I cannot verify the exact circumstances of his death, perhaps given this Jesuit tradition Murayama was treated more harshly because of his religion than he otherwise might have been. For a detailed discussion of Japanese attempts to attack Taiwan, see Iwao Seiichi, "Shiqi Shiji Riben ren zhi Taiwan Qinlue Xingdong," *Taiwan Yanjiu Cong Kan* 71: 1–23.
19. Shiryō Hensan-jo. *Nihon Kankei Kaigai Shiryō: Igirisu Shōkanchō Nikki, Vol. I* (Tokyo: Tokyo Daigaku Shiryō Hensan-jo, 1974), 21–31.
20. Coolhaas, ed., *Generalle Missiven, Deel I*, 136.
21. Cheng Shaogang, *De VOC en Formosa, 1624–1662: Een Vergeten Geschiedenis* (Leiden: Ridderkerk, 1995), 113.
22. Nagazumi and Takeda, *Hirado Oranda Shōkan Igirisu Shōkan Nikki*, 31.
23. John Wills relates an account of the Portuguese and Chinese taking Dutch heads to Peking in an effort to ingratiate themselves with the emperor. While it seems that the emperor was indeed pleased with the defense of Macao, it was of no practical gain to the Portuguese in their often-cold relations with the Chinese court. See Wills, John, *Pepper, Guns, and Parlays: The Dutch East India Company and China, 1622–1681* (Cambridge: Harvard University Press, 1974), 8.
24. Goodrich, L. Carrington and Chaoying Fang, eds., *Dictionary of Ming Biography, 1368–1644* (New York: Columbia University Press, 1976), 872–873.
25. Wills, "Maritime China from Wang Chih to Shih Lang," 216–217.
26. In chapter 3 of John Shepherd's *Statecraft and Political Economy on the Taiwan Frontier*, he undertakes an exhaustive discussion of Dutch territorial designs on the island as well as their taxation policies toward the natives and Chinese settlers. He argues convincingly that these policies helped make Taiwan one of the more profitable VOC factories.
27. Katō, "Unification and Adaptation," 222.

28. A good description of Dutch efforts to draw Chinese settlers to the island can be found in Andrade, Tonio, "Pirates, Pelts, and Promises: The Sino-Dutch Colony of Seventeenth-Century Taiwan and the Aboriginal Village of Favorolang," *The Journal of Asian Studies* 64: 2 (2004): 299–301.
29. Nagazumi and Takeda, *Hirado Oranda Shōkan Igirisu Shōkan Nikki*, 38.
30. Coolhaas, ed., *Generalle Missiven, Deel I*, February 3, 1624.
31. Nagazumi, *Shuinsen*, 174.
32. NKKS, Vol. I, 38.
33. Coolhaas, ed., *Generalle Missiven, Deel I*, 240.
34. NKKS, Vol. I, 107.
35. Nagazumi Yoko uses the term *wanzei* (literally "harbor tax") in her work on the *shuinsen* and emphasizes that it was used for maintenance, while other scholars (Charles Boxer, for example) emphasize that it was meant as an onus, making it unprofitable for Japanese merchants to trade in Taiwan. See Nagazumi, *Shuinsen*, 180.
36. This decision was taken against the advice of the factory president at Hirado. Van Nijenroode warned Pieter Nuijts in 1625 that the Japanese must be treated with respect and discretion lest there be great difficulties in Hirado. This prediction proved to be entirely accurate. See Watanabe, *Kinsei Nihon Bōeki Ron*, 63.
37. Ibid., 62.
38. William Campbell, *Formosa Under the Dutch: Described from Contemporary Records* (Taipei: Ch'eng Wen Publishing Company, 1972), 41.
39. Watanabe, *Kinsei Nihon Bōeki Ron*, 63.
40. Nagazumi, *Hirado Oranda Shōkan no Nikki*, 147.
41. The following account of "the action" is taken from Pieter Nuijts' diary, which has been translated into Japanese by Nagazumi Yoko and published with other Dutch diaries under the title *Hirado Oranda Shōkan no Nikki (Diaries of the Dutch Factory at Hirado)*. For this particular diary see Volume I, pp. 147–156.
42. The history of these prisoners is an interesting one; sixteen of them were taken by Yamada to Japan in order to ask the shogun for Japanese protection against the Dutch. This blatantly contrived effort to get the shogunate to invest itself militarily in Taiwan failed, and the party was returned to Taiwan in 1628 only to be thrown immediately in prison by the Dutch. Some of the prisoners escaped, and the remaining eleven were precisely the prisoners bargained for in the treaty between Nuijts and the Japanese. See Leonard Blussé, "Dutch Protestant Missionaries as Protagonists of the Territorial Expansion of the VOC on Formosa," in *Conversion, Competition, and Conflict: Essays on the Role of Religion*

in Asia, ed. Dick Cooiman, et al. (Amsterdam: Free University Press, 1984), *162*. For Dutch accounts of these narratives, see Colenbrander, ed., *Jan, Pietersz. Coen, Bescheiden Omtrent Zijn Bedrijf in Indië, Deel V*, 63–84.

43. Although the term *Shinkō* clearly refers at times to a specific place in Taiwan such as a town, at other times it seems to refer to an entire region, or indeed to the island in its entirety; the Dutch, for example, often refer to the natives simply as "Sinkanese" regardless of where on the island they were from.
44. The total value of the silk and money given to the Japanese was 13,540 *taels* of silver. This was later supplemented by fifteen *picols* of silk that had earlier been confiscated by Sonck, president of the Taiwan factory before Nuijts.
45. Willem Jansen made two trips to Japan to try to resolve the situation. Initially unsuccessful, he returned to Batavia only to be sent back by the new Governor-General Jacques Specx. This time, along with Francois Caron, the Dutch succeeded in resolving the conflict and restoring trade. Jansen has left a fascinating diary of his time in Japan that has been translated into Japanese by Nagazumi Yoko. See *Hirado Oranda Shōkan no Nikki, Volume 2*.
46. Kawajima, *Shuinsen Bōeki Shi.*
47. This demand is found in the records kept in the Taiwan factory for March 31, 1630. In this version, Taiwan is to be ceded to the Japanese and Fort Zeelandia destroyed. See Blussé, et al., eds., *Dagregisters Taiwan, Deel I*, 25.
48. Nagazumi, *Shuinsen,* 195.
49. Asao Naohiro, *Nihon no Kinsei 1: Seikai Shi no naka no Kinsei* (Tokyo: Chūo Kōron-sha, 1991), 137. Asao also includes an eminently readable (in Japanese) version of the entire Nuijts affair, and suggests that sending Nuijts to Japan was the deciding factor in the resolution of the conflict.
50. Nagazumi credits the patience of Jansen and the foresight of Specx for the ultimate resolution of this affair. I would amend this slightly, however, because the Japanese authorities most likely realized that the Japanese merchants were just as much to blame as the Dutch and so were relieved to find the convenient "way out" described here. See Nagazumi, *Shuinsen*, 195–196.
51. Blussé, et al., eds., *Dagregisters Taiwan, Deel I*, 65.
52. Copie Resolutie van Goveneur Putmans ende Raad op het Vertrek van Willem Jansen Genomen, January 28, 1633, VOC 1109, 220–222.
53. In these diaries, Couckebacker often writes longwinded entries in which he summarizes the state of the company in Japan. Almost invariably, he

mentions the continued incarceration of Nuijts as one of the foremost problems to be resolved. Also, when the Dutch undertook the yearly *hofreis* (court journey) to Edo, a petition to free Nuijts was invariably presented to the authorities. See, for example, NKKS, Vol. 1, 30–31: November 7, 1633.

54. There were cases in which the shogun died without an heir. In such an event, an heir would be chosen from amongst the three collateral houses of the Tokugawa located in Owari, Kii, and Mito provinces and known collectively as the *sanke*. See Marius Jansen, *The Making of Modern Japan* (Cambridge: Harvard University Press, 2000), 34.
55. A complete list of all presents given to the shogun and his major councilors for the year 1636 can be found in Couckebacker's diary entry for March 21. Included in this list is a "copper chandelier with thirty arms," a possible reference to the lantern that had such an effect on Iemitsu. See NKKS, Vol. II, 18–22.
56. *Coolhaas, ed., Generalle Missiven, Deel I*, 369.
57. Nagazumi, *Shuinsen*, 196.
58. Coolhaas, ed., *Generalle Missiven, Deel I*, 490.
59. The *Tokugawa Jikki* provides us with a brief biography of Zhilong, stating that he made the journey to Sumpu in Keichō 17, where he received a *shuinjō* from Ieyasu to trade in Japan. Shortly thereafter, he left Hirado to "become a pirate with several tens of thousands of followers." Also noted is the fact that he and his son had an intimate connection with Taiwan, and that they represented the last remains of the Ming Empire. See the KTTJ, Vol. III, 459–460.
60. For a detailed account in English of the Life of Zheng Zhilong, see Charles Boxer, "The Rise and Fall of Nicholas Iquan," *T'ien Hsia Monthly* 11 (1941): 401–439.
61. Hung, *A History of Taiwan*, 17.
62. As an endnote (literally) to the Chinese exodus to the island, Taiwan became one of the very few areas in the Dutch commercial empire targeted for missionary work. By the end of Dutch rule on the island, there were several Dutch missionaries living in native and Chinese villages. Although the missionaries enjoyed a degree of success, their efforts eventually came to naught when the Zheng forces took Taiwan in 1662. For several reprinted primary accounts of missionary work on the island, see Campbell's *Formosa Under the Dutch.*
63. This arrangement seems to have suited everyone involved. The Dutch note somewhat sourly that the whole sea between Japan and China is infested with pirates, so having the Chinese come to Taiwan actually saved them much trouble and potential loss. In the same manner, the

Dutch themselves were not above preying on Chinese ships, so Zheng must have found a de facto "safe passage" to Taiwan an attractive offer. For early cooperation with Zheng, see Blussé, et al., eds., *Dagregisters Taiwan, Deel I.*

64. The "treaty" between the Dutch and the Zheng was at best a very loose agreement. Soon after its implementation, the Zheng routinely flouted it by sending ships directly to Nagasaki, as well as ships from Taiwan to Tonkin. See Asao, *Nihon no Kinsei: Sekai Shi no naka no Kinsei*, 145–146. In the diaries of the presidents of the factory at Deshima, there are many complaints of Zheng breaking his agreement with the Dutch. For example, this subject is one of the major themes for the months August and September of 1643. See NKKS, Vol. V.
65. NKKS, Vol. I, 107.
66. Ibid., 194.
67. This edict is found in the Kan'ei 10/2/28 entry of the *Tokugawa Jikki*. It states that if any Japanese go abroad secretly, they will be executed, and likewise if any Japanese living abroad return, the same punishment will result. See KTTJ, Vol. II, 590.
68. Governor-General Carpenter writes that if the Portuguese could be cut off from their trade in Nagasaki, not only would it result in a virtual Dutch monopoly, but also the Portuguese settlement at Macao would probably have to be abandoned. While the first prediction was not too far off the mark (there was never a complete Dutch monopoly), the second proved to be totally wrong: the Portuguese never left Macao, even when the city was in dire straits as a direct result of the Portuguese expulsion from Japan. See Cheng, *De VOC en Formosa*, 59.
69. The *Tokugawa Jikki* refers to the uprising as a "Christian *ikki*," likening it to the uprisings of religious powers such as the Honganji that defied Oda Nobunaga so effectively for so long, as well as the *ikki* that Ieyasu put down only with great difficulty in Mikawa province. See KTTJ, Vol. III, 72: Kan'ei 14/1/9 (February 3, 1637).
70. Ibid., 81.
71. F. R. J. Verhoeven, *Bijdragen tot de Oudere Koloniale Geschiedenis van het Eiland Formosa* ('s-Gravenhage: J. C. van Langen, 1930), 73. See also Couckebacker's diary in NKKS, Vol. III, 61.
72. In May of 1626, a Spanish fleet arrived in a harbor that they promptly named La Sanctissima Trinidad and where they erected a fort named San Salvador. The Dutch, romanizing the Chinese name, called the harbor Keelung. See Blair and Robertson, *The Phillipine Islands, 1493–1898*, Vol. 23, 80. For contemporary Dutch accounts of the building of the

fort, see Coolhaas, ed., *Generalle Missiven, Deel I*, 240–242. The Dutch believed that the Spanish were going to attempt to re-enter the Japan trade using Taiwan as a central base for trade between Manila, China, and Japan.

73. A good example of this is an interview recorded in Couckebacker's diary with both the daimyo of Hirado and the governor of Nagasaki in 1637. The Dutch president is asked about taking the fort, to which Couckebacker responds positively, saying that the Dutch would do it to "serve Japan." See NKKS, Vol. III, 41.
74. Valentijn, Francois. *Oud en Niew Oost-Indiën, Vervattende een Naaukeurige en Uit-voerige Verhandelinge van Nederlands Mofentheyd in die Gewesten, Benevens eene Wydlustige Beschryvinge der Moluccaos, Amboina, Banda, Timor, en Solor, Java, en alle de Eylanden onder Deselve Landbestieringen Behoorende; het Nederlands Comp-toir op Suratte, en de Levens der Groote Moguls; als ook een Keurlyke Verhandeling van 'tWezentlyskste, dat men Behoort te Weten van Choromandel, Pegu, Arracan, Bengale, Mocha, persien, Malacca, Sumatra, Ceylon, Malabar, Celebes, of macassar, China, Japan, Tayouan, of Formosa, Tonkin, Cambodia, Siam, Borneo, Bali, Kaap der Goede Hoop en van Mauritius* (Te Dordrecht: Joannes van Braam te Amsterdam, 1724–1726). *Deel IV*, "Beschryvinge van Tayouan of Formosa," 72–73.
75. Cheng, *De VOC en Formosa*, 206: December 12, 1642.
76. These persistent rumors were believed even as late as 1662. The fact that repeated attempts to find the gold mines had failed doesn't seem to have diminished belief in their existence.
77. Pieter Nuijts recommended the takeover of the fort because he saw it as an effort by the Spaniards to regain the trade that the Dutch had interrupted between Manila and the Chinese coast. Nuijts was in fact wrong, but his logic is compelling. See Donald Lach and Edwin van Kley, *Asia in the Making of Europe, Vol. III: A Century of Advance, Book 4* (Chicago: The University of Chicago Press, 1993), 1749.
78. NKKS, Vol. III, 152, 168–169.
79. The details of the loan and the process of borrowing such a large quantity of silver are found in the diary of Nicholas Couckebacker for October and November of 1637. No single merchant could be found to lend such a large quantity of capital, so the loan was arranged among three separate merchants. See NKKS, Vol. III, 50–77.
80. Cheng, *De VOC en Formosa*, 188.
81. NKKS, Vol. II, 180.

82. Suzuki also deals extensively with the different types of silver in Japan and their relation to the Dutch trade. See *Kinsei Nichi-Ran Bōeki Shi no Kenkyū*, 44.
83. Cheng, *De VOC en Formosa*, 188.
84. Ibid., 192.
85. Hayami Akira sees the period from 1570 to 1630 as Japan's transformation to modernity. This transformation entailed factors such as the increasing commercialization of the economy and the increasing circulation of goods from all over Asia. Hayami, "A Great Transformation," 5.
86. Saitō Yoshiyuki has pointed out in his own work, as well as in an edited volume, the extensive nature of local trade patterns in the Edo period, especially trade carried out by sea and river. In a chapter called "Baku-han Shijo no Tenkanten" (Changes in Baku-han Markets), he deals with the rapidly developing commercialization of Edo society, and with how society was markedly changed by such trends. See Yoshiyuki Saitō, ed., *Atarashi Kinsei Shi 3: Shijo to Minkan Shakai* (Tokyo: Shin Jinbutsu Oraisha, 1996), 22–67. Mark Ravina also discusses the commercialization of foodstuffs and other commercial products such as indigo and cloth in his *Land and Lordship in Early Modern Japan.* For example, the Yonezawa domain adopted policies that forced the peasantry to grow the lacquer tree and mulberry bushes, making it illegal to uproot either. Ravina, Mark, *Land and Lordship in Early Modern Japan* (Stanford: Stanford University Press, 1999), 57–58.
87. One of the many factors that contributed to the success of the factory on Taiwan in the first place was the willingness of Japanese patrons to invest silver in Dutch ships bound for the island. On this point, see Nagazumi, *Shuinsen*, 176.
88. NKKS, Vol. I, 200.
89. NKKS, Vol. II, 8.
90. Couckebacker records this four-article petition in an entry dated May 4, 1634, and states that the fourth article is directed specifically at the Dutch attack of Portuguese ships containing a great quantity of Japanese capital. He then goes on to recommend, several days later, that the Dutch not molest Portuguese ships trading in Japan because it will do great harm to the VOC in its relations with the Japanese authorities. See NKKS, Vol. I, 152, 192.
91. Ibid., 152.
92. Another set of records that is at times useful for the connection between Japan and the rest of Asia are the Dagregisters kept at Batavia. These are records of the day-to-day workings of that factory and therefore are not a particularly good reflection of Asian trade as a whole, although to be

sure there were some ships that journeyed directly from Batavia to Japan and vice versa. These ships carried mainly rice and wheat to Batavia.

93. James Davidson, *The Island of Formosa: Past and Present* (Oxford: Oxford University Press, 1988), 24.
94. Cheng, *De VOC en Formosa*, 226.
95. NKKS, Vol. I, 202.
96. The information for these ships and their cargoes is found in the diary of Nicholas Couckebacker from November 3, 1636 to February 17, 1637. See NKKS, Vol. II, 138–163.
97. Ibid., 140. The Dutch often counted the silver taken away from Japan in terms of cases (*kisten*). One case contained 1,000 *taels* of silver, so that 150 cases translated into 150,000 *taels*.
98. Blussé, et al., eds., *Dagregisters Taiwan, Vol. I*, 381.
99. Ibid., 485.
100. Coolhaas, ed., *Generalle Missiven, Deel II*, 278–282.
101. For both the departure of the *Oudewater* and the debt of the daimyo of Hirado, see NKKS, Vol. I, 195, 198.
102. Yao Keisuke, *Kinsei Oranda Bōeki to Sakoku* (Tokyo: Yoshikawa Kōbunkan, 1998), 12–13. Professor Yao has collected a great deal of invaluable data relating to the sale of rice to the company and collated that data into a number of useful tables throughout his work.
103. Ibid., 21.
104. Ibid., 29.
105. NKKS, Vol. III, 184, 188, 191.
106. Cheng, *De VOC en Formosa*, 127. For a general idea of the volume of goods shipped to Japan, consider that in 1634 Dutch ships carried over 400 *picols* of raw silk, over 13,000 pieces of Chinese porcelain, 100,000 pounds of sugar, 111,840 deerskins, and over 500 *catties* of sandalwood. Furthermore, 1634 was not a particularly profitable year compared to the late 1630s and 1640s.
107. NKKS, Vol. III, 27–33.
108. Blussé, et al., eds., *Dagregisters Taiwan, Deel I*, 498–499.
109. For the shogunal decrees concerning the departure time of foreign ships, see KTTJ, Vol. I, 590. For a Dutch translation of this directive, see NKKS, Vol. III, 9. Another factor infringing on the company's circumscribed time was a sort of delay tactic used by the *Itowappu Nakama* in the yearly determination of the silk price. In an effort to get the Portuguese and Dutch to sell cheaply, they often stalled until the last minute, knowing that the foreigners would rather sell cheaply than leave with their silk unsold. The clause mandating that the Dutch leave twenty days after the Portuguese was a point of contention every

year when the head of the factory made his trip to Edo, although this naturally became moot when the Portuguese were expelled from the country in 1639.

110. KTTJ, 590.
111. Donald Keene, *The Battles of Coxinga: Chikamatsu's Puppet Play, Its Background and Importance* (London: Taylor Foreign Press, 1951), 44.
112. Ralph Croizier, *Koxinga and Chinese Nationalism: History, Myth and the Hero* (Cambridge: Harvard University Press, 1977), 11.
113. Ibid., 65.
114. A brief summary of the battles between the Zheng and the Qing Empire, as well as Qing policies concerning the coastal provinces, can be found in Gernet, *A History of Chinese Civilization*, 470–471.
115. *Realia: Register op de Generale Resolutien van het Kasteel Batavia,1661* (Bataviaasch Genootshap van Kunsten and Wetenschappen, 1882–1886), 489.
116. Both the *Tokugawa Jikki* and the *Edo Bakufu Nikki* report the loss of Taiwan to Zheng. Apparently, two Dutch ships arrived in Nagasaki after the cession of the island, prompting the Nagasaki *bugyō* to report to Edo on Kambun 1/4/2 why there were two unexpected ships in Japan.
117. An English version of this treaty can be found in Inez de Beauclair's *Neglected Formosa: A Translation from the Dutch of Frederick Coyett's Verwaerloosde Formosa* (San Francisco: Chinese Materials Center Inc., 1975), 85.
118. Ibid., xv.
119. Ibid., 70.
120. Wills, *Pepper, Guns and Parleys*, 32.
121. For the change in the Japanese silk trade with Tonkin, see P. W. Klein, "De Tonkinees-Japanse Zijdehandel van de Vereenigde Oost-Indishe Compagnie en het Inter-Aziatische Verkeer in de 17de Eeuw," in *Bewogen en Bewegen. De Historicus in het Spanningsveld Tussen Economie en Culture* (Tilburg: J.J. Voskuil, 1986).
122. Suzuki, *Kinsei Nichi-Ran Bōeki Shi no Kenkyū*, 67.
123. Johan Maetsuycker noted that in 1655, twenty-three Chinese junks carrying a total of 1,316 *picols* of silk arrived in Japan, most of them sent by Zheng. Furthermore, company officials often complained in their diaries that Zheng was completely circumventing the Dutch on Taiwan by sending junks directly from Tonkin to Japan. See Coolhaas, ed., *Generalle Missiven, Deel III*, 65, and *Deel II*, 778.

124. Antonio van Diemen wrote from Batavia as early as 1639 that Japanese copper fetched an extremely high price in India and that tin should be sent to Japan in exchange for it. With the shogunal ban on copper, however, shipments to India ceased. They were resumed when the bakufu again allowed the export of copper at roughly the same time that silver was banned. This enabled the VOC to resume its lucrative trade in copper with the Indian coast. See Coolhaas, ed., *Generalle Missiven, Deel II*, 60, and *Deel III*, 625.
125. Sakurai Eiji and Nakanishi Satoru, "Bōeki no Tenkai," in *Shintaikei Nihon Shi 12: Ryūtsū Keizai Shi* (Tokyo: Yamakawa Shuppansha, 2002), 361.
126. Tonio Andrade, "Pirates, Pelts and Promises," 305.
127. Robert Antony, *Like Froth Floating on the Sea: The World of Pirates and Seafarers in Late Imperial South China* (Berkeley: Institute of East Asian Studies, Center for Chinese Studies, 2003), 72.
128. Ibid., 33.
129. Hung, *A History of Taiwan*, 35. According to Hung, in 1649 the factory on Taiwan accounted for 26 percent of total VOC profits in Asia.
130. Wills, "The Seventeenth-Century Transformation," 93.
131. For a more detailed analysis of these restrictions and of the depletion of precious metals, see chapter 4 on the role of silver in Japanese trade.
132. Watanabe, *Kinsei Nihon Bōeki Ron*, 120.
133. Wills, *Embassies and Illusions*, 148–151.

Chapter 5

Imports and Exports in Seventeenth-Century Japan

Femme Gaastra, the prolific Dutch historian of the VOC, has described the company's trading system in Asia as a series of lines emanating from Batavia, stretching westwards to Persia, Ceylon, Malacca, and Southeast India in one direction, and eastwards to China and Japan in the other.[1] Along these lines that represent major VOC trade routes, goods from places as far apart as India and Japan were regularly transported back and forth across the Indian Ocean and the China Sea. It was not uncommon, for example, for the company to ship Japanese precious metals to the Indian subcontinent, and conversely Indian textiles to Japan. By employing this type of paradigm to describe the Asian economic situation in the seventeenth century, it is readily apparent that there were no true areas of isolation; every region was in some way inextricably linked to other, often disparate, economic zones, regardless of the politics of that region.

A case in point is Japan; there is no doubt that before the *sakoku* edicts of the 1630s, Japan was a major factor in the economic world of Asia. Japanese ships were plying the waters of Southeast Asia with yearly regularity; at the onset of the Tokugawa era Japanese merchants maintained official commercial ties with no fewer than nineteen different countries. What is less commonly conceded, however, is that even after the shogunate chose to prohibit direct Japanese participation in overseas trade, the country still maintained a prominent position in the economic life of the region. Not only were powerful Japanese such as daimyo and bakufu officials investing silver in Chinese and Dutch ships, but there was also a lively trade in the foreign products that arrived in these ships at Nagasaki. The quantity of foreign goods imported into Japan in terms of their value in silver is truly staggering. The Dutch, in fact, for more than forty years used Japan primarily as a "bank" from which to finance their operations in other parts of Asia. In return for the silver, gold, and copper obtained in Japan, the VOC imported goods from all over the world to satisfy the insatiable desire of the Japanese elite for luxury goods. As Hamashita Takeshi has observed, one should not view the Tokugawa era as one of isolation, but rather as one of "selective openness."[2] Nowhere is this truer than in Japan's consumption of foreign goods in the seventeenth century.

Despite a number of governmental prohibitions, both political and economic in nature, Japan remained a major consumer of goods from across Asia, and indeed from around the world. Far from attempting to restrict the flow of goods into and out of Japan during the seventeenth century, the Tokugawa government adopted measures to ensure that access to foreign markets remained open to the Japanese by cultivating relations with the Dutch, Chinese, Koreans, Siamese, and the Ryūkyū Islanders.[3] In fact, when the Japanese authorities were debating the contentious issue of expelling the Portuguese, they took special care to make sure that the Dutch would be able to supply Japan with the same quantity of goods that their Iberian rivals did. The bakufu, despite a continued trend towards political centralization and withdrawal from direct foreign contact, was clearly interested in maintaining the flow of merchandise into the country. Therefore, the economic and political restrictions enforced by the bakufu should not be seen as a withdrawal from "the world," but rather as an effort to create a new international system that placed Japan at the center. The continuing desire to maintain at least limited ties to the wider world is nowhere better illustrated than in the vast array of goods that were flowing into and out of Japan. Whereas the preceding chapter addressed Japan's role in the world market in terms of precious metals, this chapter will address the goods that were imported into and exported out of Japan. This steady flow of goods was not only remarkable for its sheer quantity, but it was also of enormous consequence for the emerging world economy of the seventeenth century.[4]

Goods Imported into Japan

Raw Silk

In any discussion of imports into early modern Japan, silk must rank as the first and the most important of the vast array of goods brought from around the world. The Japanese market represented a huge demand for silk, usually of the raw, undyed variety. As the seventeenth century progressed, quantities of imports rose steadily, as did the number of places from which it was imported. The cargo of the Portuguese galleons from Macao that were of such value to that country's trade empire consisted almost solely of raw Chinese silk. Michael Cooper maintains that were it not for the Europeans' ability to import this into Japan, contact between the two would have been much more brief, and of far less significance. He also states that silk played a role in the initial development of Christianity in Japan because the Kyushu daimyo were willing to tolerate a missionary presence in their domains, and in fact often used interest in Christianity to lure the Portuguese ships to their harbors, in order to control the large imports of silk.[5]

In 1604 the Japanese demand for Chinese silk was between 300,000 and 400,000 *kin*, much of which the Portuguese brought from Macao.[6] The Portuguese, aside from the *shuinsen*, had a virtual monopoly on foreign silk imports until 1612 when a number of Chinese ships from Canton arrived at Nagasaki and were given permission by Ieyasu to trade in Japan. Trade between the Ming Empire and Japan was, of course, officially forbidden largely because of the recurring raids of the *wakō*, who ravaged the coast of China in a strange combination of illicit trade and piracy. Although Ieyasu tried on several occasions to reopen commercial relations with China through both Satsuma and Korea, the Ming steadfastly refused.[7]

Because of the rapidly deteriorating situation in China, one by-product of which was the loss of effective central governmental control in the southeast, the Chinese from areas such as Fujian Province were relatively free to trade abroad, even in Japan. Thus it is that merchants such as Li Tan make frequent appearances in western sources, especially in the diary of Richard Cocks. The Zheng family was also a product of this de facto semiautonomous nature of the Chinese coastal provinces. Zheng Zhilong was originally a merchant who rose through the ranks of Li Tan's commercial operations and who eventually took over his trade network upon Li's death. Zheng had a Japanese wife and his son, the famous "Coxinga," was born in Hirado before Zhilong moved his base of operations to Amoy (Xiamen). When Chinese merchants received official permission to trade at Hirado and Nagasaki, it was Li Tan and later the Zheng family who were responsible for most of this trade. Subsequently, the Chinese began to import silk in earnest with the arrival of sixty ships in 1614, effectively challenging the Portuguese hold on silk imports.[8]

The Dutch tried in vain for many years to gain access to the lucrative Chinese market so that they could import silk into Japan, as did the Portuguese and Chinese. When diplomatic attempts to this end failed, the Dutch resorted to outright violence against Portuguese and Chinese ships. One of the first Dutch "prizes," for example, was a Portuguese ship called the *Santa Catharina* that was taken off the coast of Johore in 1603. The ship contained 1,200 bales of Chinese silk, which was subsequently sold on the Amsterdam market for a handsome profit of 2,250,000 *gulden*.[9] This sort of piratical activity suited the Dutch perfectly in that the VOC was not only a trading company bent on the pursuit of profit, but also an instrument of the Dutch state authorized to carry the war against the Spanish and Portuguese to the Indian Ocean.

The VOC had, from the very beginning, obtained its initial foothold in Asia by attacking Portuguese settlements in the Spice Islands such as Fort Victoria. When it became apparent that the fantastic profits the Portuguese derived from Japan were primarily a result of the Chinese silk that they obtained in Macao, the Dutch did not hesitate to attack as many of these ships as possible. This, however, could only last so long; the bakufu, concerned about the loss of Japanese investments in the Portuguese ships, ordered the VOC not to attack the ships from Macao involved in the Japan trade. Similarly, the shogun issued an edict declaring the seizure of Chinese ships in Japanese waters illegal.[10] With the seizure of Portuguese and Chinese ships now forbidden, the VOC leaders soon recognized that in order to compete in Japan, they would have to find a way to tap into the Chinese silk market. The Governor-General of the VOC at Batavia wrote to his superiors in the Netherlands in December of 1626 that if the company was to be profitable in Japan, it would have to find a way to imitate the Portuguese by importing both raw silk and silk piece goods.[11] Not only would they have to find a way to obtain the silk, but they would have to obtain it in suitable quantities, because the miniscule quantity that they were able to obtain previously brought almost no profit since the large quantities brought by the competition drove down the market value of silk. While the Chinese and Portuguese were able to deal with this low price by importing higher volumes, the Dutch had no recourse to such measures. Antonio van Diemen, the VOC Governor-General at Batavia, for example, wrote in 1637 that six Portuguese galleons from Macao and sixty-four Chinese junks had come to Japan that year richly laden with silk goods. As a result, the selling price was so low that the small Dutch imports were rendered insignificant.[12]

That situation changed in 1622 when the VOC, in an unsuccessful attack on Macao the year before, was forced to fall back on the

Pescadores, where Ming naval forces threatened to attack unless they left. An agreement was subsequently reached with the Chinese, stipulating that if the Dutch left the Pescadores for the more distant island of Taiwan, then Chinese merchants would be allowed to trade with the Dutch there. This was an unexpected boon to the Dutch, who now faced the prospect of obtaining direct access to Chinese silk. In order to jumpstart this process, the *opperhoofd* (chief merchant) at Hirado borrowed 400,000 *taels* of silver from Japanese merchants from Kyoto and Osaka at 3 percent interest.[13] This was then used to improve Fort Zeelandia and its harbor as well as to purchase a stock of silk to be sold in Japan. With a steady supply of Chinese silk for the Japanese market, the Dutch were now able to compete more effectively with the Portuguese, Chinese, and Japanese merchants. The VOC was also now in a position to realize the tremendous wealth that such trade with Japan made possible. The precious metals obtained from Japan in return for products such as silk allowed the VOC to support its other factories throughout Asia without the huge shipments of silver from Europe that characterized the trade of other European companies.

The early years of the VOC's involvement with the Japan trade saw a continuing effort to exclude the Chinese and Portuguese from that market. In the case of the Chinese, the Dutch attacked their junks without provocation all along the coast of China, thereby obtaining by force a supply of silk. The junks sailing from China to Manila were particularly vulnerable; it was only within Japanese waters that they were relatively safe from VOC attacks.[14] The shogun repeatedly stressed that these attacks were no concern of the Japanese and that the Dutch would not be punished for them so long as they did not violate Japanese sovereignty. In an entry dated the twelfth of September 1643, the *opperhoofd* of the factory on Deshima wrote that while Dutch attacks on Chinese ships made the *bugyō* of Nagasaki angry because he often had silver invested in them, the shogun refused to interfere, stating explicitly that such attacks did not affect the Japanese.[15] The Chinese, however, were granted a request to be able to leave ten days after the departure of the Dutch ships so as not to be molested as they departed Japan laden with silver and other precious metals.[16] Richard Cocks, far from condemning these Dutch attacks, wrote a letter to the company directors in London in which he advocated taking the same measures as the VOC. According to Cocks, English ships should attack Chinese junks in order to obtain silk for the Japan trade.[17]

The attacks on Chinese ships became somewhat less frequent when a deal was reached between the VOC and Zheng Zhilong whereby the Chinese would sell their silk to the Dutch at Taiwan, whence it would be sold in Japan by the VOC.[18] This agreement was more or less effective for a time, but eventually it could not prevent the Chinese from sailing directly to Nagasaki, to the great consternation of the Dutch. In 1641, in fact, Zheng made it standard policy to send junks directly to Nagasaki to sell silk and other goods, thereby realizing a higher profit than simply using the Dutch as a middleman. The situation only worsened for the VOC when Zhilong's son, Zheng Chenggong, took control of his commercial empire in the 1640s. It was under the leadership of Chenggong that the company was forced to abandon Taiwan in February 1662.[19]

Japanese trade with the Ryūkyū Islands was another source of Chinese silk, obtained from the twenty or so of the boats that traveled yearly to China from the Ryūkyū Islands to pay tribute to the emperor in Beijing. Before the advent of the European powers and during the Ming commercial ban on Chinese trade with Japan, the Ryūkyū Islands enjoyed a privileged position astride the main trading routes between Japan and Southeast Asia.[20] Ryūkyū trade declined sharply, however, with the increased number of Japanese ships sailing directly to Southeast Asia and the increase in Chinese ships trading with Japan. Although raw silk imports into Japan during the early Edo period remained consistent at between one thousand and two thousand *kin*, it was not enough to affect the hundreds of thousands of *kin* coming in at Nagasaki, and therefore the trade between Satsuma and the Ryūkyū Islands was maintained more for political reasons having to do with shogunal legitimacy.

Although the quantity of silk imported from the Ryūkyū Islands was never particularly large, it did serve in the 1630s to keep the prices low by increasing the supply. In fact, when trade disputes arose between Japan and the West that served to temporarily curb foreign trade, the bakufu turned to the Ryūkyū Islands as an alternative source of silk, regardless of its small yield.[21] In this respect the islands played an important role as a backup to the main sources of silk imports. When commerce between the Qing and Japan was normalized in the late seventeenth century, however, there was no longer any fear of silk imports being cut off unexpectedly, and accordingly the commercial importance of the Ryūkyū Islands decreased dramatically.[22]

The Dutch believed with good reason that if the Portuguese could be cut off from trade in Japan, their entire Asian trade empire would be in jeopardy. Instead of confronting the Portuguese in Japan and possibly incurring the displeasure of the shogun, however, the company decided to attack them at Macao. In 1622 a fleet of twelve warships was sent to attack the city but ended in utter failure, and the Dutch were forced to retreat first to the Pescadores and later to Taiwan.[23] After this fiasco, there were no more large-scale attacks on Macao, although Portuguese junks continued to be attacked more or less regularly. Eiichi Katō argues, in fact, that one of the primary functions of the VOC factory at Hirado was to serve as a redistribution center for confiscated goods taken from Portuguese and Chinese "prizes." The high point of attacks on Portuguese shipping was in the 1620s when the English and Dutch formed an alliance as part of a 1619 treaty in which Hirado was to be used as the headquarters for combined attacks on Iberian shipping in Asia.[24] That this alliance was superlatively effective can be seen in the successes of July 1621, when a combined Anglo-Dutch fleet destroyed a Portuguese ship carrying the new Governor-General to his post at Goa.[25] Richard Cocks, the head of the English Factory at Hirado, noted in his diary that by attacking Portuguese galleons the "Dutch will drive them out of this region."[26] Cocks also wrote (most likely with some pleasure) that in June 1617 a huge typhoon destroyed two Dutch ships and a

Spanish "prize," attributing the loss to "divine vengeance" for Dutch looting and piracy![27]

Ironically, it was the Dutch failure to capture Macao that put them in a more advantageous position to import Chinese silk into Japan. By retreating to Taiwan, the Dutch were able to serve as the middleman between Japan and China in the silk trade, especially during the years when the Zheng family abided by its agreement to refrain from sending ships directly to Nagasaki and to trade instead with the VOC at Fort Zeelandia. While the VOC factory on Taiwan did not afford the Dutch the tremendous profits that the Portuguese enjoyed with their base on the Chinese mainland, it nevertheless gave them indirect access to the Chinese silk market. Furthermore, with the exception of a few years surrounding the fall of the Ming and the rise of the Qing dynasty, the Dutch were never able to compete with the Chinese in terms of volume of silk imports. Instead, the company became quite successful in finding alternative sources of silk in Asia.

In 1622 the annual Portuguese ship to Nagasaki carried a letter addressed to the shogun's senior advisors.[28] The purpose of the letter was essentially to complain of VOC piracy against the Portuguese throughout Asia. Of special concern, of course, was the trade between Macao and Nagasaki since the silk cargoes were extremely valuable and the proceeds derived from them served to finance a good part of their Asian trade empire. Doi Tadakatsu, perhaps the most influential shogunal advisor at this time, drafted a reply that was recorded in Sūden's *Ikoku Nikki*.[29] Doi's main thrust was that Dutch attacks on Portuguese ships involved in the Japan trade would not be tolerated. This was only a partial victory for the Portuguese, however, for, as events would prove, attacks on both Portuguese and Chinese ships outside of Japanese waters were of no consequence to the shogun. Portuguese losses therefore continued unabated throughout Asia and served to hasten the decline of their once flourishing trade empire.

Although the Dutch were able to gain limited access to the Chinese market on Taiwan, the quantity of silk they were able to procure was severely limited by the increased commercial activities of the Zheng family. Under the leadership of Zheng Zhilong and later of his son Chenggong, this family came to dominate the silk trade with Japan, especially after the expulsion of the Portuguese in 1639. Jan van Elseraq, the *opperhoofd* of the Dutch factory at Deshima, complained that although the Dutch had an agreement with Zhilong whereby he would send his junks to Taiwan rather than to Nagasaki, he soon recognized that this was not in his own interest and he effectively ignored the treaty by sending more and more ships to Japan with every passing year.[30] When van Elseraq took his complaints to the Nagasaki *bugyō*, citing the broken agreement as well as the Ming prohibition of trade with Japan, he was all but ignored, and the Chinese continued to send a considerable number of ships to Nagasaki.[31]

In the year 1658, Chinese junks coming to Nagasaki from the Chinese mainland, Siam, Quinam, Cambodia, and Tonkin brought a total of 1,360 *picols* of raw silk and 50,000 silk piece goods.[32] We are able to observe this remarkable increase in Chinese commercial activity in part because VOC officials kept meticulous records of how many ships arrived in Japan, as well as of their cargoes and the profits derived from them. To cite just a few examples, in 1650, sixty-nine Chinese junks arrived at Nagasaki bearing a total of 963 *picols* of raw silk followed the next year by forty-six junks bringing 937 *picols* of silk. Needless to say, these figures represented serious competition for Dutch imports.[33] The increased Chinese competition would plague the company for the remainder of the Edo period. Even when the bakufu, in an effort to curb the outflow of silver from Japan, limited the quantity of imports by foreign merchants, the Chinese were allowed to bring in twice as many goods as the Dutch.

To counter the problem of silk shortages on Taiwan—a result of the Chinese merchants' increasing tendency to bypass the VOC and trade directly with Nagasaki—the Dutch began to turn to Southeast Asia and India to obtain silk, and while this variety was never as profitable as Chinese silk, Tonkinese and Indian silk came to represent an important source of profit for the Dutch in Japan. In 1645 the Dutch became so desperate to obtain a supply of silk that they attacked Qishm Island in the Persian Gulf and forced the rulers there to grant the VOC a monopoly on the export of Persian silk.[34] As the 1650s progressed, more and more silver (much of it from Japan) found its way to Persian markets in return for valuable goods such as silk and sugar. Because these products were readily availability in Persia, and because silver, and later gold, was quite valuable in Persia relative to other places in Asia, the VOC trade with Japan ultimately made their operations in Persia extremely profitable.

In addition to the VOC factory in Persia, Southeast Asia and India also became prominent in the Dutch intra-Asian trade as a result of the search for alternative sources of silk to sell on the Japanese market. In 1655, for example, all of the silver exported from Japan by the VOC was sent to Tonkin and India in order to purchase the necessary quantities of silk.[35] When a factory was established at Tonkin in 1637, it immediately became profitable because of its ability to supply Japan with raw silk and other luxury commodities that were in demand in Japan. At the high point of Tonkin's importance, 300,000 to 350,000 *kin* of Tonkinese silk was exported to the Japanese market every year, much of that in VOC ships.[36] In the VOC diaries kept by the president of the factory in Hirado, we can see a dramatic increase in the quantity of Japanese silver sent to Tonkin; on the thirteenth of February 1637, for example, the *Grol* delivered 50,000 *taels* of silver and 300 *picols* of copper to Tonkin via Taiwan, and just eleven days later another 60,000 *taels* were sent to Tonkin in order to purchase goods there for the Japanese market.[37]

Conditions in Tonkin became especially favorable for the Dutch in 1641 when the King of Tonkin sent a letter to the president of the Dutch factory on Deshima (le Maire) offering free trade between his kingdom and the VOC.[38] Furthermore, at the end of the year, the Japanese government banned the arrival of native junks from Cambodia and Tonkin because they had previously brought Christian artifacts to Japan, a grave offence in the eyes of the Tokugawa government.[39] Shortly thereafter, in September of 1643, the company sent 100 cases of silver (100,000 *taels*) with which to buy Tonkinese goods for the Japanese market because the demand was found to be so great.[40] In 1645 the *opperhoofd* on Deshima declared that Tonkinese raw silk realized in a 143 percent profit.[41] It is apparent from VOC sources, therefore, that factories such as those in Tonkin and Persia played an increasingly important role in supplying Japan with the raw silk that was in such demand there. Here again we see that the Dutch were able to exploit the "country trade" to such effect. In this case the VOC used Japanese demand for goods from disparate areas such as Tonkin and Persia to realize tremendous profits in Japanese precious metals, subsequently using a portion of those precious metals to reinvest in goods for the Japanese market.

After the Japanese authorities prohibited the export of silver in 1668, it was quickly replaced with the gold *koban*, which the bakufu allowed to be exported for the first time. Because there was a consistent profit of over thirty percent by exchanging the gold *koban* for various Indian currencies, most notably the *pagoda* and the *rupee*, and because Indian textiles were gradually becoming popular in Japan, there was a steady flow of silver and then gold to places such as Coromandel, Surat, and Persia. In a letter to the *Herren Zeventien* written in December of 1662, for example, we learn that three ships were sent from Japan directly to "Hindustan" with 1,561,455 *gulden* in precious metals.[42] After about 1650 in particular, the flow of precious metals from Japan to India is well documented in the *Generale Missiven* and the *Dagregisters* of the factories concerned.

Conversely, large shipments of textiles from the subcontinent to the archipelago attest to the increased VOC trade between Japan and India. In 1667, for example, three ships sailed from India for Japan with 560 bales of silk. Furthermore on the fifth of October of the same year, Johan Maetsuyker expected that at least 1,200 bales of Indian silk would be sold in Japan that year.[43] In return for the often-substantial shipments of silk, so much gold and copper was sent to the subcontinent that nine ships were needed to transport it![44] Maetsuyker, in fact, wrote in a letter to the *Herren Zeventien* that Japan and India supplied enough gold and silver that there was no need to send any from the Netherlands.[45]

According to Yamawaki Teijirō, Tonkinese silk served as a "pinch hitter" for Chinese silk, and in return, the VOC exported mainly copper coins to Tonkin. After 1679, however, Japanese coins were debased and became almost worthless for international use, rendering the further purchase of Tonkin silk goods unprofitable for the company.[46] Similarly, the Governor-General at Batavia referred to Bengalese silk in 1657 as the "pillar of Japanese trade," and he was instructed by the *Herren Zeventien* to send it first and foremost to Japan, even though demand at home was considerable. In 1659 the company realized a profit of 80 percent on 1,600 bales of Bengalese silk in Japan, whereas for the Tonkinese silk, profits were a meager 25 percent. In 1667 Bengalese silk again brought in a handsome profit of 100 percent in Japan, second only to Persian silk, which realized a 106 percent profit.[47] Clearly, profits on silk imported to Japan from India, Southeast Asia and Persia were generally quite high, often soaring above 100 percent. This is in stark contrast to previous years when Japanese demand for silk from these areas was far from overwhelming, with profits ranging from a mere 60 to 70 percent. In 1656, for instance, Bengalese silk brought 62 percent profit, Tonkinese silk 60 percent, and Siamese silk 75 percent profit.[48]

Towards the end of the 1650s, profits from Southeast Asian and Indian silk were consistently around 80 percent, and by the mid-1660s were occasionally at or above 100 percent. In 1667, for example, the VOC sent most of its silk to Batavia, thus creating a shortage in the Japanese market, a strategy that brought them a 144 percent profit in that year.[49] Bengalese silk in particular seems to have found a ready market in Japan. Om Prakash estimates that between 1656 and 1672, Bengalese silk accounted for an average of 48 percent of the total cargo sent to Japan.[50] Silk from Bengal, Persia, and Tonkin continued to be sent to Japan in huge quantities until 1684 when the bakufu set a limit of 3,400 *kan* of goods allowed to be imported. This restriction represented a severe blow to the company's activities in Asia, a testament to the role that the Japanese market played in the Asian economy as a whole, and in the VOC's trade in particular.

Sugar

Sugar was grown throughout Southeast Asia and was therefore not particularly hard to come by. It was also grown in both Batavia and Taiwan, a situation that resulted in a low overhead cost because the middleman was eliminated. Because its cost of production was so low and because it was suitable as ballast on the ships that sailed for Japan, profits of only 20 to 30 percent were acceptable, whereas for other goods this would have been far too low.[51] Because of this the *Herren Zeventien*, in their instructions to Batavia, emphasized that sugar should be marketed in Japan as much as possible.[52]

Sugar had played a relatively minor role in the Japanese *shuinsen* trade. Until the arrival of the Portuguese and Dutch, in fact, its consumption was limited to upper class warriors and the nobility.[53] The Portuguese were soon importing it in bulk, however, so that by the time of their expulsion in the late 1630s, they were importing 6,000 to 7,000 *kin* of white sugar per year and 11,000 to 20,000 *kin* of black sugar per year. Profits of 60 to 100 percent made sugar second only to silk in importance for the Portuguese merchants. The Dutch and the Chinese soon followed the Portuguese lead, and by the middle of the seventeenth century were importing a combined 100,000 *kin* per year.[54] The sheer volume of sugar imports is a reflection of the fact that consumption had spread from the upper classes of society to the commoners.

Taiwan served as a staging area for sugar imports into Japan. Sugar from Batavia, India, Persia, and elsewhere was shipped to Taiwanese storehouses whence it was transported as needed to ports throughout the Indian Ocean. Because of its usefulness as ballast in both Chinese and Dutch ships, the records of the VOC on Taiwan report that sugar was shipped on many of these ships in such a capacity. Throughout the 1630s, Chinese junks bringing silk goods from the mainland and goods from Southeast Asia were almost always loaded with sugar as well. In January of 1637, for example, a junk from Amoy (Xiamen) arrived in Taiwan with the usual cargo of silk, but was also carrying 200 *picols* of rock sugar and 400 *picols* of powdered sugar. In February of the same year a junk arrived from the coast of China with 700 to 800 *picols* of powdered sugar, followed shortly thereafter by a junk from Anhui carrying 2000 *picols* of powdered sugar.[55] Although these are just a few random examples, they are nonetheless indicative of a general pattern of large sugar shipments that would ultimately end up on the Japanese market.

Sugar was consistently one of the most important goods in the Indian Ocean trade, partly because it was shipped throughout the year and on all types of vessels. There seem to have been no restrictions on its shipment in terms of season or demand; and because it was used as ballast on ships that would return with their cargo holds full of Japanese precious metals, that country received a large share of the sugar produced throughout the region. For the Dutch, the only factor that served to limit their shipments to Japan was Chinese competition. As with silk, Chinese ships plied the seas from Japan to Southeast Asia, acquiring goods such as sugar and spices and shipping them to Japan in great volumes. In August of 1641, for example, the president of the VOC factory on Deshima (Le Maire) wrote in his log that the Chinese were bringing so much sugar to Japan that he feared the market would be flooded and the price would bottom out.[56] As with the silk trade, however, the Dutch found an effective countermeasure to Chinese competition in Southeast Asia in their factories in India and Persia. These areas were a prime area of sugar production and, most importantly, were outside of the range of Chinese vessels. In return, sugar (along with silk) from these areas helped to facilitate the flow of Japanese capital to the subcontinent and the Middle East.

In the late 1660s, VOC shipments of sugar from India and Persia increased considerably. In 1667, for example, 2,500 to 3,000 packages of sugar were exported from these areas; between 1,000 and 1,500 of these were sent to Japan as ballast while the remainder went to the Netherlands.[57] In the following year, moreover, it was reported that sugar from Persia brought a 140 percent profit in Japan.[58] Whereas sugar from India and Persia became important later in the seventeenth century, regular shipments of Taiwanese sugar were sent to Japan a decade before sugar from these areas; in 1655, for example,

Pieter Van Dam records that the company sent 18,000 *picols* of Taiwanese sugar to Japan, an extraordinary quantity.[59] Here again we see the importance of the extensive Dutch network of factories in Asia; when goods from a certain region were no longer profitable or available, the VOC was able to simply obtain them from another area without disrupting the overall flow of trade within Asia.

Animal Hides

It can be argued persuasively that factories such as Siam and Cambodia were maintained almost entirely in order to support the Japan trade. As demonstrated throughout this work, goods from these regions were of immense importance to Japan and served to maintain the steady flow of precious metals out of that country. Tonkinese silk, as noted earlier, was the "pinch hitter" in place of Chinese silk and helped the Dutch maintain a foothold in the lucrative Japanese silk market when it became difficult for the company to obtain Chinese silk and before their Indian and Persian sources became fully viable. In the same way, Siamese and Cambodian deerskins, along with a number of other products, served to supply Japan with the luxury goods that were in such demand there. The Japanese were willing to pay dearly for these goods (especially deerskins and sandalwood), and this in turn helped the VOC to support its commercial empire in Asia.

In an important study of the VOC in Siam, George Vinal Smith argues that the fortunes of the factory at Ayuthia went hand in hand with those of the Japan trade. When trade with Japan was temporarily disrupted in 1628–1629, for example, the factory in Ayuthia was closed because of exceedingly low profits.[60] Similarly, the factories in Cambodia and Cochin were supported mainly because of their capacity as trading partners with Japan. And after the *sakoku* edicts prohibited Japanese merchants from traveling to these areas, the Dutch took over a great deal of this trade and actively promoted Southeast Asian goods in Japan, thereby driving up demand, and thus of course profits. The factory in Cambodia began to be truly profitable after the Japanese demand for sandalwood, deerskins, and ray skins took off from the 1640s onward. Tonkin as well began to be immensely profitable with mass Chinese and Dutch exports (mainly to Japan) of several types of silk. The Cochin factory was also invigorated by the Dutch trade with Japan. In 1633 Francois Caron and Paulus Tradenius traveled to Cochin where they met a Japanese resident by the name of Domingo living in the old *nihonmachi.* The two VOC officials quickly established good relations with him and subsequently rented his house in order to set up a factory.[61] It is a somewhat ironic situation that it was only after the shogunate banned Japanese merchants from traveling to ports in Southeast Asia that these ports became so important to the Japanese market.

Deerskins

Next to silk, deerskins were the most valuable item imported into Japan. The number of skins arriving at Nagasaki often reached hundreds of thousands, an almost unbelievable number considering that the skins were harvested purely through hunting rather than through raising deer. Japanese demand was insatiable, and remained so for virtually the entirety of the seventeenth century. Deerskins were considered first and foremost an item of military value in Tokugawa Japan, and therefore appealed particularly to the large samurai class. The armor worn by the warriors in battle was not extremely comfortable, and since deerskins were soft and absorbed moisture, warriors used them to fashion undergarments.[62] Moreover, they were also used to make *tabi*, or two-toed socks that were worn throughout Japan (and that can still be seen in Japan today, albeit not generally fashioned out of hides). Deerskins were also used to make the *hakama*, or Japanese divided skirt, and were additionally used in the construction of shields as well as on the armor itself. And finally, deerskins were used to make bags and, because of their nonabrasive qualities, wrapping for rifle storage. Interestingly, the market for these hides was controlled by the *Eta*, the caste of people in Japan who were considered to be ritually unclean (outcast) because of their involvement with occupations such as butchery and leatherworking. Valentijn, in his account of Japan, describes the *Eta* merchants flocking to the Dutch factory during the sale of deerskins and buying them in huge quantities.[63]

As in the case of sugar, Taiwan again proved invaluable in the deerskin trade with Japan; the island was home to a great number of deer that were hunted by the indigenous population and sold to various merchants for export. Siam, Tonkin, and Cambodia were also areas from which these hides were purchased. During the three decades of the *shuinsen* trade, merchants from Japan regularly visited Siam, Cambodia, and later Taiwan in order to procure these deerskins for the Japanese market. When six Japanese ships arrived in Siam and bought 70,000 deerskins, Martin Houtman, the head of the VOC factory in Siam, recognized the Japanese demand and wrote to his superiors advocating company involvement in the trade. Similarly, Governor-General Peter de Carpentier reported to the *Herren Zeventien* on January 17, 1625, that Siam exported 250,000 deerskins per year, most of which found their way to the Japanese market.[64] When the bakufu discontinued the *shuinsen* trade, the Dutch found themselves in an advantageous position from which to corner the Japanese market for deerskins. Not only did they obtain a monopoly on deerskin export from the Siamese king, but they also used their position on Taiwan to obtain the skins that were hunted by the natives.

The natives on Taiwan had hunted the deer that lived in the mountainous interior of the island for centuries. The deer seems to have played a role in Taiwanese aboriginal culture analogous to the role of the buffalo in the Native American culture of the American west. These animals were a source of food, clothing, and shelter, and therefore provided the aborigines with the basic necessities of life. When the Japanese, Dutch, and Chinese merchants arrived, however, the hunting of deer shifted from a purely utile function to one of commercial profit. The skins were sold and shipped to Japan, while the meat was primarily sent to the coast of China on Chinese junks.[65] In 1642, for example, ninety-seven Chinese ships arrived in Nagasaki bringing a total of 52,950 deerskins, many of them obtained on Taiwan.[66] The following year, the Chinese sent their ships to Cambodia whence they shipped 50,000 deerskins to Japan in three ships.[67] That number had fallen somewhat by 1650, but was still relatively high at 38,773.[68] With only a cursory glance at these statistics, therefore, we can see that the Chinese were a considerable source of competition to the VOC in the import of deerskins to Japan.

The Dutch, however, remained the primary importers of deerskins for two reasons. First of all they maintained a continuous presence on Taiwan, where they attempted with varying success to act as middlemen in the Chinese trade with Japan. Secondly, they were able to obtain a monopoly on the export of deerskins from the king in Siam. Nevertheless, there was a continuing problem with illicit trading on Taiwan by both the Chinese and the Spanish in their garrison at Keelung. On the twenty-ninth of September, for example, the head of the VOC factory on Taiwan issued a proclamation to the Chinese living on the island that they were not allowed to sell deerskins to the Japanese, even if they had a permit from the shogun.[69] Furthermore, after 1642 the Dutch began to seriously clamp down on Chinese competition by declaring that Chinese vessels without a Dutch trade permit would not be allowed to trade on Taiwan. Governor-General van Diemen wrote from Batavia, "We order with this letter that you will allow no Chinese without knowledge of license to go about in Formosa, much less live among the natives."[70] While the Dutch control of Taiwan gave the VOC a decided advantage in the deerskin trade, Chinese competition was always a factor, despite repeated proclamations such as the one noted previously.

In 1656 the king of Siam granted the Dutch a monopoly on the export of deerskins, a concession that allowed them to exclude their Chinese rivals from this lucrative trade. The monopoly lasted until 1688, and during the entire thirty-two year period the Dutch jealously guarded this right by sending frequent ambassadors to the Siamese court in order to remain in the king's good graces.[71] Because of the VOC monopoly, Japanese silver was sent to Siam either directly or (more often) through the company's factory on Taiwan. In return, Siamese deerskins and other exotic goods were shipped to the

Japanese market via either Batavia or Taiwan.[72] In August of 1639, for example, two ships arrived in Taiwan carrying, among other things, deerskins from Siam; the *Castricum* came from Batavia with almost 8,000 Siamese deerskins on the eleventh of August, and the *Otter* arrived from Siam with another 8,000 deerskins on the twenty-second.[73] As an indication of how large the trade in deerskins could be, in 1637 the *opperhoofd* (chief merchant) on Taiwan complained to the *Herren Zeventien* that in that year the company would not be able to send any more than 61,000 deerskins to Japan because of problems between the Dutch and the Siamese authorities![74]

The year 1656 was the high point in the deerskin trade, with a total of 195,574 hides sent to Japan from various regions.[75] This number fell drastically, however, when the Dutch lost Taiwan to the forces of the Zheng family in 1662. Moreover, after trade with Cambodia was suspended in 1667, Siam became the sole provider of deerskins to the VOC. Because the Dutch now had no other source for this commodity, they tried repeatedly to exclude Chinese and Siamese ships from trading directly with Japan. In 1663–1664, for example, the Dutch set up a blockade of Siamese ports specifically to stop these ships from traveling to Japan. The situation was finally resolved when a treaty between the king and the VOC was signed whereby the Siamese agreed not to employ any Chinese as pilots on their ships to Japan.[76] The major blow to the VOC deerskin trade came, however, when the forces of Zheng Chenggong made the VOC abandon Taiwan. Because the Chinese on the island now had unfettered access to Nagasaki, the Japanese market for deerskins was soon glutted, thereby driving down the price. Nonetheless, throughout the seventeenth century deerskins remained a profitable venture, and for the Siamese it represented a valuable source of much needed Japanese copper for use in their coinage.[77]

Ray Skins

Although ray skins were also used in a military capacity, these products (much moreso than deerskins) were valued for their aesthetic appeal. Ray skins were used primarily in the decoration of sword hilts and sheaths. They were also commonly used in the construction of cases and boxes of various types and for various functions.[78] The Japanese believed that these skins, with their rather exotic patterns, contained magical powers, and that a sword was somehow supernaturally strengthened by their incorporation.[79] Often simply called shark skins in the Japanese sources, they were imported to Japan from Southeast Asia, namely from Siam and Cambodia, but also from India and Africa, specifically from the area of Sao Tomé. While the number of ray skins imported never reached that of deerskins, imports were nevertheless significant in Japan, and because of their intricate patterns they fetched high prices on the Japanese market.

As with other goods, the Dutch often had to face stiff competition with the Chinese over the import of ray skins. This competition became especially intense in the mid-1640s when there was a large increase in the number of Chinese ships arriving at Nagasaki. The immediate reason for this increase in Chinese shipping can be found in the diary of Pieter Overwater, head of the VOC factory at Deshima. On June 11, 1645, he notes that because of the great civil war raging in China, there was no central control over commerce, and that consequently, Chinese merchants who wanted to trade at Nagasaki were able to do so with little or no interference from Beijing, which had hitherto prohibited trade with Japan.[80] Although merchant families such as the Zheng had routinely violated the Ming prohibition for years, they were an exception because of their immense power base in Southeastern China. Be that as it may, a number of Chinese vessels appeared in Japan throughout the 1640s carrying a great quantity of goods, including ray skins. Needless to say, this increase in Chinese shipping to Japan represented a source of great competition for the VOC.

According to Dircq Snoecq, the *opperhoofd* on Deshima in 1649, the price of Sao Tomé ray skins was very favorable, and because the company faced no Chinese competition there, the Dutch had a virtual monopoly as far as the Japan trade was concerned. On October twentieth, for example, the company sold 20,000 to 25,000 Sao Tomé ray skins on the Japanese market for a considerable profit, a reflection of the fact that skins from this area were generally prized above all others.[81]

Cowhides/Water Buffalo Hides

Cowhides were imported into Japan with some regularity, albeit with much less profit than deerskins or ray skins. These hides were either imported in an unfinished state, or they could be dyed a variety of colors before being brought to Japan. Spanish skins were usually dyed white or black, while those bought in Persia and Coromandel could be dyed white, black, yellow, red, or dark grey. The major use for cowhides was to make what the Japanese called "horse implements," or more specifically saddles and equestrian armor. The number of imports was never particularly large, but they were generally consistent, with about 3,000 pieces brought per year.[82] In addition to cowhides, the hides of water buffalo were, like deerskins, imported into Japan mainly from Siam. In 1650, for example, the Dutch ship *de Vrede* arrived in Japan on the twenty-sixth of August with a number of water buffalo hides, although the number of deerskins on the ship dwarfed that of the other hides. This was primarily because deerskins were significantly more profitable and much more in demand in Japan.[83]

Spices, Herbs, and Dyestuffs

While the import of spices and fragrances into Japan never approached the monumental quantities obtained for the European markets, Japanese *shuinsen* merchants, the Chinese, and the Dutch all brought these goods to Japan in greater or lesser quantities, and all of them realized a consistent profit over the years. It is easy to overlook these goods insofar as they never brought in the fabulous profits that other items such as deerskins and raw silk did, nor were they imported in such staggering quantities. With the exception of sandalwood, which as we will see was in very high demand and became extremely profitable for the foreign merchants, spices, dyes, and fragrances represented a modest but steady import item, which is reason enough for us to consider them here.

Until 1661, the VOC's base at Fort Zeelandia on Taiwan was extremely important for Dutch trade with Japan. As we have already noted, the island was invaluable for its supply of deerskins; but also, and more importantly, it served as a staging area for company activity to and from Japan. Considering only the category of spices, fragrances, and dyestuffs as an example, one can see a regular pattern of ships arriving at Taiwan from all over Southeast Asia and India laden with sandalwood, pepper, nutmeg, and a variety of other goods. The volume of trade was so great in the region that ships sailing between Taiwan and Southeast and South Asia often crossed paths within a matter of days; in August of 1637, for example, the *Noortwijk* departed Taiwan for Cambodia with 10,000 *taels* of Japanese silver, just as another ship richly laden with goods for Japan was departing in the opposite direction. Taking as an example the year 1639, there was a tremendous flow of goods from the factories in Southeast Asia to Japan via Taiwan; pepper, sandalwood, alum, sugar, and of course goods such as deerskins, silk, lead, elephant tusks, and rhinoceros horns all flowed towards Taiwan on their way to Nagasaki. In exchange for these goods, several ships departed Japan laden with silver for Taiwan, whence much of that silver was redirected to these Southeast Asian factories. Because Taiwan was ideally situated astride the trade routes between Asia and Japan, the Dutch were able to efficiently supply Japan with goods from all over the region, and nowhere is this more evident than in the great variety and quantity of spices and dyestuffs that made their way to Nagasaki in VOC ships

Within the category of spices and dyestuffs, sandalwood was without a doubt the most sought after item on the Japanese market. This wood came mainly from Siam and Cambodia and was often imported in large quantities in both Dutch and Chinese ships. The Japanese used sandalwood primarily as a dye for the raw, white silk that was imported into Japan in such great quantities. Since there was no suitable dying agent in Japan that had the same brilliant color as sandalwood, the Japanese had to rely solely on imports to support its substantial weaving industry. Furthermore, because the color obtained from sandalwood was very much in vogue throughout the seventeenth century, great quantities of the substance were imported. From 1624 to 1661, for example, one tenth of all VOC imports to Japan consisted of sandalwood, and by 1689 company warehouses in Batavia recorded that 1,165,858 *kin* of the product was stored for future shipment to Japan.[84] Such a devaluation in the market value of sandalwood occurred several times in the early seventeenth century. In 1624 the price of sandalwood was thirty-seven *taels* of silver per *picol*, but in the next year it had dropped to a mere five *taels* because of an overabundance. The pattern repeated itself in the next two-year period, with the price dropping from twenty-two *taels* in 1626 to less than five *taels* the following year.[85] Therefore, because sandalwood was relatively abundant in Southeast Asia, and because there was a finite market for it in Japan, it was stored in places such as Batavia so as to avoid this sort of price fluctuation.

The Dutch faced stiff competition not only from Chinese junks operating out of Siam, but also from the Siamese king himself. In 1657, recognizing the huge profits to be made on items such as deerskins and sandalwood, the king began to send his own junks to Japan. VOC officials were understandably upset since the prosperity of the Siamese factory depended almost wholly on the Japan trade. Shortly thereafter, the VOC and the king reached an agreement whereby the Dutch would maintain their monopoly on the export of deerskins while the king would limit his ships to Japan to only a few each year.[86] Chinese sandalwood exports from Siam, however, continued to prove a considerable source of competition to the company. In 1641, ninety-seven Chinese junks brought a total of 98,700 *kin* of sandalwood to Nagasaki. Despite this, the Japanese demand for this commodity was apparently not fulfilled even with increased Chinese trade. In August of 1648, Frederick Coyett wrote that even though 1,300 *picols* of sandalwood had arrived in Japan, the full demand could not be met that year because of a lack of space on VOC ships.[87] Sandalwood therefore was perhaps the most consistently imported good in the VOC's trade with Japan insofar as it was imported in steady quantities and with steady profits until the very end of the company's existence in the late eighteenth century.

Of all of the spices imported by the VOC, pepper was on the whole the most profitable in Japan. Contrary to modern culinary habits, the Japanese and Chinese used pepper not so much as a spice, but rather as a medicinal herb. It was first ground into a fine powder and then dissolved in hot water to make a drink not unlike tea. It was, of course, also used to liven the flavor of food, as in Europe, but by and large it was consumed in the form of a drink.[88] During the first Dutch audience with Tokugawa Ieyasu in 1609, Jacques Specx and Melchior van Sandtvoort recorded that Ieyasu himself bought the entire stock of pepper imported that year.[89] Furthermore, according to Pieter van Dam, because the Dutch in Europe began to scale back their demand for pepper, the company started to look for an alternative market, a market that it found in Japan. Van Dam states that the high point of pepper imports into Japan came during the 1670s; in 1674, for example, the VOC brought 3,346,500 *kin* of pepper to Nagasaki, a truly staggering amount.[90]

Although pepper was imported in relatively modest quantities from the earliest years of Dutch trade at Hirado, Japanese demand increased gradually until, by the second half of the seventeenth century, Japan was one of the largest consumers of VOC pepper, a fact that is easy to overlook since pepper never realized the fantastic profits of other, more exotic goods.[91] The price of pepper remained between ten and fifteen *taels* per *picol* and never seems to have fluctuated much, making it a valuable import because the company could usually rely on a steady profit.[92] After the Japanese purchased the pepper, a good portion of it was redistributed to Korea through the mediation of the Sō house on Tsushima. In fact, when trade between Tsushima and Korea slackened, the VOC was directly affected as it was forced to drastically cut back pepper imports to Japan.[93] The Chinese also imported a consistently large quantity of pepper, with quantities often exceeding 30,000 *kin* per year. In 1650, for example, Chinese junks brought in a combined total of 31,900 *kin*, thereby offering a considerable source of competition to the Dutch.

Finally, it should be noted that the nobility and the Buddhist clergy in Japan were significant consumers of spices, herbs, and fragrances of all types. Some Buddhist ceremonies in fact could not proceed without certain substances, and because the Japanese were forbidden to go abroad in the 1630s, priests relied on the Dutch and the Chinese to obtain the necessary spices and fragrances.[94] The Japanese nobility at the imperial court in Kyoto made a pastime out of experimenting with different fragrances derived from exotic substances only found in Southeast Asia.[95] Although the quantities of these herbs and spices were never extremely high, they nonetheless fetched a rather high unit price, and so were usually profitable for Dutch and Chinese merchants.

Exotic Goods

There were a whole host of goods imported into Japan that can be classified under the rather generic heading of "exotic goods." These items came primarily from two areas, namely Europe and Southeast Asia. Their value to the VOC lay not so much in their capacity to realize large profits, although certainly items such as elephant tusks and "unicorn horns" were quite valuable; rather they were important in satisfying the desire for curiosities and luxury goods that primarily characterized the wealthy strata of Japanese society. Many of these exotic goods were used in "official" gift giving, a practice that often cost the VOC upwards of 10,000 *gulden* per year. There were countless numbers of Japanese officials to "thank," and countless others who, with the proper "donation," could make life for company officials much easier. The requisite gratitude was invariably expressed through the presentation of lavish gifts or, as was sometimes the case, gifts disguised as a legitimate sale, but at a ridiculously low price. The latter practice was especially applicable for many of the higher officials within the bakufu, perhaps because of the seeming impropriety of accepting too many gifts from foreigners.

Gifts were by no means limited to those holding official office, but were also given to people who could simply make life easier for VOC merchants as well as to those people who might one day hold important office, such as sons of prominent officials.[96] The bewildering diversity and the oftentimes strange nature of the exotic goods brought to Japan can be seen in the "eis-boek" kept at the Dutch factory. This book is a list of goods that the Japanese authorities had ordered during the year, ranging from the commonplace, such as silk and woven cloth, to the extraordinary, such as various species of animals, scientific instruments, and weapons.[97] Even though the sum total of these gifts was relatively low compared to that of any of the other "staple" imports such as silk, animal skins, sugar, and so forth, their function was often very important and cannot simply be weighed in terms of their profit or intrinsic value.[98]

Three animal products that fall into the category of exotic goods are elephant tusks, buffalo horns, and rhinoceros horns. They were acquired primarily from Southeast Asia and Ceylon and were always in high demand in Japan. In 1643, for example, the *Hoge Regering* specifically ordered that rhinoceros horns and elephant tusks be sent to Japan because at that time these items were fetching a particularly high price on the Japanese market.[99] Rhinoceros horns were thought to be the horns of unicorns (as reflected in the Dutch word *eenhorn*) and were believed to have powerful magical qualities.[100] They were also thought to be a powerful aphrodisiac when ground up into a powder and consumed.[101] Of these three animal products, elephant tusks were the most frequently imported and were valued in Japan, as in the West, for their ivory. The records kept on Taiwan and in Japan invariably indicate that elephant tusks were present on almost all ships from Siam and Cambodia. In 1636, for example, the *opperhoofd* of the factory in Taiwan noted that the Dutch, Siamese, and Chinese had all sent elephant "teeth" to the island for ultimate shipment to Japan. He also noted on the ninth of November of that same year that the company sold four *picols* of Siamese elephant tusks in Japan for a hefty profit.[102] The Taiwanese records indicate that in every year (until the loss of the island in 1661) elephant tusks bound for Japan arrived on the island, albeit almost never in appreciable quantities. Trade continued, however, because of the great value per unit that elephant tusks brought.

Although not exotic to Europeans, the Japanese considered European cloth to be a novelty and were eager to spend often-large sums on it. In fact, cloth of all types was generally in high demand in Japan and played a huge role in the economy from the earliest times right down to the era of Meiji industrialization. In 1626 the Dutchman Conraad Kramer participated in the yearly VOC journey to Edo to pay respects to the "old" and the "young" shogun. En route to Edo, the party sojourned in Kyoto and witnessed a huge procession of daimyo and their innumerable retainers, all resplendently clothed, on the occasion of Hidetada's audience with the emperor. Kramer remarked that ceremonial occasions such as these made Japan a good market for Dutch cloth because the nobility, daimyo, and bakufu officials all strove to outdo each other for the most exotic colors and patterns of dress.[103]

The Dutch cloth that was often popular in Japan was woven in the city of Leiden and from there was sent all over the world in VOC ships. Pieter van Dam included black "Leiden cloth" on his lists of goods regularly sent to Japan and stated that it consistently fetched around twenty *taels* per *picol*, a much greater profit than it would fetch on the European market.[104] Although this particular type of cloth was often popular with the Japanese nobility, other European cloth was not in demand at all. In fact, one factor usually cited in the early closure of the English factory at Hirado is that the Japanese were simply not interested in English woolen cloth (called broadcloth). Because the English lacked the extensive intra-Asian structure of the VOC whereby the Dutch could simply "redirect" unwanted merchandise to other factories, the English factory was forced to close when its goods consistently went unsold.

The officials with whom the Dutch came into contact, including of course the shogun and all of his senior councilors, were all presented with gifts every year during the requisite journey to Edo. These gifts were not spontaneous expressions of Dutch goodwill, but were rather part of the diplomatic process that served to facilitate relations between Japan and the VOC. On the seventeenth of January 1642, van Elseraq, the *opperhoofd* at Deshima, included in his journal a list of people to whom gifts were to be presented that year.[105] The list is fabulously long, and includes brothers and sons of officials as well as the officials themselves. Almost without exception the most important items presented were cloth of varying origins and colors. It is hard to overstate the importance of cloth in Edo-period Japan; despite periodic sumptuary laws in which it was decreed that fine silk was contrary to the samurai ethic, it was common practice (if not socially requisite) for high-ranking warriors such as daimyo and their retainers to dress lavishly. This was all the more so when there was an official state function such as the reception of a Korean or Ryūkyūan embassy, or even just the regular attendance on the shogun that was required of all daimyo during their stay in Edo. On occasions such as these, daimyo spared no expense in dressing as lavishly as possible, and had personal clothiers for this very purpose. This goes a long way in explaining why the most valuable VOC gifts to shogunal counselors were invariably cloth of various designs, colors, and origins.

Apart from gifts of silk and other types of cloth, presents were at times truly bizarre, especially those given to the shogun.[106] The *Edo Bakufu Nikki*, *Tokugawa Jikki*, and *Tōdaiki* all contain lists of the "tribute" items presented to the shogun and his officials. These mostly consisted of cloth from around the world—silk from Asia, cotton from India, and woven cloth from the Netherlands—but many of the gifts were more personal and often represented the whims of the ruling class in Japan. In 1660 (Manji 2/2/28), for example, the Dutch arrived at court and brought with them a gift not only of the usual dyed silk, raw white silk, and European woven goods, but also two European swords, elephant tusks, rhinoceros horns, tortoise shells, two oxen, and a map of the world drawn in Europe.[107]

It was not uncommon for the Dutch to bring several species of exotic animals to Edo as presents for various officials during audiences. In 1640, for example, the president of the Dutch factory took along with him to Edo two dogs as well as the skin of a red bear to present to the shogun.[108] Two years later, the Dutch were in Edo again, this time with a present of several types of live birds, including a goldfinch.[109] For the next several years, birds made frequent appearances amongst the shogunal gifts since they proved to be great favorites among the elite in Edo. The shogun's officials, in fact, inquired if European falcons would be able to survive the trip to Asia so that the shogun might have one in his possession, all Tokugawa shogun being great connoisseurs of falconry.

In 1646 the Dutch brought to Edo what must be accounted one of the strangest gifts recorded: the liver of a rhinoceros, fat from an elephant, several Cockatoos, and a number of camels![110] Another favorite of both the shogun and his officials seems to have been the buffalo; these animals were therefore brought to court with relative frequency for several high-ranking officials.[111] In addition to live animals, animal products such as elephant tusks, hides and pelts of various species, and rhinoceros horns were also brought in considerable quantities to Edo for the gratification of the shogunal officials. These gifts should not be seen as mere trifles, but rather as serious political tools in the ongoing effort to maintain the favor of the Japanese authorities.

Another luxury item that was imported into Japan and valued very highly by those with an interest in tea was "rusun jars" from Manila.[112] It may at first seem strange to include such a seemingly mundane item in the category of "luxury goods," but these jars were highly prized pieces of art. Their importation began at the time when Hideyoshi began to authorize Japanese merchants to journey to the Philippines. When Japanese merchants began to bring the jars back from Manila, Hideyoshi valued them so much that he monopolized their purchase.[113] This is not so surprising since the main use of these jars in Japan was to store tealeaves for the tea ceremony, and as Hideyoshi was an ardent patron and practitioner of *chanoyu* ("Tea Ceremony"), he prized these vessels accordingly. Charles Boxer states that these jars from Manila took the place of similar jars from Song China that had previously been used; because relations with China had been severed for over a century, the jars from Manila served as a substitute for the Chinese goods.[114] Whatever the reason for the attraction, the Japanese were willing to pay high prices for the jars, and subsequently a brisk trade arose between Japan and Manila. After the death of Hideyoshi, however, the jars no longer appear in any of the Japanese sources, and the Dutch certainly make no mention of them. Perhaps the fetish for them died with their biggest patron, or perhaps, as with so many other fads, interest simply waned. At any rate, after Ieyasu issued an edict banning trade with Manila, all goods from the Philippines were declared contraband, bringing to an end the role of Spanish and Luzon luxury goods in early modern Japan.

A group of exotic goods that were always highly sought after by the Japanese officialdom was a vast array of Western scientific implements and maps. There were endless requests for these items, which the Dutch genuinely tried their best to fulfill. In 1657, for example, the Dutch brought two large maps of the "entire world" for the shogun's perusal.[115] These maps served as a supplementary response to the barrage of questions about international affairs that the Dutch were subjected to by officials both high and low. It is not uncommon, for example, to read in the Dutch diaries about interviews that lasted four or five hours during every day of their stay in Edo. The shogunal officials mainly questioned the Dutch about foreign politics, the wars that the Netherlands was endlessly engaged in against the Spanish, Portuguese, and English in both Europe and Asia, and of course Christianity. For these interviews, maps and globes were helpful visual aids, and especially after the midpoint of the seventeenth century, they were brought to court ever more frequently. Telescopes and spectacles were also very much in demand by the Edo elite and were shipped to Japan in considerable quantities, mainly as gifts. In 1641, for example, the shogun "requested" that the Dutch bring a telescope to court the following year, which was subsequently done.[116] The Dutch also brought mortars, grenades, clocks, and a whole host of other such curiosities to Japan from around the world in an effort to maintain friendly relations with the Japanese authorities.

The shogun particularly appreciated gifts of a military nature such as canons and mortars, and by the end of the seventeenth century, both Japanese and Dutch records suggest that the shogun must have had quite an arsenal of western artillery, although the only people with the knowledge and skills to use these weapons effectively were westerners. One particular gift of arms seems to have been very effective in placating the Japanese authorities. In 1649 a special ambassador was sent to Japan to thank the shogun for his kind treatment of Dutch castaways who were apprehended in the northern domain of Nambu several years before. Accompanying Andreas Frisius, the Dutch ambassador sent from Batavia, were two large pieces of ordinance that were intended as gifts for the shogun.[117] In addition to the artillery, a Dutchman skilled in the use of mortars and canons was left behind in Edo in order to instruct a number of *hatamoto* (literally "bannerman," or more generally a lower rank of shogunal retainer) in the use of western artillery.[118] We read that in the following year, the Dutch gunner was able to successfully fire the pieces in Edo, to the great pleasure of the shogun and his officials.[119] These gifts helped to smooth over an increasingly tense situation in which the Japanese were disturbed by the apparent lack of gratitude by the Dutch for the safe return of their compatriots.

ITEMS EXPORTED FROM JAPAN

As noted in the previous chapter, Japan's major items of export consisted of precious metals. Silver, gold, and copper made up almost the entirety of VOC exports to both Asia and (at times) to Europe itself. Apart from the great quantities of these precious metals that left Japan in VOC ships, this section will deal with five main export products from Japan. One item in this list, Japanese porcelain, was only of international importance for a brief period in which the Japanese product was substituted for Chinese porcelain as an item for export to the European market. During the Manchu war of conquest on the Asian continent, the number of pieces of Japanese porcelain leaving the country was often quite large. This, however, was only a stopgap measure, and once the Manchu solidified their hold on China, the export from Japan dropped to its previous unremarkable levels. Japanese porcelain is included here not only because it was temporarily quite important as a product on the European market, but also because it served to stimulate the growth of the porcelain industry in Japan. The other four commodities exported in appreciable quantities were weapons, rice, camphor, and lacquer ware, the latter sought after even in Europe because of its fine workmanship. As early as 1610, the Dutch ship *Rode Leeuw met Pijlen* returned to the Netherlands with, among other goods, 9,227 pieces of porcelain and nine cases of lacquer ware from Japan, both items that often sold well on the European market in limited quantities.[120]

Weapons

Governor-General Gerard Reynst, in a letter to the *Herren Zeventien,* noted that a Japanese ship arrived on the island of Amboina in 1615 loaded with "ammunition of war."[121] For years, the Japanese islands had been known in East and Southeast Asia as a place from which high-quality swords could be obtained. In fact, in the early years of Japanese trade with China, one of the chief patterns of exchange was Chinese copper coinage for Japanese swords. Similarly, swords were also exported to Southeast Asia, especially to areas such as Siam and Cambodia in which perennial warfare was the norm. Antonio Morga, the Spanish governor of the Philippines, claimed that Japanese ships came to Manila regularly laden with such military items as swords, helmets, and shields.[122] It is evident that in the early seventeenth century, the export of Japanese weapons was a well-established pattern of trade in Asia. The Dutch, while not particularly interested in Japanese weapons in and of themselves, were quite interested in another kind of weapon: Japanese soldiers.

The Japanese of the seventeenth century were generally considered fierce and effective soldiers. A rather large contingent of warriors served in the army of the king of Siam until factional divisions at court drove them out of the country. Similarly, the Dutch and English employed Japanese soldiers at their factories and settlements, most notably at Batavia. In 1620, for example, 10 percent of all foreigners in the employ of the English at Batavia were Japanese.[123] The Dutch, English, and

Portuguese also found that Japanese sailors were some of the best in all of Asia because they had a much lower mortality rate than either Europeans or Southeast Asians. Therefore, the 1621 ban prohibiting the use of Japanese citizens on foreign ships came as a blow to the European companies.[124] Soon thereafter, the use of Japanese soldiers would also be banned, as would the export of weapons from Japan.

In 1621 the bakufu forbade the export of all war materiél from Japan. This was partially in response to the disorder then prevalent on the Asian continent; with the Manchu subjugation of Korea, Japanese weapons were making their way to the Qing armies through the peninsula via its trade with Tsushima.[125] Japanese weapons were also being supplied to "Ming loyalist" forces in Southeast China, especially during the Revolt of the Three Feudatories.[126] The bakufu took the export and use of Japanese weapons on the continent very seriously, and the subsequent crackdown on the trade was quite severe. Couckebacker, in a diary entry for August 1634, notes that seven Japanese and twenty-six Chinese were executed for smuggling weapons out of the country.[127] Similarly, the bakufu discovered that a Hakata merchant, in collusion with a Nagasaki *machidoshiyori,* was smuggling arms to Korea through Tsushima in 1664. In this particular incident, almost 100 people were severely punished for this blatant disregard for the shogun's order.[128] Although Couckebacker noted that the ban was regularly flouted, exports of weapons would never reach the high levels they had enjoyed before 1621.

Camphor

Although camphor was cultivated in the Malay Peninsula and on the islands of Sumatra and Borneo, it also began to be grown commercially in Japan beginning in the late sixteenth century. The primary areas of production within Japan were the domain of Satsuma (in the west) and Sado Island (in the Sea of Japan). Camphor was used primarily as a tea-like drink because of its purported medicinal qualities and also as an ingredient in the production of fireworks. Dirk Gerritszoon Pomp, perhaps the first Dutchman to visit Japan, served as an artillery specialist with the Portuguese on a voyage to Nagasaki in 1585 and has left us an account of his impression of the country. Among his many observations, he states that Japan is one of the few places where camphor is grown, indicating that by this date production of the tree had already reached a relatively large scale.[129] Knowledge of camphor cultivation was apparently obtained in Korea and subsequently spread throughout the archipelago, until the beginning of the seventeenth century when it was being cultivated widely in western Japan. To produce the desired product, the camphor tree was sapped, cut down, and further cut into chips. The chips were subsequently boiled to produce a resin that was placed in a vat with a hole at the bottom, through which the desired product escaped. This oil was usually collected and sold in bags of one *picol*.[130] In addition to the resin produced from the camphor tree, Joao Rodrigues states that the wood was of unusual durability and so was often used in the construction of ships, although he does not elaborate any further on this use.[131] At any rate, while the Japanese *shuinsen* merchants took it to various ports in Southeast Asia, export increased dramatically with the ban on the Japanese international trade and the resulting increased activity of the VOC and the Chinese.

Because the account books were rather neglected during the first ten years of the VOC factory at Hirado, we have almost no surviving data on the exact amount of goods brought in or taken out of Japan by the Dutch. It is only with the increased assiduousness of company officials in the early 1620s, therefore, that we can say with any certainty how much camphor was exported. According to the *Negotie Journaal* for 1621 and 1622, there were nine purchases of camphor by the VOC, four of which were over 14,000 *catties*.[132] In 1636, over 20,000 *kin* of camphor was exported from Japan and sent to various factories around Asia.[133] In 1643, furthermore, president Overwater urged Japanese merchants to send as much camphor as possible to the Dutch at Nagasaki; Southeast Asian demand for the resin had increased to the extent that two years later the company exported 204,002 *kin* from Nagasaki.[134] This quantity, however, represents a peak in camphor export; after the 1640s the export leveled off to a more modest quantity. One of the factors working against the company was that the daimyo of Satsuma (Satsuma was the chief region of camphor production) often placed bans on its growth in an attempt to force farmers to produce more food and less "cash crops." In 1648, for example, the daimyo of Satsuma banned all production of the product and uprooted many camphor trees, thereby sending the price so high that the company was unable to buy an appreciable amount.[135] Although production was resumed soon thereafter, there were several more periodic bans so that export was never very regular from year to year. A good example of this can be seen in the 1670s when, for several years throughout the decade, there was no export of camphor at all because of the vagaries of production in Satsuma.[136]

While most Japanese camphor went initially to various Southeast Asian ports such as Siam, Cambodia, and Tonkin, starting in the 1650s, more and more of it was sent to areas in India such as Surat, Bengal, and the Coromandel Coast, as well as to places in the Middle East, with Persia being the primary destination.[137] Whereas in China camphor was used as a medicinal, tea-like drink, in India it was highly regarded as a type of lubricant for the body.[138] The shift in camphor distribution towards India in particular reflects the shift in the importance of Indian goods in Japan. While the export of camphor as a whole was not very large, profits from its sale were consistently very high. From 1655 to 1684, for example, VOC profits on Japanese camphor rarely dipped below 100 percent, and in fact often reached over 200 percent, with the high point coming in 1676 when 4,000 pounds of camphor brought in an amazing 616 percent profit.[139] While it is true that company profits on camphor sales paled in comparison with the fabulous earnings derived from the export of precious metals, camphor nonetheless brought a handsome return in several areas of Asia, and therefore cannot be ignored in terms of Japanese influence on the Asian economy.

Lacquer Ware

Black lacquer was a valuable raw material that was imported into Japan from areas in Southeast Asia such as Siam and Cambodia. Japanese craftsmen used this resin to create the famous Japanese lacquer ware products, including sword sheaths, bowls, tables, and a whole host of other products. According to Joao Rodrigues, "The Japanese stand supreme in this art, for they are so skillful that they can make a varnished object look as if it were made of smooth, shiny ivory."[140] These handicrafts were subsequently exported to several areas ranging from Southeast Asia to India, and even at times to Europe. In fact, apart from a few years in which Japanese porcelain was exported to Europe in large quantities, Japanese lacquer ware was probably the most consistently exported Japanese product to the West. In a letter to the *Herren Zeventien* in 1636, Governor-General Hendrick Brouwer stated that there was a considerable demand for Japanese lacquer ware in Persia, Surat, and Coromandel, in addition to the perennial demand for silver and camphor.[141] On October 15, 1643, two Dutch ships, the *Oranjeboom* and *Capelle*, left Japan for Taiwan with a considerable quantity of lacquer ware on board, whence it was then shipped to other factories throughout Asia.[142] Similarly, president Overwater wrote in 1645 that he was sending a large shipment of lacquer ware (in addition to 80,000 *taels* of Japanese silver) to Coromandel.[143] It appears that lacquer ware was especially in demand on the Coromandel Coast, a situation that was surely beneficial to the company insofar as they were able to supplement the local demand for silver with other products in return for desired Indian goods such as cotton cloth and silk.

Not only was Japanese lacquer ware prevalent in the inter-Asian market, but it was also sent to the Netherlands in often-large quantities. In October of 1645, for example, Overwater recorded in his journal that there were intense negotiations over the price of the lacquer ware until the twenty-second of October, when an agreement was reached and the ships *Henriette Louise* and *Leeuwerik* departed Japan for Holland laden with the handicrafts and other commodities.[144] In a convenient and somewhat ironic situation, the VOC, especially after the issuance of the *sakoku* edicts in the 1630s, found itself in the position of both importing the raw, black lacquer from Southeast Asia and also exporting the finished product to those same areas, as well as India, Persia, and Europe.

As with almost every other commodity in Japan, however, the Dutch faced rather stiff competition from the Chinese. On the eighteenth of December 1639, for example, a Dutch report states that a Chinese junk arrived in Nagasaki carrying a number of goods for the Japanese market, including black lacquer.[145] Every year a number of Chinese ships arrived in Nagasaki with this raw material, but as far as at least the Dutch sources reveal, Chinese junks did not usually export the finished products, perhaps because the Chinese were usually more concerned with the acquisition of Japanese silver. Products such as lacquer ware were more profitable for the Dutch because of their ability to exploit the "country trade," in which a complex system of inter-Asian trade (with Batavia at the center) made the export of goods such as lacquer ware profitable.

Porcelain

The ability to produce fine porcelain, as with the knowledge of camphor production, was in part a product of Hideyoshi's invasions of Korea in the late sixteenth century. Within a few short years thereafter, Japan, with the help of potters kidnapped from the peninsula, was producing high-grade porcelain. The Japanese product rivaled that of the Chinese in quality, although it was never able to replace, or even seriously rival, the Chinese product on the European market. There were two periods in the seventeenth century, however, when Japanese porcelain played a large role in the European market. The first was in the 1640s during the Manchu invasion of Ming China; because production and distribution on the continent was severely disrupted, the VOC turned to the Japanese product to fill both Asian and European demand. The second period came in the 1660s when the Dutch were forced to abandon their factory on Taiwan to the forces of Zheng Chenggong. With the VOC's access to the Chinese porcelain market effectively denied, it was primarily Japanese porcelain that filled the gap until the Dutch found alternative means of procuring the Chinese product.

In September 1661, Hendrik Indijk, the head of the Dutch factory in Nagasaki, wrote that there was a great quantity of fine porcelain produced at Imari and Arita in the province of Bizen.[146] Because at this time the Dutch had no direct way of obtaining Chinese porcelain, Japan became a net exporter of the very product that was formerly imported into the country in large quantities.[147] In 1653 the first shipment of Japanese porcelain was sent to Batavia, whence it was sent to the European market.[148] From this date, regular shipments of Japanese porcelain were sent to Batavia as well as to other factories in India and the Middle East such as Surat and Mocha. Volker estimates that between 1653 and 1682, 1.9 million pieces of Japanese porcelain were shipped to factories around Asia.

While Japanese ware fared much better in Asia than in Europe, there was nonetheless a considerable quantity shipped to the European market in the three decades from the 1650s to the 1680s, after which exports dropped to their previous low levels. Governor-General Maetsuyker wrote in 1662, for example, that Japanese porcelain, especially lamps, was becoming somewhat fashionable in the Netherlands and that he would therefore begin to ship greater quantities of it home on the *Retourvloot*.[149] The Amsterdam chamber of the VOC subsequently reported that it had received thirty-three cases of Japanese porcelain on that year's fleet from Batavia.[150] The lasting result of the Japanese porcelain production of the seventeenth century was not due to the quantity exported, for this international trade flourished for only a few decades in the seventeenth century, but in its effect on the domestic Japanese market. This effect was indeed profound and was responsible for the longevity of the industry, an industry that is in fact very much alive and well today. Furthermore, in 1668 the shogun issued another edict in a long series of "sumptuary laws" in which it was forbidden to import foreign porcelain.[151] This was a boon to the new centers of production in Bizen and elsewhere and served to perpetuate the prosperity that these areas enjoyed during the brief period of increased demand by the VOC.

Rice and Other Foodstuffs

In a letter dated the twenty-seventh of January 1625, the ship *'t Wapen van Zeelandt* was instructed to obtain from Japan five or six hundred *lasten* of rice for Batavia.[152] Similarly, Governor-General de Carpentier wrote in February 1626 that Japan was one of several places in Asia from which the VOC obtained foodstuffs (such as rice) that were of such material value to its factories in Asia.[153] Hendrick Brouwer elaborated on this trade in foodstuffs when he noted in 1636 that rice and wheat from agriculturally rich areas such as Japan, Aracan, Surat, Persia, and the Coromandel Coast were sent to places that grew little food such as Batavia, Banda, Amboina, and the Moluccas.[154] Ironically, islands that grew tremendous quantities of spices were poor producers of foodstuffs and hence had to rely on outside sources for a sufficient supply of food. In a letter to William Nealson in 1617, Richard Cocks stated that one of the main functions of Japan for the VOC was as a "storehouse" for the Spice Islands.[155] Before Japan began to be such a large treasure trove of silver, the VOC used their position in the islands as a source of food for other parts of their trade empire in Asia.

Rice became increasingly important once the Dutch established Fort Zeelandia on Taiwan. In the diaries kept by the heads of the factory on the island, it is not at all uncommon to find references to rice and wheat being included in the shipments of precious metals to Taiwan. On the twenty-eighth of November, just to cite a single example, the president notes that four ships arrived from Japan with 450,000 *gulden* in silver intended for various factories around Asia, as well as 400 bales of white rice for Taiwan.[156] Pieter Nuijts, in fact, stated that deerskins from Taiwan were traded in Japan specifically for Japanese silver and rice.[157] This rice was valuable to the Dutch in their initial years on Taiwan because there were very few Chinese living on the island, and therefore very little organized agriculture. Furthermore, the Dutch had not yet established sufficient control over the population of the island to enable them to levy taxes. It was only after the disturbances on the mainland, precipitated by the Manchu invasion, that Chinese settlers fled to Taiwan and began to grow enough rice to support the Dutch. Furthermore, as the Dutch became more entrenched on the island, their control became more pervasive, allowing them to tap into the resources of the farming villages that lay some distance from the VOC factory. Until that time, however, much of the rice that was needed on Taiwan came from Japan.[158]

There is one other aspect of Japanese rice that was of importance to the Dutch, and that is the fact that it was used by various daimyo as a means of repaying debts owed the VOC. Yao Keisuke has studied the role of rice in lieu of silver as a medium of repayment in the domains of both the Matsuura and Hosokawa families.[159] According to Yao, the Matsuura began repaying their debts in rice as early as 1626 and continued doing so until after the Dutch were relocated to Deshima in 1641. In 1635, for example, 97 percent of all rice exported from Japan by the VOC was received from the Matsuura family, and rice constituted 91 percent of all goods that the Dutch received from that family. The total rice exported in 1635 amounted to 2,898 *koku*, an extraordinary figure, since in order to qualify as a daimyo, one had to have an income of at least 10,000 *koku* (one *koku* being equivalent to the quantity of rice needed to feed one person for a year). Clearly, then, the VOC was exporting a tremendous quantity of rice; one wonders what effect this rice export had on the people of the Matsuura and Hosokawa domains since the rice productivity for at least the Matsuura family was never particularly large.

After the company was forced to move to Deshima in 1641, the Hosokawa family became the leading supplier of rice to the VOC. Because the Hosokawa lands bordered on the Inland Sea, transport to Nagasaki was a relatively easy matter. In 1656, a total of 3.7 percent of all rice produced on Hosokawa lands was delivered to the Dutch, no mean feat considering that the total yield was 299,657 *koku.* This trade in rice, however, rapidly declined after the Dutch were forced off of Taiwan in 1662. For the first five decades of the VOC's presence in Japan, however, rice was an extremely important commodity, and the "storehouse" that was Japan made it much easier for the Dutch to maintain several of their factories in Asia.

There were many other commodities brought to and taken away from Japan than these few listed here, but they are too numerous to count, and in terms of value and quantity are of comparatively little consequence. Before the bakufu banned the export of all war materiél, for example, the Dutch obtained large quantities of sulfur and saltpeter in Japan which, when shipped to India, was used in the production of gunpowder, an advantageous situation given the constant military encounters with the Portuguese, Spanish, and at times the Chinese.[160] Other Japanese goods that found their way to Europe were the official gifts that the shogun gave to the "king" of the Netherlands and several other European monarchs. Japanese suits of armor, for example, can still be seen today in museums in The Hague as well as London and Lisbon.[161] In 1663, moreover, the wife of Samuel Pepys was given a Japanese "gown," a gift of some significance since fine Japanese handicrafts were much esteemed by the wealthy classes of Europe.[162] Although somewhat trivial, these few examples serve to demonstrate that the flow of goods over vast distances was considerable both in Asia and Europe in premodern times.

What is of much more consequence for us, however, is the fact that even after the bakufu instituted the *sakoku* decrees in the 1630s, there remained a considerable demand for foreign goods. This demand was satisfied through several channels, namely the Sō house on Tsushima, the Dutch and Chinese at Nagasaki, the Matsumae in Ezo, and the Satsuma overlordship of the Ryūkyū Islands. In this indirect way, Japan was able to play a major role in the international economy of the seventeenth century while at the same time maintaining a policy of "selective openness." The Dutch for their part were able to achieve the resounding success they did throughout Asia in part because of the dominant commercial position they held within Japan. The *Herren Zeventien*, in a letter dated November 1640, admitted as much when they stated that the Japanese-Chinese trade was of the utmost importance to the company.[163] Through this trade the Dutch were able to obtain the vast quantities of precious metals that helped to finance their operations in Asia, while the Japanese were able to obtain from around the world the goods of which they were such avid consumers.

Endnotes

1. Femme Gaastra, *De Geschiedenis van de VOC* (Zutphen: Walburg Press, 2002), 124. Although there were many more factories than the ones listed here, these represent the major nodes of VOC trade, to which the smaller factories were tied in a complex web of trade routes. A prime example is Taiwan (not an unimportant factory in its own right), whose most important aspect was its relation to the trade between Japan and the various VOC factories in Southeast Asia and India.
2. Hamashita Takeshi, *Kindai Chūgoku no Kokusaiteki Keiki: Chōkō Bōeki Shisutemu to Kindai Ajia* (Tokyo: Tokyo Daigaku Shuppan Kai, 1990), 44.
3. Kazui Tashirō, "Tokugawa Jidai no Bōeki," in *Nihon Keizai Shi Ichikeizai Shakai no Seiritsu, 17–18 Seiki, Vol. I*, ed. Hayami Akira and Miyamoto Matau (Tokyo: Iwanami Shoten, 1988), 156.
4. Some have argued that an important side effect of the large-scale import of goods from across the globe, and the drain on Japanese precious metals that it produced, was the rise of several Japanese industries to offset reliance on foreign products. This phenomenon of "import substitution" was most notable in the sugar and silk industries, although it can also be seen earlier in the porcelain and camphor industries. The main proponents of Japanese proto-industrialization through "import substitution" are Kawakatsu Heita, Tessa Morris Suzuki, and Christian Daniels.
5. Cooper, "The Mechanics of the Macao-Nagasaki Silk Trade," 423.
6. Yanai Kenji, *Nagasaki* (Tokyo: Shibundō, 1959), 78.
7. The destructive *wakō* raids were still fresh in the minds of the Chinese rulers, as were Hideyoshi's invasions of Korea in the 1590s.
8. Iwao, *Nihon no Rekishi 14: Sakoku*, 148.
9. Furber, *Rival Empires of Trade*, 239.
10. To the great delight of the Dutch, the bakufu repeatedly implied that what happened outside of Japanese waters was none of its concern. Dutch ships could therefore freely take Chinese, Portuguese, and Spanish ships without fear of Japanese reprisal, as long as the captured ships were not involved in the Japan trade.
11. Coolhaas, ed., *Generalle Missiven, Deel I*, 588.
12. Ibid., 659.
13. Blussé, et al., eds., *Dagregisters Taiwan, Deel I*, 384.
14. Scammell, G. V., "European Exiles, Renegades, and Outlaws and the Maritime Economy of Asia c.1500–1750," *Modern Asian Studies* 26: 4 (1992): 651.

15. *Nederlandse Factorij in Japan* (hereafter NFJ), *57*, Dagregister van Elseracq, September 12, 1643. My thanks to Leonard Blussé and Cynthia Viallé for translating the dagregisters from 1641 to 1660; they have been enormously helpful in my own work and are a notable contribution to the field in general. See Blussé, Leonard, and Cynthia Viallé (trans.), *The Deshima Dagregisters Volume XI: 1641–1650* (Leiden: Institute for the History of European Expansion, 2001).
16. NFJ 55, Dagregister Le Maire, Oct. 4, 1641.
17. Thompson, ed., *Diary of Richard Cocks*, Vol. II, 271.
18. Blussé, "No Boats to China," 64.
19. Ibid., 67–68.
20. Tomimura Shinen, "Ryūkyū ni okeru Min-Nihon to no Kankei," *Rekishi Kyōiku* 8 (1960): 13–14.
21. Takeno Toshi, "Sappan Ryūkyū Bōeki to Shōnin Ishimoto-ke no Kankei," *Kyūshō Keizai Shi Ronshū* 2 (1956): 98.
22. Sakai, "The Satsuma-Ryūkyū Trade and the Tokugawa Seclusion Policy," 396.
23. Van Dam, *Beschryvinge*, 369.
24. Katō, "Early Shogunate and Dutch Trade Policies, 220–221.
25. Furber, *Rival Empires of Trade*, 44.
26. Thompson, ed., *Diary of Richard Cocks*, Vol. I, 25.
27. Ibid., 262.
28. Nakamura, ed., *Ikoku Nikki*, 86.
29. Ibid., 87.
30. NFJ 57, Dagregister van Elseracq, August 2, 1643.
31. In December 1642, Antonio van Diemen wrote that Zhilong's trade with Japan amounted to over 500,000 *taels* of silver, mainly in silk and silk piece goods. He also complained that the Dutch could not hope to compete with silk imports of this magnitude. It was precisely this reasoning that compelled the Dutch to "turn south and west" in order to obtain increased supplies of silk in Tonkin, India, and Persia. See Coolhaas, ed., *Generealle Missiven, Deel II*, 176.
32. Van Dam, *Beschryvinge, Deel II, Part I*, 409.
33. Ibid., 394.
34. Abdul Aziz Awad, "The Gulf in the Seventeenth Century," *Bulletin (British Society for Middle Eastern Studies)* 12: 2 (1985): 127.
35. Yao, *Kinsei Oranda Bōeki to Sakoku*, 161–163.
36. Murakami, *Bōeki Shijō no Hirado*, 103. The Chinese imitated the Dutch by importing large quantities of Tonkinese silk into Japan.
37. Blussé, et al., eds., *Dagregisters Taiwan, Deel I*, 305, 310.

38. NFJ 55, Dagregister Le Maire, September 14, 1641.
39. NFJ 56, Dagregister van Elseracq, November 15, 1641.
40. NFJ 57, Dagregister van Elseracq, September 23, 1643.
41. Charles Boxer, "Jan Compagnie in Japan, 1672–1674," *Transactions of the Asiatic Society of Japan, Second Series* 7 (1931): 138–203.
42. Coolhaas, ed., *Generale Missiven, Deel III*, 440. To cite two additional examples, on the thirtieth of January, 1666, four ships left Nagasaki bound for Malacca with 1,376,066 *gulden* in silver and copper (p. 495), and a little more than a year later, on the eighth of December 1668, five more ships sailed for Bengal and Coromandel with 2,261,232 *gulden* in gold, silver, and copper (p. 625).
43. Ibid., 544, 586.
44. Ibid., 644.
45. Ibid., 625.
46. Yamawaki, *Nagasaki no Oranda Shōkan*, 56–58.
47. Van Dam, *Beschryvinge, Deel II, part I*, 418–419.
48. Ibid., 403.
49. Coolhaas, ed., *Generalle Missiven, Deel III*, 545.
50. Prakash, "The Dutch East India Company in the Trade of the Indian Ocean," 198.
51. In December of 1649 the Governor-General recorded that of 5,300 *picols* of sugar sent to Taiwan, 1,000 *picols* were subsequently sent to Japan as ballast. Coolhaas, ed., *Generalle Missiven, Deel II*, 392.
52. Furber, *Rival Empires of Trade in the Orient*, 247.
53. Iwao, *Sakoku*, 273.
54. Ibid., 274.
55. Blussé, et al., eds., *Dagregisters Taiwan*, 298, 309, 342.
56. NFJ 55, Dagregister Le Maire, August 4, 1641.
57. Coolhaas, ed., *Generalle Missiven, Deel III*, 606.
58. Ibid., 658.
59. Van Dam, *Beschryvinge*, 398.
60. George Vinal Smith, *The Dutch in Seventeenth Century Thailand* (Dekalb: Northern Illinois University Special Report No. 16, 1977), 49.
61. Iwao, *Shuinsen Bōeki Shi no Kenkyū*, 394.
62. Yamawaki, *Nagasaki no Oranda Shōkan*, 79.
63. Valentyn, *Beschryvinge van Japan*, 40.
64. Coolhaas, ed., *Generalle Missiven, Deel I*, January 17, 1625.
65. Iwao, *Sakoku*, 269.
66. Yamawaki Teijirō, *Nihon Rekishi Gakkai Henshū 6: Nagasaki no Tōjin Bōeki* (Tokyo: Yoshikawa Kōbunkan, 1964), 244.

67. NFJ 57, Dagregister van Elseracq, August 11, 1643.
68. Murakami, *Nagasaki Oranda Shōkan no Nikki*, 321–323.
69. Blussé, et al., eds., *Dagregisters Taiwan, Deel I*, 194.
70. As quoted in Tonio Andreade, "Pirates, Pelts and Promises," 314.
71. Smith, *The Dutch in Seventeenth Century Thailand*, 46.
72. The existence of a monopoly did not mean that all Chinese competition came to an end, however. In January of 1651, for example, the Governor-General at Batavia noted that in the previous year, ten Chinese ships took away a considerable number of deerskins from Siam to sell in Japan. If this was indeed the case, it represented a gross breach of the VOC's monopoly. Coolhaas, ed., *Generalle Missiven, Deel II*, 448.
73. Blussé, et al., eds., *Dagresgisters Taiwan, Deel I*, 473.
74. Ibid., 358.
75. Yamawaki, *Nagasaki no Oranda Shōkan*, 79.
76. Dhiravat Pombejra, *Court, Company, and Campong: Essays on the VOC Presence in Ayutthaya* (Phra Nakhon Sri Ayutthaya: Ayutthaya Historical Study Center, 1992), 27.
77. Ibid., 80.
78. Iwao, *Sakoku*, 272.
79. Wennekes, *Gouden Handel in de Eerst Nederlanders Overzee*, 332.
80. NJF 59, Dagregister Overtwater, June 11, 1645.
81. NFJ 62, Dagregister Snoecq, October 20, 1649.
82. Yamawaki, *Nagasaki no Tōjin Bōeki*, 82.
83. NFJ 63, Dagregister van Brouckhorst, August 26, 1650.
84. Yamawaki, *Nagasaki no Oranda Shōkan*, 76.
85. Van Dam, *Beschryvinge*, 414–18.
86. Blussé, "No Boats to China," 69.
87. NFJ 61, Dagregister Coyett, August 4, 1648.
88. Murakami, *Nagasaki Oranda Shōkan no Nikki, Volume II*, 321–323.
89. Arnoldus Montanus, *Gedenkwaerdige Gesantschappen der Oost-Indische Maetschappy in't Vereenigde Nederland, aen de kaisaren van Japan: Vervaetende Wonderlijke Voorvallen op de togt der Nederlandsche Gesanten: Beschryvinge van de Dorpen, Sterkten, Steden, Landschappen, Tempels, Gods-Diensten, Dragten... Vereeuwde en Niewe oorlogs-Daeden der Japanners: Verciert met een Groot Getal Afbeeldsels in Japan Geteikent: Getrokken uit de Geschriften en Reis-Aentekeningen Derselve Gesanten* (Oost-Indische Maetschappy in 't Vereenigde Nederland 'tAmsterdam: Jacob Meurs, 1669), 197.
90. van Dam, *Beschryvinge, Deel II, part I*, 450.

91. Glamann, *Dutch-Asiatic Trade, 1620–1740*, 85.
92. In 1638 the price of pepper in Japan soared to twenty-seven *taels* per *picol*. The company sold 1,300 picols from Batavia, Taiwan, Siam, Cambodia, and Tonkin, and realized a good profit. Incidentally, pepper sales in Japan for this year nicely illustrates the effectiveness of Dutch inter-Asiatic trade; the company was able to rapidly assess demand in various areas of the world and ship the appropriate goods accordingly. Coolhaas, ed., *Generalle Missiven, Deel I*, 736.
93. Yamawaki, *Nagasaki no Oranda Shōkan*, 71.
94. Ariga Yōen, *Kō to Bukkyō* (Tokyo: Kokusho Kankōkai, 1990), 278.
95. For a detailed study of the role of spices in Buddhist ceremony, see Sanjōnishi Kinkōsa, *Kōdō: Rekishi to Bungaku* (Kyoto: Tankōsha, 1985).
96. NFJ 60, Dagregister Versteeghen, January 2, 1647.
97. Itazawa Takeo, *Nihon to Oranda: Kinsei no Gaikō, Bōeki, Gakumon* (Tokyo: Shibundō, 1955), 117.
98. Johan Maetsuyker states in a letter dated the twenty-sixth of January 1655 that the company should do its best to honor the Japanese requests for rarities in order to maintain favorable relations with the bakufu. Coolhaas, ed., *Generalle Missiven, Deel II*, 788.
99. Algemene Rijksarchief, VOC 1145, folio 454.
100. NFJ 61, Dagregister Coyett, November 8, 1648.
101. Wennekes, *Gouden Handel*, 332.
102. Blussé, et al., eds., *Dagregisters Taiwan, Deel I*, 280.
103. Konraad Cramer, *Journaal Gehouden bij Sr. Coenraedt Kramer, Gecommiteerd wegens d'oost-Indische Compagnie uit Firando naar Miaco aan de Keizerlijke Majesteit en de Raden des Rijks van Japan*, as quoted in Pieter Rietbergen, *Japan Verwoord: Nihon door Nederlandse Ogen* (Amsterdam: Hotei Publishing, 2003), 68.
104. Van Dam, *Beschryvinge, Deel II, part I*, 414–418.
105. NFJ 56, Dagregister van Elseracq, January 17, 1642.
106. Wennekes, *Gouden Handel*, 233–234.
107. *Edo Bakufu Nikki*, (Tokyo: Nogami Shuppan, 1985), Manji 2/2/28 (April 19, 1659).
108. KTTJ, Vol. 3, 135.
109. Ibid., 248.
110. NFJ 59, Dagregister van Tzum, January 26, 1646 and NFJ 60, Dagregister Versteeghen, December 18, 1646.
111. NFJ 61, Dagregister Coyett, November 20, 1648; KTTJ, Vol. 4, 527.
112. For a concise art historical analysis of these jars, see Tokugawa Yoshimune, "Ruzon no Tsubo no Imi suru Mono," in *Nihon Rekishi*

9: Shuinsen to Minami e no Senkisha, ed. Ōishi Shinzaburō (Tokyo: Gyōsei, 1986), 62–75.
113. Hayashi Motoi, "Luzon no Tsubo," *Shigaku* 21: 2.
114. As quoted in Iwano, "Firipin Bōeki to Sukezaemon/Kiemon," 38.
115. *Edo Bakufu Nikki: Meireki Nenroku*, 36.
116. NFJ 55, Dagregister le Maire, October 28, 1641.
117. van Dam, *Beschryvinge*, 384.
118. NFJ 63, Dagregister van Brouckhorst, November and December, 1649.
119. NFJ 63, Dagregister van Brouckhorst, September 23, 1650.
120. Oskar Nachod, *Die Beziehungen der Niederländischen Ostindischen Kompagnie zu Japan im Siebzehnten Jahrhundert* (Leipzig: Rob. Friese, 1897), 115.
121. Coolhaas, ed., *Generalle Missiven, Deel I*, 47: October 26, 1615.
122. Asao, *Nihon No Kinsei, Vol. I: Seikai Shi no naka no Kinsei*, 138.
123. Hidetoshi Kato, "The Significance of the Period of National Seclusion Reconsidered," *Journal of Japanese Studies* 7: 1 (1981): 97.
124. Thompson, ed., *Diary of Richard Cocks*, Vol. II, 191: September 3, 1621. Cocks includes an English translation of the shogunal edict in his diary.
125. Uehara, *Bakuhan-sei Keiseiki no Ryukyu Shihai* (Tokyo: Yoshikawa Kōbunkan, 2001).
126. Yamawaki, "Tōjin Bōeki to Nukini," in *Shuinsen to Minami e no Senkisha*, 137.
127. NKKS, Vol. 1, 168: August 7, 1634.
128. Yamawaki, "Tōjin Bōeki," 137.
129. Wennekes, *Gouden Handel*, 225.
130. The process of extracting the oil from the camphor tree is described in Robert Swinhoe's article "Notes on the Island of Formosa," 6–18.
131. Cooper, ed., *Joao Rodrigues's Account of Sixteenth-Century Japan*, 108.
132. *Algemeen Rijksarchief, Archief Japan, No. 829: Negotie Journalen 1636–1666. Het Archief van de Nederlandse Factorij in Japan, 1609–*1860, folios 836–860.
133. Suzuki, *Kinsei Nichi-Ran Bōeki Shi no Kenkyū*, 279.
134. NFJ 57, Dagregister van Elseracq, June 30, 1643.
135. Nagazumi, *Hirado Oranda Shōkan no Nikki, Volume 3*, 16–17.
136. Suzuki, *Kinsei Nichi-Ran Bōeki Shi no Kenkyū*, 286.
137. Coolhaas, ed., *Generalle Missiven, Deel III*, 665.
138. Swinhoe, "Notes on the Island of Formosa," 17.

139. Suzuki, *Kinsei Nichi-Ran Bōeki Shi no Kenkyū*, 300.
140. Cooper, ed., *Joao Rodrigues's Account of Sixteenth-Century Japan*, 326.
141. Coolhaas, ed., *Generalle Missiven, Deel I*, 549.
142. NFJ 57, Dagregister van Elseracq, October 15, 1643.
143. Algemene Rijksarchief: VOC 1156, folio 50: Missive Overwater to Caron.
144. NFJ 59, Dagregister van Tzum, October 21–November 1, 1645.
145. Coolhaas, ed., *Generalle Missiven, Deel II*, 78.
146. Iwao, *Sakoku*, 448.
147. Daimyo placed their yearly orders for Chinese porcelain with the Dutch when the VOC president came to Edo for his annual audience with the shogun. We know that in 1634, for example, the daimyo of Hizen ordered pottery from the Dutch, as did the daimyo of Arima in 1645. See Tijs Volker, *Porcelain and the Dutch East India Company, as Recorded in the Dagh-Registers of Batavia Castle those of Hirado and Deshima, and other Contemporary Papers, 1602–1682* (Leiden: Brill, 1954), 118. I cannot help but wonder if the reason why these daimyo consistently ordered pottery from the VOC was so that their native potters could more effectively imitate it. It is perhaps not surprising that in the 1650s, shortly after the orders mentioned here, the artisans of Hizen and Arima finally perfected the manufacture of porcelain.
148. Volker, *Porcelain and the Dutch East India Company*, 125.
149. Coolhaas, ed., *Generalle Missiven, Deel III*, 389.
150. Ibid., 440.
151. Volker, *Porcelain and the Dutch East India Company*, 155–156.
152. Coolhaas, ed., *Generalle Missiven, Deel I*, 161–63: January 27, 1625.
153. Ibid., 195–196: February 3, 1626.
154. Ibid., 508: January 4, 1636.
155. Thompson, ed., *Diary of Richard Cocks*, Vol. II, 311.
156. Blussé, et al., eds., *Dagregisters Taiwan, Deel I*, 381: November 28, 1637.
157. Ibid., 48: April 29, 1631.
158. For an overview of the role of Japanese rice in VOC factories in Asia, see Maehira Fusaaki, "Bōeki no Tenkai," in *Shintaikei Nihon Shi 12: Ryūtsū Keizai Shi*, ed. Sakurai Eiji and Nakanishi Satoru (Tokyo: Yamakawa Shuppansha, 2002), 361–363.
159. Yao, *Kinsei Oranda Bōeki to Sakoku*, 13–55. Much of the information that follows is based on this detailed study.
160. Wennekes, *Gouden Handel*, 229.
161. Jacques Specx, on an embassy to Sumpu in 1611, received from Ieyasu three suits of armor intended for Prince Maurits in the Netherlands.

In the same year, John Saris, on a similar embassy for the English, received a suit of armor for the English king. See Zandfleet, *The Dutch Encounter with Asia*, 100.

162. Corr, *Adams the Pilot*, 5.
163. Algemene Rijksarchief: Kolonial Archief No. 488, November 9, 1640.

Conclusion

An accurate evaluation of the impact of Japanese trade on the economy of Asia, particularly in the seventeenth century, is difficult to formulate since many of the fundamental premises upon which the historiography of the period is based are flawed. Nowhere is this truer than in our historical understanding of *sakoku.* The way that we approach the study of this phenomenon will necessarily color our view of the Japanese international economy and the role that Japan played in Asia. For example, if we view *sakoku* as a policy aimed at cutting Japan off as far as possible from the wider world, then we must necessarily conclude that Japan was not at all interested in maintaining commercial relations with foreign powers, to say nothing of diplomatic relations.

That Japan was not isolated is in part the point of the present research. Japan was never isolated politically, although to be sure political contact with Europe was severely curtailed after the *sakoku* decrees were promulgated. The issue of isolation, however, can also be viewed from an economic standpoint, and here the issue becomes thorny indeed, for the economic influence of Japan on Asia and vice versa has been difficult to asses since there was little direct contact between the two after about 1635. Yet the truth of the matter is that the economy of

Japan had a substantial effect on the Asian mainland. The converse of this argument is also true: Asian influence on Japanese society was considerable, mainly in the form of luxury goods imported into the country from all over the region. We must, however, recognize the role of intermediate agents to fully comprehend this influence.

The primary means of examining the impact of Japanese trade on the Asian continent in this study has been to examine the records of the Dutch East India Company, a product of a close economic relationship with Japan for most of the seventeenth century. Dutch sources are particularly helpful because the VOC was not limited to simply trading with Japan, but was also involved commercially with almost the whole of Asia, from the Indian subcontinent through Southeast Asia to Taiwan. This fact alone makes it easy to see that Japanese goods, mainly precious metals, were being distributed throughout the region and that goods from these areas were at the same time making their way to Japan. The volume of this trade was often enormous, and as such should be considered one of the most important commercial patterns of the early modern period.

It is well known that the Asian maritime scene before the penetration of Western merchants was a highly developed one. We know of course that significant trade in the form of tribute missions to China occurred very early on in the history of Japan. Only in the Muromachi period, however, do we have definitive records of ships that were given *shuinjō* to trade abroad, primarily in China. Accordingly, the Ming Empire issued *kangō* to the Japanese merchants as a means of controlling illicit trade. It is interesting to note that Hideyoshi, as one of the justifications for his plan of conquering the Ming Empire, cited the resumption of this lapsed *kangō* trade in response to Japanese pirate attacks along the coast of China. The *wakō* had caused a tremendous amount of destruction along the coast, particularly from the later sixteenth century onwards, and this more than any other reason served to alienate the Ming against trade with Japan. It was not until the 1680s, in fact, that China would again officially allow its merchants to trade in Japan, although to be sure this did not stop ships from provinces such as Fujian from calling regularly at Nagasaki.

After the turbulence of the *sengoku* period had given way to the stability of the Toyotomi regime, Hideyoshi moved to put foreign commerce under his control by issuing *shuinjō* to prominent merchants from the great commercial cities of Sakai, Nagasaki, and Kyoto. Although Hideyoshi is thus credited with making these permits a part of his policy of centralization, it was his successor Tokugawa Ieyasu who really institutionalized the *shuinjō* into a coherent system of commercial control. Ieyasu built on the foundations that Hideyoshi had laid and began the systematic issuance of trading privileges to a number of people in Japanese society: wealthy merchants, daimyo (particularly those from the western domains), bakufu officials, foreigners, and even two women. The people who obtained these passes sailed to several ports throughout Southeast Asia, including most prominently Siam, Manila, Taiwan, Tonkin, Cochin, and Cambodia. And while the number of people who obtained *shuinjō* and sent ships abroad dwindled rapidly from about the mid-1620s, there were still a number of powerful families, almost all of them with connections to the central government, still able to consistently send ships overseas. This too, however, was brought to an end in 1635 when the bakufu, after a number of restrictions on the system, finally abolished it outright with the fifth and final version of the *sakoku* decrees. With the issuance of this decree, no Japanese ships (or in fact Japanese people) were allowed to go abroad. This measure effectively brought to an end the long and often extremely active period of Japanese commercial activity in China and Southeast Asia.

The history of the *shuinsen* trade illustrates a theme that runs throughout the first half of the seventeenth century: increasing bakufu control at the expense of the individual daimyo. This control was directed mainly at the western daimyo who represented an extremely powerful segment of Japanese politics, and who were, to varying degrees, implicitly anti-Tokugawa. Many of these powerful families, the Shimazu of Satsuma for example, had fought against the Tokugawa at the Battle of Sekigahara in 1600, or had at least changed allegiance at the last moment, and so were also considered untrustworthy. After Sekigahara these erstwhile enemies swore allegiance to Ieyasu, but that allegiance must have been small comfort to the Tokugawa who were, for all their military prowess, still quite vulnerable in their new role as military overlords of a recently reunited country. Therefore, it is no surprise that the Tokugawa should attempt at every turn to undermine the strength of families such as the Shimazu; and one of the primary sources of these families' wealth and power lay in foreign trade.

At the beginning of the formal system of *shuinsen* trade, the western daimyo were heavily involved in foreign commerce and as such accounted for a large number of the *shuinjō* issued by the bakufu. This changed quite rapidly, however, to the point that two decades later not a single western daimyo still participated in overseas trade.[1] In the meantime, the bakufu had forbidden the construction of oceangoing ships over 500 *koku* in capacity (a measure again aimed primarily a the western daimyo) and had also required their vassals to spend half of their time at Edo. This seemingly unrelated measure ensured that the daimyo, especially those with domains located far from Edo, spent huge sums to maintain themselves and their relatives (virtual hostages to the shogun) in Edo. Therefore, there was precious little money left to invest in the *shuinsen* trade, a venture that required a large capital investment for a protracted period of time (often over a year). By the end of the *shuinsen* period, in fact, only seven families were allowed to send ships abroad, and needless to say none of them were western daimyo.[2] The bakufu had effectively managed to divorce the western daimyo from one of their principal sources of wealth, and in the process they strengthened the position of the central government.

It is important to note that when the bakufu prohibited its own merchants from traveling abroad, this did not have the effect of lowering the quantity of foreign merchandise coming into the country. On the contrary, the combined efforts of the Dutch, Portuguese, and Chinese merchants served to increase the quantity of goods imported into Japan. This was not a coincidence; rather it was the bakufu's intention to ensure the continued import of luxury goods. This policy can be most clearly seen by examining the often-complex relationship among the Portuguese, Japanese, and the Dutch. When the bakufu became increasingly disillusioned about the continued presence of Portuguese merchants in the country, rather than simply expel them outright, the bakufu chose to wait until it could be absolutely sure that the Dutch would be able to import the same quantity of goods, particularly silk, as had their Portuguese rivals. The president of the VOC factory recorded these "interviews" with shogunal officials in which the deep concern for the continued inflow of foreign goods is quite obvious. Only after the government felt secure that the Dutch would be able to accommodate the Japanese demand for foreign merchandise did it take the drastic step of expelling the Portuguese.

Trade in foreign goods in Japan was big business, and there were several segments of society that had invested heavily in it, even after the *shuinsen* system was abolished. Shogunal councilors, lesser bakufu officials such as the Nagasaki *bugyō*, and of course prominent merchants all invested silver in Chinese, Dutch, and Portuguese ships. In fact, when the bakufu reprimanded the Dutch for attacking Portuguese and Chinese ships, it was not because of any great affection for the latter, but rather because there was a considerable Japanese investment in many of these ships, an investment that often involved the highest echelon of the Edo political structure.

Although the most important item in Japan's foreign trade was undoubtedly silk, there was a host of other goods that brought an extremely high profit in Japan. While the Portuguese brought primarily silk obtained from Macao, the Chinese and Dutch brought a great range of products from throughout Asia. The Dutch were especially well-placed to do this in that they exploited to the fullest their several factories throughout Asia. The VOC, for example, had factories in Siam, Tonkin, Cochin, Bengal, Persia, Surat, the Coromandel Coast, Taiwan, and a number of other places, from which they obtained goods that were consistently profitable on the Japanese market. Similarly the Chinese, especially the Zheng family under first Zhilong and then Chenggong, had a vast trading network that included most of the major ports of Southeast Asia, but did not extend as far as the Indian subcontinent. Both the Chinese and the

Dutch used their relationships with these disparate areas to supply Japan with the luxury goods that were in such demand.

The Chinese obviously had a clear advantage over other foreigners, as they were the foremost producers of high quality silk in Asia. The Dutch, with the establishment of a factory on Taiwan in the early 1620s, were themselves finally able to tap into the Chinese silk market, and this made their profits in Japan skyrocket. It is particularly telling that until a steady source of silk was obtained, the VOC realized only very modest profits in Japan, and much of that was because of silk confiscated from captured Chinese and Portuguese ships. From the 1630s, however, Dutch profits soared, partly because of their newfound ability to bring a sizeable quantity of silk to Japan. Moreover, the Dutch had one advantage over the Chinese when it came to silk imports: the VOC, because of its factories in Persia and Bengal, was able to obtain a large quantity of silk from those areas when Chinese and Tonkinese silk became less profitable in Japan. Therefore, from the late 1640s, we see a marked shift in VOC trade with Japan from Southeast Asia west to Persia and the Indian subcontinent.

Silk was not the only product brought to Japan in great quantities; sugar, sandalwood, deerskins, ray skins, and a variety of other luxury goods were also imported. Deerskins in particular brought the VOC a huge profit since the Japanese bought them in often-staggering quantities. Imports of 100,000 hides per year were not uncommon, while ray skins, although imported in more modest numbers, were also bought in great quantities. Similarly, sugar, before being grown in Japan at the end of the seventeenth century, was imported in huge quantities. Sugar was a particularly easy product to ship to Japan since it was often used as ballast in ships that carried other products from the same region. A great variety of other luxury goods such as rhinoceros horns, elephant tusks, spices, incense, and raw lacquer were also brought to Japan aboard Dutch and Chinese ships. One final category of goods that deserves mention is goods that were brought primarily as gifts for the shogun and his officials. Examples include rare items such as white buffalo, camels, microscopes, telescopes, spectacles, and military items such as mortars and guns. The Dutch in particular used the bakufu officials' craving for foreign curiosities to great effect when dealing with them on their yearly journey to Edo to pay homage to the shogun.

The island of Taiwan played an extremely important, often-overlooked role in Dutch trade between Japan and Asia. The island was able to serve in such a capacity because of its strategic location astride the main trading routes between Japan and Southeast Asia. Originally used to supply silk, deerskins, and sugar for the Japanese market, the island came to play an indispensable role as an entrepôt for goods destined for Japan as well as a redistribution center for Japanese precious metals.

Commercial relations with Japan were so highly prized because of its seemingly inexhaustible supply of precious metals, especially silver and copper. Japanese mines had begun to be developed in earnest in the late sengoku period when the various warring daimyo such as the Takeda, Uesugi, Hōjō, and others began to exploit the mines in their provinces by diverting huge workforces to the sites. This, combined with new innovations in the smelting of the ore (largely learned from either the Chinese or the Portuguese), made Japanese mines among the most productive in the world. By the time the Tokugawa brought the country's mines under its own direct control, Japan was producing roughly one-third of the world's silver, an astonishing figure considering that New World mines in Mexico and Peru were also operational at this time. The sheer quantity of silver produced in Japan, combined with an increasingly urban society that demanded foreign luxury goods, made the country an ideal trading partner. Therefore, even when its own merchants were prohibited from trading abroad, the economy of Japan still exerted a profound impact on Asia.

The Dutch position on Taiwan gave the VOC a special advantage with respect to the Japan trade. Because goods from all over Asia were being sent to Japan, and because new shogunal restrictions limited the time allowed for trade in the country, the VOC used Taiwan as an entrepôt in which to collect the various goods destined for Nagasaki. This was particularly beneficial to the company because no goods could remain in Japan after the season's commercial activity had been concluded. Similarly, if the market in Japan was saturated for a particular product, that product could be stored on the island until such a time as it became more profitable to send it on to Japan. The real benefit of Taiwan to the company, however, was as a redistribution center for Japanese precious metals. We have very detailed information preserved in Dutch records about how much Japanese silver, gold, and copper was sent to each factory from Taiwan. This was particularly useful because each factory could send its demand to Batavia, and that demand would be fulfilled as much as possible from the precious metals collected at Taiwan. This obviously made the VOC much more efficient and, accordingly, made the profits of the company that much higher.

Finally, this research has tried to evaluate the so-called *sakoku* decrees not from the standpoint of an irrational bakufu, but rather from the viewpoint of a government still rather insecure in its own political position, and which perceived a number of viable threats to its supremacy. The prime example of this is the bakufu's early response to Christianity. There is no denying that the bakufu rigorously enforced a policy of calculated terror in order to stamp out the new religion. Nor were the government's threats idle: we have a number of horrific accounts from Dutch, Portuguese, and Japanese observers who testify to the barbaric tortures and executions visited upon believers and propagators.

The purpose of this work is certainly not to deny the inhumanity of the Christian purges, as the sheer horror of the atrocities committed against Christians is well documented. Rather, the purpose of this work is to show that the Japanese authorities were never interested in divorcing themselves entirely from the outside world, but rather wanted to reshape that contact in a way that placed the bakufu at the center. In this system, there was no room for a religion that had as its main power base an area dominated by the (real or imagined) enemies of the bakufu. It is no secret that the Tokugawa placed little trust in the western daimyo; the absolute loyalty of these powerful houses was always in doubt. Therefore, it is not surprising that Christianity was at the center of bakufu concerns. While the Kyushu daimyo had repudiated the religion at the onset of the Tokugawa government, there was still a sizeable Christian population in the western domains. It would not be difficult to imagine an uprising against the Tokugawa that used Christianity to garner support. The fact that this seems absurd to us today does not mean that it was not a valid concern of the Tokugawa authorities in the early seventeenth century. One need look no further than Ieyasu's campaign against the last of the Toyotomi in 1615 and realize that many of his enemies were in fact Christian samurai. Similarly, many of the leaders and peasants in the Shimabara Rebellion, a revolt that took an embarrassingly long time to quell, were Christian. (The fact that neither of these incidents was a Christian uprising is quite beside the point, for they were widely believed to be so). Therefore, the bakufu's suppression of Christianity was initially not the result of a deep doctrinal hatred, but was rather entirely an issue of political expediency.

The other items in the *sakoku* decrees were also not arbitrary prohibitions but rather specific responses to political or economic stimuli. The *Itowappu* system, for example, was not instituted to ensure a big profit for the bakufu or even for the merchants involved, but was simply a way to ensure a fair distribution of silk throughout the country at a fair price. Ieyasu and subsequent shogun displayed a consistent concern with establishing an orderly market system in Japan. Indicative of this is the phenomenon known as "the emperor's silk." By maintaining a large supply of silk in bakufu storehouses, Ieyasu was able to release the silk onto the market when there was a severe shortage so that the price did not become prohibitively high. There was apparently no motive of profit in this system, only a concern with the smooth operation of the markets and the inherent motive of increased bakufu control over the machinery of the state.

This work has tried to show that even after the shogun implemented a series of strict prohibitions regulating almost every aspect of commercial activity within Japan, there was still a keen desire to maintain the level of foreign imports that society had come to expect. There was no drop in the quantity of silk or of dozens of other foreign luxury goods after the *sakoku* decrees, or indeed after the Portuguese were expelled. The government consistently emphasized the steady flow of goods from overseas, and to that end the Dutch, Chinese, Koreans, Ryūkyū Islanders, and even the Ainu on Hokkaido all played an important role in Japan's economy in the seventeenth century. It was only when shogunal councilors such as Arai Hakuseki brought to the bakufu's attention the impending crisis in precious metal supply that foreign trade was truly restricted. Perhaps it is not a coincidence that it was exactly at that time that the VOC began to experience serious problems in its previously flourishing commercial empire. Certainly there were problems inherent in the company that led it to experience a period of gradual but steady decline, but the loss of Japanese precious metals undoubtedly dealt a severe blow to the VOC's operations in Asia.

The Japanese economy of the seventeenth century was intimately tied to the economy of Asia, especially when it came to the large-scale consumption of luxury goods. Through the agency of the Dutch and Chinese merchants, huge quantities of Japanese precious metals, especially silver and gold, made their way to places as far apart as the Indian subcontinent and Taiwan. In fact, for the few years in which the Dutch were at war with Sweden, Japanese copper played a large role in the European copper market. With the large-scale import of Japanese copper, Sweden lost its monopoly, and the price of Swedish copper accordingly plummeted. In return for this precious metal, Asian goods from throughout the region arrived in Japan in staggering quantities and had a profound impact on Japan. Therefore, it is clear that Japan and the Asian continent shared an important economic tie for the better part of the seventeenth century. The fact that it was a third party that made this relationship possible serves to hide the true nature of this connection, but it existed nonetheless.

Endnotes

1. The single exception was the Shimazu, who maintained a tributary relationship with the Ryūkyū Islands. Even this relationship, however, served more as a legitimating capacity for the Tokugawa (who entertained Ryūkyū tribute embassies regularly) than as an economic boon for the Shimazu.
2. In fact, there were probably not very many families that were able to shoulder the burden of paying for *shuinsen.*

APPENDIX I

CHARACTER INDEX

Ainu	アイヌ
Akita Han	秋田藩
Amakusa	天草
Amakusa Shigehisa	天草重久
Anhui	安徽
Arai Hakuseki	新井白石
Araki	荒木
Arima	有馬
Arima Harunobu	有馬晴信
Arita	有田
Ashikaga	足利
Ashikaga Yoshimitsu	足利義満
Bakufu	幕府
Bateren Tsuihō no Bun	伴天連追放の文
Beijing	北京
Bizen	備前
Bōeki-ke	貿易家
Bugyō	奉行
Buke Shohatto	武家諸法度
Chanoyu	茶の湯
Chaya	茶屋
Chaya Shirōjirō	茶屋四郎次郎
Chikugo	筑後
Chokkatsuchi	直轄地
Chūgoku	中国
Chūgoku Yashiki	中国屋敷
Daikan	代官
Daimyō	大名
Date	伊達

Date Masamune	伊達正宗
Deshima	出島
Doi Tadakatsu	土井只勝
Doi Toshikatsu	土井利勝
Edo	江戸
Edo Bakufu Nikki	江戸幕府日記
Eta	穢多
Ezo	蝦夷
Fujian	福建
Funamoto	船本
Fuzhou	福州
Genna Kōkai-ki	元和航海記
Ginza	銀座
Go-nin gumi	五人組
Gotō (Islands)	五島
Gotō Mitsusugu	五島三津
Guangzhou	広州
Hachiman (Bawan)	八幡
Haibukihō	灰吹法
Hakama	袴
Hakata	博多
Han	藩
Hara-jō (castle)	原城
Hasegawa Gonroku	長谷川藤广
Hashimoto	橋本
Hatamoto	旗本
Hirado	平戸
Hirano	平野
Hirayama (Incident)	平山
Hizen	肥前
Hōjō	北条
Hokkaidō	北海道
Honda Masazumi	本多正純
Hōshojō	奉書状
Hōshosen	奉書船

Hosokawa	細川
Hyakushō	百姓
Ikeda Kōzaemon (Kōun)	池田好運
Ikki	一揆
Ikoku Nikki	異国日記
Ikuno	生野
Imari	伊万里
Inoue Masashige	井上政重
Itakura Katsushige	板倉勝茂
Iteian (hermitage)	以酊庵
Itowappu Nakama	糸割符仲間
Iwami	岩見
Iwashū	岩州
Ji'in Shohatto	寺院諸法度
Jingtai Emperor	景泰
Jōdaka	上高
Jōkamachi	城下町
Kai	甲斐
Kaikin	海禁
Kamiya Jūtei	神谷宗湛
Kan	貫
Kanayama	金山
Kangō	勘合
Kangxi	康熙
Kanme	貫目
Kantō	関東
Karō	家老
Katō	加藤
Katō Kiyomasa	加藤清正
Kawahara	川原
Keelung	基隆
Kii	紀伊
Kin	斤
Kinai	畿内
Kinsei	近世

Kiyomizudera	清水寺
Koban	小判
Kobayakawa Hideaki	小早川秀秋
Koku	石
Konchi'in	金地院
Kōsatsu	高札
Kōzangyōsha	鉱山業者
Kuge Shohatto	公家諸法度
Kuo Hsing-yeh	国姓爺
Kuroda	黒田
Kyoto	京都
Kyushu	九州
Li Tan	李旦
Machidoshiyori	町年寄り
Matsumae	松前
Matsumae Yoshihiro	松前義弘
Matsuura	松浦
Matsuura Shigenobu	松浦鎮信
Meiji	明治
Mikawa	三河
Minamoto no Ieyasu	源の家康
Ming	明
Mito	水戸
Mōri	毛利
Murayama Tōan	村山等安
Muromachi Bakufu	室町幕府
Nabeshima	鍋島
Nagasaki	長崎
Nagasaki Jitsuroku Taisei	長崎実録体制
Nagasaki-ki	長崎記
Nagegane	投げ金
Naitō	内藤
Nakatsu Masaie	名勝将家
Nambu	南部
Nan Chu-I	南居益

Nanjing	南京
Nanzenji	南禅寺
Nihonmachi	日本町
Nikkō	日光
Nishi	西
Oda Nobunaga	織田信長
Odawara	小田原
Ogura	小倉
Ōkubo Nagayasu	大久保長安
Ōmetsuke	大目付
Ōmura	大村
Orandafusetsugaki	阿蘭陀風説書き
Osaka	大阪
Ōshu	奥州
Ōtomo	大友
Ōuchi	大内
Owari	尾張
Penghu	澎湖
Pusan	釜山
Qing	清
Rangaku	蘭学
Rōju	老中
Rōnin	浪人
Ryō	両
Ryūkotsusen	竜骨船
Ryūkyū (Islands)	琉球
Sado (Island)	佐渡
Sakai	境
Sakai Tadakatsu	酒井忠勝
Sakai Tadayo	酒井忠世
Sakoku	鎖国
Samurai	侍
Sanke	三家
Sankin-kōtai	参勤交代
Satsuma	薩摩

Sei-i tai shōgun	征夷大将軍
Sekigahara	関ヶ原
Sengoku daimyo	戦国大名
Seppuku	切腹
Shaku	尺
Shih Lang	施瑯
Shihō baibai	司法売買
Shikoku	四国
Shimabara	島原
Shimazu	島津
Shimazu Yoshihiro	島津義弘
Shinano	信濃
Shinkō	新港
Shōgun	将軍
Shuinjō	朱印状
Shuinsen	朱印船
Shūmon Aratame	宗門改め長
Sō	宗
Sō Yoshinari	総吉成
Sūden	崇伝
Suetsugu	末次
Suetsugu Heizō	末次平蔵
Sueyoshi	末吉
Suminokura	角の倉
Suminokura Yoichi	角の倉与一
Sumpu	駿府
Sumpu-ki	駿府記
Suruga	駿河国
Tabi	足袋
Tagawa	田川
Taikō	太閤
Tainan	台南
Taiwan	台湾
Takasago	高砂
Takayama	高山

Takeda	武田
Takeda Shingen	武田信玄
Takenaga Masashige	竹長政重
Takenaka Masasugu	竹中重義
Tana'ita	棚板
T'ang Wang	唐王
Terasawa Hirotaka	寺沢広高
Tōdai-ki	当代記
Tōfukuji	東福寺
Tōjinmachi	唐人町
Tokugawa Hidetada	徳川秀忠
Tokugawa Iemitsu	徳川家光
Tokugawa Ieyasu	徳川家康
Tokugawa Jikki	徳川実記
Toyotomi Hideyori	豊臣秀頼
Toyotomi Hideyoshi	豊臣秀吉
Tōzama	外様
Tsūkō Ichiran	通航一覧
Tsushima	対島
Tsubo	坪
Ueda	上田
Uesugi	上杉
Uesugi Kagekatsu	上杉景勝
Uesugi Kenshinn	上杉謙信
Umi no katana-gari	海の刀狩り
Usuki	臼杵
Wakō	倭冦
Wang Chih	王直
Wanzei	湾税
Yamada Nagamasa	山田長政
Yamada Yahyōe	山田屋兵衛
Yamana	山名
Yamashi	山師
Yama no rei gojyūsan ka-jō	山の令五十三か条
Yanagawa Shigeoki	柳川茂男

Yangtze (River)	揚子
Yonezawa Han	米沢藩
Yoshida Bonshun	吉田梵舜
Zheng	鄭
Zheng Chenggong	鄭成功
Zheng Zhilong	鄭芝龍

Appendix II

Japanese Era Names, 1555–1704

1555–1558	Kōji	弘治
1558–1570	Eiroku	永禄
1570–1573	Genki	元亀
1573–1592	Tenshō	天正
1592–1596	Bunroku	文禄
1596–1615	Keichō	慶長
1615–1624	Genna	元和
1624–1644	Kan'ei	寛永
1644–1648	Shōhō	正保
1648–1652	Keian	慶安
1652–1655	Jōō	貞応
1655–1658	Meireki	明暦
1658–1661	Manji	万治
1661–1673	Kanbun	寛文
1673–1681	Enpō	延宝
1681–1684	Tenna	天和
1684–1688	Jōkyō	貞享
1688–1704	Genroku	元禄

Appendix III

Presidents of the VOC Factory in Japan, 1609–1700

At Hirado

Jacques Specx	September 20, 1609–August 28, 1612
Hendrijk Brouwer	August 28, 1612–August 6, 1614
Jacques Specx	August 6, 1614–January 1621
Leonard Camps	January 1621–November 21, 1623
Cornelis van Neijenroode	November 1623–January 1633
Willem Jansen	Early January 1633–January 17, 1633
Pieter van Santen	January 17, 1633–September 6, 1633
Nicolaas Couckebacker	September 6, 1633–February 3, 1639
Francois Caron	February 4, 1639–February 14, 1641

At Deshima (Nagasaki)

Maximiliaen Le Maire	February 14, 1641–October 31, 1641
Jan van Elseracq	August 1, 1641–November 23, 1644
Pieter Overwater	November 24, 1644–November 29,1645
Reijner van't Zum	November 30, 1645–October 27, 1646
Willem Verstegen	October 28, 1646–November 3, 1647
Frederick Coijet	November 3, 1647–December 9, 1648
Dircq Snoecq	December 9, 1648–November 5, 1649
Anthonio van Brouckhorst	November 5, 1649–October 25, 1650
Pieter Sterthemius	October 25, 1650–November 1, 1651
Adriaen van der Burgh	November 1, 1651–November 3, 1652
Frederick Coijet	November 4, 1652–November 10, 1653
Gabriel Happart	November 10, 1653–October 1, 1654
Leonard Winnincx	October 1, 1654–October 23, 1655

Joan Bouchelijon	October 23, 1655–November 1, 1656
Zacharias Wagenaer	November 1, 1656–October 27, 1657
Joan Bouchelijon	October 27, 1657–October 23, 1658
Zacharias Wagenaer	October 22, 1658–November 4, 1659
Joan Bouchelijon	November 4, 1659–October 26, 1660
Hendrijck Indijck	October 26, 1660–November 21, 1661
Dirk van Liter	November 11, 1661–July 12, 1662
Hendrijck Indijck	August 10, 1662–October 20, 1663
Willem Volger	October 19, 1663–November 7, 1664
Jacob Gruijs	November 7, 1664–October 27, 1665
Willem Volger	October 28, 1665–October 18, 1666
Daniel Six	October 18, 1666–November 6, 1667
Constantin Ranst	November 6, 1667–October 25, 1668
Daniel Six	October 25, 1668–October 14, 1669
Francois de Haese	October 14, 1669–November 2, 1670
Martinus Caesar	November 2, 1670–October 21, 1671
Johannes Camphuijs	October 22, 1671–November 12, 1672
Martinus Caesar	November 13, 1672–October 29, 1673
Johannes Camphuijs	October 29, 1673–October 19, 1674
Martinus Caesar	October 20, 1674–November 7, 1675
Johannes Camphuijs	November 7, 1675–October 27, 1676
Dircq de Haas	October 27, 1676–October 16, 1677
Albert Brevincq	October 16, 1677–November 4, 1678
Dircq de Haas	November 4, 1678–October 24, 1679
Albert Brevincq	October 24, 1679–November 11, 1680
Isaacq van Schinne	November 11, 1680–October 31, 1681
Hendrick Canzius	October 31, 1681–October 20, 1682
Andries Cleijer	October 20, 1682–November 8, 1683
Constantin Ranst de Jonge	November 8, 1683–October 28, 1684
Hendrick van Buijtenhem	October 28, 1684–October 18, 1685
Cornelis van Outhoorn	October 17, 1685–November 5, 1686
Balthasar Sweers	November 5, 1686–October 25, 1687
Hendrick van Buijtenhem	October 25, 1687–October 13, 1688
Cornelis van Outhoorn	October 13, 1688–November 1, 1689
Hendrick van Buijtenhem	November 1, 1689–October 21, 1690

Gerrit de Heere	October 21, 1690–November 9, 1691
Hendrik Dijkman	November 9, 1691–October 29, 1692
Cornelis van Outhoorn	October 29, 1692–October 19, 1693
Hendrik Dijkman	October 19, 1693–November 7, 1694
Pieter de Vos	November 7, 1694–October 27, 1695
Hendrik Dijkman	October 27, 1695–October 15, 1696
Pieter de Vos	October 15, 1696–November 3, 1697
Hendrik Dijkman	November 3, 1697–October 23, 1698
Abraham Douglas	October 23, 1698–October 12, 1699
Ferdinand de Groot	October 12, 1699–October 31, 1700

Bibliography

d'Albuquerque, Alfonso. *The Commentaries of the Great Alfonso d'Albuquerque, Second Viceroy of India, Volume III*. Translated by Walter Gray Birch. London: Hakluyt Society, 1880.

Ames, Glenn. "Colbert's Indian Ocean Strategy of 1664–1674: A Reappraisal." *French Historical Studies* 16: 3 (1990): 536–559.

Anderson, Gary, and Robert Tollison. "Adam Smith's Analysis of Joint-Stock Companies." *The Journal of Political Economy* 90: 6 (1982): 1237–1256.

Andrade, Tonio. "Pirates, Pelts, and Promises: The Sino-Dutch colony of Seventeenth-Century Taiwan and the Aboriginal Village of Favorolang." *The Journal of Asian Studies* 64: 2 (2005): 295–321.

Anesaki Masaharu. *Kirishitan Dendō no Kōhai.* Tokyo: Dōbunkan, 1930.

Antony, Robert. *Like Froth Floating on the Sea: The World of Pirates and Seafarers in Late Imperial South China.* Berkeley: Institute of East Asian Studies, Center for Chinese Studies, 2003.

Arai Hakuseki. "Honchō Hōka Tsūyō Jiryaku." In *Arai Hakuseki Zenshū, Vol. III*, edited by Imaizumi Teisuke. Tokyo: Yoshikawa Hanshichi, 1907.

Arano Yasunori. "Sakoku Ron kara Kaikin/Ka-I Chitsujo." In *Nihon Rekishi 14: Kaikin to Sakoku*, edited by Kamiya Nobuyuki and Kimura Naoya, 51–65. Tokyo: Tokyo-Dō Shuppan, 2002.

———, Ishii Masatoshi, and Murai Shōsuke, eds. *Ajia no Naka no Nihonshi, III: Kaijō no Michi.* Tokyo: Tokyo Daigaku Shuppan Kai, 1992.

———, eds. *Nihon no Jidai Shi 14: Edo Bakufu to Higashi Ajia.* Tokyo: Yoshikawa Kōbunkan, 2002.

Ariga Yōen. *Kō to Bukkyō*. Tokyo: Kokusho Kankōkai, 1990.

Asao Naohiro. "Sakoku-sei no Seiritsu." In *Nihon Rekishi 14: Kaikin to Sakoku*, edited by Kamiya Nobuyuki and Kimura Naoya, 18–37. Tokyo: Tokyo-Dō Shuppan, 2002.

———. *Nihon no Kinsei 1: Seikai Shi no naka no Kinsei*. Tokyo: Chuo Kōronsha, 1991.

———. *Nihon Kinseishi no Jiritsu*. Tokyo: Azekura Shobō, 1988.

Attman, Artur. *American Bullion in the European World Trade, 1600–1800.* Goeteburg: Acta Regiae Societatis Scientiarum et Litterarum Gothoburgensis Humaniora, 1986.

———. *Dutch Enterprise in the World Bullion Trade, 1550–1800.* Goeteborg, Almqvist and Wiksell, 1983.

Atwell, William. "International Bullion Flows and the Chinese Economy circa 1530–1650." *Past and Present* 95 (1982): 68–90.

———. "Ming Observers of Ming Decline: Some Chinese Views of the Seventeenth Century Crisis." *The Journal of the Royal Asiatic Society* 2 (1988): 316–348.

Awad, Abdul Aziz. "The Gulf in the Seventeenth Century." *Bulletin (British Society for Middle Eastern Studies)* 12: 2 (1985): 123–134.

Ayusawa Shintarō. "Geography and Japanese Knowledge of World Geography." *Monumenta Nipponica* 19: 3/4 (1964): 275–294.

Bassett, D. K. "The Trade of the English East India Company in the Far East, 1623–1684." *The Journal of the Royal Asiatic Society* (1960), 32–57.

de Beauclair, Inez. *Neglected Formosa; A Translation from the Dutch of Frederic Coyett's* 't Verwaerloosde Formosa. San Francisco: Chinese Materials Center, Inc., 1975.

Berg, G. L. "Schatgravers naar De Liefde." *Spiegel Historiael* 3 (1968): 355–360.

Berry, Mary Elizabeth. *Hideyoshi*. Cambridge: The Council on East Asian Studies and The Harvard University Press, 1989.

Beylen, J. van. "Scheepstypen." In *Maritieme Geschiedenis der Nederlanden, Vol. 2: Zeventiende Eeuw.* Bussum: De Boer Maritiem, 1976–1978.

———. *Schepen der Nederlanden. Van de Laate Middeleeuwen tot het Einde van de Zeventiende Eeuw*. Amsterdam, van Kampen, 1970.

Blair, Emma Helen, and James Robertson, eds. *The Philippine Islands 1493–1898, Vol. 9–11*. Cleveland: The Arthur H. Clark Company, 1904.

Blakewell, P. J. *Silver Mining and Society in Colonial Mexico, Zacatecas, 1546–1700.* Cambridge: Cambridge University Press, 1971.

Blitz, Rudolph. "Mercantilist Policies and the Pattern of World Trade." *The Journal of Economic History* 27: 1 (1967): 39–55.

Blussé, Leonard. "Japanese Historiography and European Sources." In *Reappraisals in Overseas History*, edited by P. C. Emmer and H. L. Wesseling. Leiden: Leiden University Press, 1979.

______, and Cynthia Viallé (trans.), *The Deshima Dagregisters Volume XI: 1641–1650* (Leiden: Institute for the History of European Expansion, 2001).

———. "No Boats to China. The Dutch East India Company and the Changing Pattern of the China Sea Trade, 1635–1690." *Modern Asian Studies* 30: 1 (1996): 51–76.

———, M. E. van Opstall, and Ts'ao Yung-Ho. *De Dagregisters van het Kasteel Zeelandia, Taiwan: Deel I, 1629–1641.* 's-Gravenhage: Martinus Nijhoff, 1986.

———, M. E. van Opstall, and Ts'ao Yung-Ho. *De Dagregisters van het Kasteel Zeelandia, Taiwan: Deel II, 1641–1648.* Den Hague: Instituut voor Nederlandse Geschiedenis, 1995.

Blussé, Leonard and Femme Gaastra, eds. *Companies and Trade: Essays on Overseas Trading Companies During the Ancién Regime.* Leiden: Leiden University Press, 1981.

——— and Jap de Moor. *Nederlanders Overzee: De Eerste Vijftig Jaar 1600–1650*. Franeker: Uitgeverij T. Weber, 1983.

———. "Dutch Protestant Missionaries as Protaganists of the Territorial Expanison of the VOC on Formosa." In *Conversion, Competition, and Conflict: Essays on the Role of Religion in Asia*, edited by Dick Kooiman,155–184. Amsterdam: Free University Press, 1984.

Bodart-Bailey, Beatrice, trans. *Kaempfer's Japan: Tokugawa Culture Observed.* Honolulu: University of Hawai'i Press, 1999.

Bogucka, Maria. "Amsterdam and the Baltic in the First Half of the Seventeenth Century." *Economic History Review* 26: 3 (1973).

Borah, Woodrow. *Early Colonial Trade and Navigation Between Mexico and Peru.* Berkeley: University of California Press, 1954.

Boxer, Charles. "Jan Compagnie in Japan, 1672–1674." *Transactions of the Asiatic Society of Japan, Second Series* 7 (1931): 138–203.

———. *The Dutch Seaborne Empire, 1600–1800.* London: Penguin Books, 1965.

———. "Notes on Early European Military Influence in Japan." *Transactions of the Asiatic Society of Japan, Second Series* 8 (1931), 67–93.

———. "The Siege of Fort Zeelandia and the Capture of Formosa from the Dutch, 1661–1662." *Transactions and Proceedings of the Japan Society of London* 24 (1927), 16–47.

———. "The Dutch East-Indiamen: Their Sailors, Their Navigators, and Life on Board, 1602–1795." In *Dutch Merchants and Mariners in Asia, 1602–1795*, 81–104, London: Valorum Reprints, 1988.

———, ed. *South China in the Sixteenth Century.* London: The Hakluyt Society, 1953.

———. *The Christian Century in Japan, 1549–1650.* Berkeley: University of California Press, 1951.

———. "The Rise and Fall of Nicholas Iquan." *T'ien Hsia Monthly* 11 (1941): 401–439.

Brading, D. A., and Harry Cross. "Colonial Silver Mining: Mexico and Peru." *Hispanic American Historical Review* 52 (1972): 545–579.

Brakel, S. van. *De Hollandsche Handelscompanieën der Zeventiende Eeuw. Hunne Onstaanm Hunne Inrichting.* 's-Gravenhage, Nijhoff, 1908.

Brown, Delmer. *Money Economy in Medieval Japan: A Study in the Use of Coins*. New Haven: Institute of Far Eastern Languages, Yale University, 1951.

Bruijn, J. R., Femme Gaastra, and I. Schoeffer. *Dutch-Asiatic Shipping in the 17th and 18th Centuries: Volume I.* The Hague: Martinus Nijhoff, 1987.

Burnell, Arthur Coke, ed. *The Voyage of John Huyghen van Linschoten to the East Indies in Two Volumes.* London: The Hakluyt Society, 1885.

Campbell, William. *Formosa Under the Dutch: Described from Contemporary Records.* Taipei: Ch'eng Wen Publishing Company, 1972.

Caron, Francois. *Beschrijvinghe van het Machtigh Koninghrijcke Japan, Dervattende Den Aerdt en Eyghenschappen van't Landt, Manieren der Volckeren, als Mede Hare Grouwelijcke Wreedtheydt Teghen de Roomsche Christenen/ Ghesteldt door Francoys Caron.* Amsterdam: Joost Hartgers, 1652.

Chang, Aloysius. *The Chinese Community of Nagasaki in the First Century of the Tokugawa Period, 1603–1688.* Ann Arbor: University Microfilms International, 1970.

Chaudhuri, K. N. "The East India Company and the Export of Treasure in the Early Seventeenth Century." *The Economic History Review* 16: 1 (1963): 23–38.

Cheng Shaogang. *De VOC en Formosa, 1624–62: Een Vergeten Geschiedenis.* Leiden: Ridderkerk, 1995.

Chijs, J. A. van der. *De Geschiedenis der Stichting van de VOC.* Leiden, Engels, 1857.

Cieslik, Hubert, S. J. "The Great Martyrdom in Edo of 1623." *Monumenta Nipponica* 10: 1 (1954).

Clark, G. N. "Early Capitalism and Invention." *The Economic History Review* 6: 2 (1936): 143–156.

Colenbrander, H. T., ed. *Jan Pietersz. Coen, Bescheiden Omtrent Zijn Bedrijf in Indië.* 's-Gravenhage: Matinus Nijhoff, 1919.

Coolhaas, W. Ph., ed. *Generale Missiven van Governeurs-Generaal en Raden aan Heren XVII der Vereenigde Oostindische Compagnie: Deel I, 1610–1638.* 's-Gravenhage: Martinus Nijhoff, 1960.

———, ed. *Generale Missiven van Governeurs-Generaal en Raden aan Heren XVII der Vereenigde Oostindische Compagnie: Deel II, 1639–1655.* 's-Gravenhage: Martinus Nijhoff, 1964.

———, ed. *Generale Missiven van Governeurs-Generaal en Raden aan Heren XVII der Vereenigde Oostindische Compagnie: Deel III, 1655–1674.* 's-Gravenhage: Martinus Nijhoff, 1968.

———. "De Vereenigde Oostindische Compagnie." In *Algemene Geshiedenis der Nederlanden 7: Niewe Tijd*, 147–182. Haarlem: Fibula van Dishoeck, 1980.

———, ed. *Pieter van den Broecke in Azië*. 's-Gravenhage: Nijhoff, 1962.

Cooper, Michael. "The Mechanics of the Macao-Nagasaki Silk Trade." *Monumenta Nipponica* 27: 4 (1972): 423–433.

———, ed. *Joao Rodrigues's Account of Sixteenth-Century Japan.* London: The Hakluyt Society, 2001.

Corr, William. *Adams the Pilot: The Life and Times of Captain William Adams: 1564– 1620.* London: Japan Library, 1995.

Crawcour, Sydney. "Notes on Shipping and Trade in Japan and the Ryūkyūs." *The Journal of Asian Studies* 23: 3 (1964): 377–381.

———. "The Development of a Credit System in Seventeenth-Century Japan." *The Journal of Economic History* 21: 3 (1961): 342–360.

Croizier, Ralph. *Koxinga and Chinese Nationalism: History, Myth and the Hero.* Cambridge: Harvard University Press, 1977.

Curtin, Philip. *Cross-Cultural Trade in World History*. London: Cambridge University Press, 1984.

Dai Nihon Kinsei Shiryō, 113 Volumes. Tokyo: Shiryō Hensanjō, 1969.

Dekker, F. *De Betrekkingen Tusschen de Oost-Indische Compagnie en Japan.* 's-Gravenhage: Boucher, 1941.

de La Court de Jonge, Pieter. *Interest van Holland, ofte Gronden van Hollandse Welvaren.* 't Amsterdam: Joan Cyprianus van der Gracht, 1662.

Dales, J. H. "The Discoveries and Mercantilism: An Essay in History and Theory." *The Canadian Journal of Economics and Political Science* 21: 2 (1955): 141–153.

Van Dam, Pieter. *Beschryvinge van de Oostindische Compagnie, 7 Volumes.* Edited by F. W. Stapel and C. W. Th. van Boetzelaer. The Hague: Rijks Geschiedenis Publicatiën, 1977.

Davidson, James. *The Island of Formosa Past and Present.* Oxford: Oxford University Press, 1988.

Departement van Koloniën. *Daghregister Gehouden in't Casteel Batavia vant Passerende Daar ter Plaetse als Over Geheel Nederlandts Indië.* 's-Gravenhage: Nijhoff, 1887–1931.

Diffe, Bailey W. and George D. Winius. *Foundations of the Portuguese Empire 1415–1580.* Minneapolis: University of Minnesota Press, 1977.

Van Dillen, J. G. "Geld en Bank Wezen." In *Zeven Eeuwen Amsterdam 2: De Zeventiende Eeuw,* edited by A. E. d'Ailley. Amsterdam: Joost van den Vondel, 1947.

_____. *Bronnen tot de Geschiedenis der Wissebanken, 2 Volumes.* 's-Gravenhage: Martinus Nijhoff, 1925.

Edo Bakufu Nikki. Tokyo: Nogami Shuppan, 1985.

Elison, George. *Deus Destroyed: The Image of Christianity in Early Modern Japan.* Cambridge: Harvard University Press, 1973.

Elisonas, Jurgis. "The Inseparable Trinity: Japan's relations with China and Korea." In *The Cambridge History of Japan, Volume 4: Early Modern Japan,* edited by John Hall, 235–300. Cambridge: Cambridge University Press, 1991.

Elliott, J. H. *Europe Divided, 1559–1598.* Oxford: Blackwell Publishers, 1968.

Emmer, P. C., and Femme Gaastra. "De Vaart Buiten Europa." In *Maritieme Geschiedenis der Nederlanden, Vol. 2: Zeventiende Eeuw.* Bussum: De Boer Maritiemm, 1976.

Fisher, Wolfram, Marvin McInnis, and Jürgen Schneider, eds. *The Emergence of a World Economy, 1500–1914 (Papers of the IX International Congress of Economic History).* Stuttgart: F. Steiner Verlag Wiesbaden, 1986.

Fitch, Ralph. *Aanmerklyke Reys van Ralph Fitch, Koopman te Londen, Gedaan van Anno 1583 tot 1591: Na Ormus, Goa, Cambaya, Bacola, Chonderi,*

Pegu, Jamahay in Siam, en Weer na Pegu: van Daar na Malacca, Ceylon, Cochin, en de Geheel Kust van Oost-Indiën nu Aldereerst uyt het Engelsch Vertaald; met Schoone Figueren, en een Volkomen Register. Leyden: Pieter van der Aa, 1706.

Flershem, Robert. "Some Aspects of the Japan Sea Trade in the Tokugawa Period." *The Journal of Asian Studies* 23: 3 (1964): 405–416.

Flynn, Dennis. "Comparing the Tokugawa Shogunate with Hapsburg Spain: Two Silver Based Empires in a Global Setting." In *The Political Economies of Merchant Empires,* edited by James D. Tracy Cambridge: Cambridge University Press 1991, 332–359.

Fujii Jōji. *Edo Kaibaki.* Tokyo: Shūeisha, 1992.

———. "17 Seiki no Nihon—Buke no Kokka no Keisei." In *Nihon Tsūshi 12: Kinsei 2*, edited by Asao Naohiro, et al., 40–41, Tokyo: Iwanami Shoten, 1993.

Fujino Tamotsu, ed. *Ronshu Bakuhan Taisei Shi 8: Taigai Kankei to Sakoku.* Tokyo: Yūzankaku, 1995.

Fumoto Saburō. *Sado Kinginzan Shiwa.* Tokyo: Mitsubishi Kinzoku Kōgyō, 1973.

Furber, Holden. *Rival Empires of Trade in the Orient, 1600–1800.* Minneapolis: University of Minnesota Press, 1976.

Gaastra, Femme. "De VOC in Azië tot 1680." In *Algemene Geschiedenis der Nederlanden, Vol. 7: Niewe Tijd.* Haarlem: Fibula van Dishoeck, 1980.

———. "De Vereenigde Oostindische Compagnie in the 17de en 18de Eeuw: de Grooie van een Bedrijf. Geld Tegen Goederen." *Bijdragen en Mededelingen Betreffende Geschiedenis der Nederlanden* 91 (1976): 244–272.

———. "The Exports of Precious Metal from Europe to Asia by the Dutch East India Company." In *Precious Metals in the Later Medieval and Early Modern Worlds*, edited by J. F. Richards, 447–476, Durham: Carolina Academic Press, 1983.

———. *De Geshiedenis van de VOC.* Zutphen: Walburg Pers, 2002.

———. "The Dutch East India Company and its International Trade in precious Metals." In *The Emergence of a World Economy, 1500–1914 (Papers of the IX International Congress of Economic History)*, edited by Wolfram Fisher, Marvin McInnis, and Jürgen Schneider, 151–166, Stuttgart: F. Steiner Verlag Wiesbaden, 1986.

Gernet, Jacques. *A History of Chinese Civilization.* Cambridge: Cambridge University Press, 1982.

Glahn, Richard von. "Myth and Reality of China's Seventeenth-Century Monetary Crisis." *The Journal of Economic History* 56: 2 (1996): 429–454.

Glamman, Kristof. *Dutch-Asiatic Trade, 1620–1740*. 's-Gravenhage: Nijhoff, 1958.

———. "The Dutch East India Company's Trade in Japanese Copper, 1645–1736." In *Metals and Monies in an Emerging Global Economy*, edited by Dennis Flynn and Arturo Giraldez., 95–134, Aldershot: Variorum, 1997.

Gonoi Tadashi. "Keichō 14 Nen Ki-ito Bōeki ni tsuite." *Shigaku Zasshi* 81: 11 (1972): 37–64.

Goodman, Grant. *The Dutch Impact on Japan, 1640–1853.* Leiden: E. J. Brill, 1967.

Goodrich, L. Carrington and Chaoying Fang, eds. *A Dictionary of Ming Biography, 1368–1644.* New York: Columbia University Press, 1976.

Gupta, Ashin Das. "Indian Merchants and the Western Indian Ocean: the Early Seventeenth Century." *Modern Asian Studies* 19: 3 (1985): 481–499.

Hall, John W. "Notes on the Early Ch'ing Copper Trade with Japan." *Harvard Journal of Asiatic Studies* 12: 3/4 (1949): 444–461.

Hamashita Takeshi. *Kindai Chūgoku no Kokusaiteki Keiki: Chōkō Bōeki Shisutemu to Kindai Ajia.* Tokyo: Tokyo Daigaku Shuppan Kai, 1990.

——— and Kawakatsu Heita, eds. *Ajia Kōeki-ken to Nihon Kōgyō-ka, 1500–1900.* Tokyo: Riburo, 1991.

Hart, S. "Amsterdam Shipping and Trade to Northern Russia in the Seventeenth Century." *Mededelingen van de Nederlandse Vereninging voor Zeegeschiedenis* 26 (1973) , 5–30.

Hayami Akira. "A Great Transformation: Social and Economic Change in Sixteenth and Seventeenth Century Japan." *Bonner Zeitschrift fur Japanologie* 8 (1986), 3–13.

Hayashi Fukusai. "Koshūki." In *Tsūkō Ichiran (8 Volumes), Vol. 4*. Tokyo: Kokusho Kankōkai, 1967.

Hazard, Benjamin. "The Formative Years of the Wakō, 1223–63." *Monumenta Nipponica* 22: 3/4 (1967): 260–77.

Hesselink, Reinier. *De Gevangenen uit Nambu: Een Waar Geschiedverhaal over de VOC in Japan*. Zutphen: Walburg Pers, 2000.

Het Archief van de Nederlandse Factorij in Japan, 1609–1860 (Identification Code 1.04.21). Den Hague: Algemeene Rijksarchief.

Hobsbawm, E. J. "The General Crisis of the European Economy in the Seventeenth Century." *Past and Present* 5 (1954): 33–53.

Horst, W. A. "De Pepperhandel van de Verenigde Oostindische Compagnie." *Bijdragen Voor Vaderlandsche Geschiedenis en Oudheidskunde* 8: 3 (1942), 95–103.

Hsieh Chiao-min. *Taiwan—Ihla Formosa: A Geography in Perspective.* Washington: Butterworths, 1964.

Hung Chien-Chao. *A History of Taiwan.* Rimini: Il Cerchio, 2000.

Hyma, Albert. *The Dutch in the Far East: A History of the Dutch Commercial and Colonial Empire.* Ann Arbor: George Wahr Publishers, 1942.

———. "Calvinism and Capitalism in the Netherlands." *The Journal of Modern History,* 10: 3 (1938): 321–343.

Ichimura Yuichi and Ōishi Shinzaburō. *Sakoku=Yuruyaka na Jōhō Kakumei.* Tokyo: Kodansha Gendai Shinsho, 1996.

Innes, Robert. "The Door Ajar: Japan's Foreign Trade in the Seventeenth Century." PhD diss., University of Michigan, 1980.

Inoue Toshio. *Kenshin to Shingen.* Tokyo: Nihon Rekishi Shinsho, 1966.

Irwin, Douglas. "Mercantilism as Strategic Trade Policy: The Anglo-Dutch Rivalry for The East India Trade." *The Journal of Political Economy* 99: 6 (1991): 1296–1314.

Ishihara Michihiro. *Nihon Rekishi Sosho 7: Wakō.* Tokyo: Yoshikawa Kōbunkan, 1964.

Ishii Kenji. *Nihon no Fune.* Tokyo: Sōgensha, 1957.

———. *Zusetsu Wasen Shiwa.* Tokyo: Shiseidō, 1983.

Israel, J. I. "A Conflict of Empires: Spain and The Netherlands, 1618–1648." *Past and Present* 76 (1977): 34–74.

———. "Mexico and the 'General Crisis' of the Seventeenth Century." *Past and Present* 63 (1974): 33–57.

———. "Spain, the Spanish Embargoes, and the Struggle for Mastery of World Trade, 1585–1660." In *Empires and Entrepots; The Dutch, the Spanish Monarchy and The Jews, 1585–1713.* London: Hambledon Press, 1990.

Itazawa Takeo. *Nihon to Oranda: Kinsei no Gaikō, Bōeki, Gakumon.* Tokyo: Shibundō, 1955.

———. *Nichi-Ran Bōeki Shi*. Tokyo: Heibonsha, 1953.

Iwano Hisashi. "Filipin Bōeki to Sukezaemon/Kiemon." In *Nihon Rekishi 9: Shuinsen To Minami e no Senkish*, edited by Ōishi, 34–47. Tokyo: Gyōsei, 1986.

Iwao Seiichi. *Shuinsen Bōeki shi no Kenkyū.* Tokyo: Kyōbundō, 1958.

———. *Nihon no Rekishi 14: Sakoku.* Tokyo: Chūo Koronsha, 1966.

———. *Kaigai Kōshōshi no Shiten*, Vol. 2. Tokyo: Nihon Shoseki, 1976.

———. *Nihon Rekishi Shinsho: Shuinsen to Nihonmachi*. Tokyo: Shibundō, 1966.

———. "Shuinsen Bōeki-ke no Seikaku." In *Ronshu Bakuhan Taisei Shi 8: Taigai Kankei to Sakoku*, edited by Fujino Tamotsu. Tokyo: Yūzankaku, 1995.

———, ed. *Oranda Fusetsugaki Shūsei (A Collection of the World News Presented Annually by the Dutch Factory at Deshima to the Tokugawa Shogunate, 1641–1857).* Tokyo: The Japan-Netherlands Institute, 1976.

———. "Sakoku." In *Taigai Kankei to Sakoku*, edited by Fujino Tamotsu. Tokyo: Yūzankaku, 1993.

———. *Kinsei ni okeru Nihonjin no Nanyō Hatten.* Tokyo: Keimeikai/Hatsubaijō Hokuryokan, 1941.

———. "Taijin no Tai Nikkoku Bōeki Hukkatsu Undō." *Tō-A Ronsō* 4: 85 (1941), 27–54.

———. "Li Tan, Chief of the Chinese Residents at Hirado, Japan, in the Last Days of the Ming Dynasty." *Memoirs of the Research Department of the Tōyō Bunkō* 17 (Tokyo: Toyo Bunko, 1958): 27–83.

———. "Shiqi Shiji Riben ren zhi Taiwan Qinlue Xingdong." *Taiwan Yanjiu Cong Kan* 71 (1959): 1–23.

Jacobs, Els. *De Vereenigde Oost-Indische Compagnie.* Utrecht: Teleac, 1997.

Jansen, Marius. *The Making of Modern Japan*. Cambridge: The Belknap Press of Harvard University, 2000.

Jones, S. R. H., and Simon Ville. "Efficient Transactors or Rent-Seeking Monopolists? The Rationale for Early Chartered Trading Companies." *The Journal of Economic History* 56: 4 (1966): 898–915.

Kaempfer, Engelbert. *The History of Japan, 3 Volumes.* Translated by J. G. Scheuzcher. New York: AMS Press, 1971.

Katagiri Kazuo. *Hirakareta Sakoku—Nagasaki Deshima no Hito, Mono, Jyōhō.* Tokyo: Kodansha Gendai Shinsho, 1997.

Katō Eiichi. "The Japanese-Dutch Trade in the Formative Period of the Seclusion Policy, Particularly in the Raw Silk Trade by the Dutch Factory at Hirado 1620–1640." *Acta Asiatica* 30 (1976), 34–84.

———. "Unification and Adaptation, The Early Shogunate and Dutch Trade Policies." In *Companies and Trade: Essays on Overseas Trading Companies During the Ancién Regime,* edited by Leonard Blussé and Femme Gaastra. Leiden: Leiden University Press, 1981.

———. "Bawansen, Shuinsen, Hōshosen—Bakuhan-sei Kokka no Keisei to Taigai Kankei." In *Nihon Rekishi 14: Kaikin to Sakoku,* edited by Kamiya Nobuyuki and Kimura Naoya, 41–51. Tokyo: Tokyo-dō Shuppan, 2002.

———. "Deshima Ron." In *Nihon Tsūshi 12: Kinsei 2,* edited by Asao Naohiro. Tokyo: Iwanami Kōza, 1993.

———. "Seiritsuki no Itowappu ni kansuru Ikkōsatsu." In *Nihon Shakai Keizaishi Kenkyū, Kinsei Hen.* Tokyo: Yoshikawa Kōbunkan, 1967.

Katō Hidetoshi. "The Significance of the Period of National Seclusion Reconsidered." *Journal of Japanese Studies* 7: 1 (1981): 85–109.

Kawaji Toshiakira. *Nagasaki Nikki.* In *Tōyō Bunkō 124: Nagasaki Nikki, Shimoda Nikki.* Tokyo: Heibonsha, 1968.

Kawajima Genjirō. *Shuinsen Bōeki Shi.* Tokyo: Naigai Shuppan Kabushikigaisha, 1922.

Kawakatsu Heita, ed. *"Sakoku" wo Hiraku.* Tokyo: Dōbunkan, 2000.

Kazui Tashirō. *Kinsei Nitchō Tsūkō Bōekishi no Kenkyū.* Tokyo: Sōbunsha, 1981.

———. "Exports of Japan's Silver to China via Korea and Changes in the Tokugawa Monetary System During the Seventeenth and Eighteenth Centuries." In *Metals and Monies in an Emerging Global Economy,* edited by Dennis Flynn and Arturo Giraldez. Aldershot: Variorum, 1997.

——— and Susan Videen. "Foreign Relations During the Edo Period: Sakoku Reexamined." *Journal of Japanese Studies* 8: 2 (1982): 283–306.

———. "Tokugawa Jidai no Bōeki." In *Nihon Keizai Shi, Ichikeizai Shakai no Seiritsu, 17–18 Seiki, Vol. 1,* edited by Hayami Akira and Miyamoto Masao. Tokyo: Iwanami Shoten, 1988.

Keene, Donald. *The Battles of Coxinga: Chikamatsu's Puppet Play, Its Background and Importance.* London: Taylor Foreign Press, 1951.

Kikuchi Junsuke, ed. *Tokugawa Kinrei Kō Kōsho.* Tokyo: Yoshikawa Kōbunkan, 1931–32.

Kishimoto-Nakayama, Mio. "The Kangxi Depression and Early Qing Local Markets." *Modern China* 10: 2 (1984): 227–256.

Kitajima Masamoto. *Edo Bakufu no Kenryoku Kōzō.* Tokyo: Iwanami Shoten, 1964.

Klein, P. W. "De Zeventiende Eeuw (1585–1700)." In *De Economische Geschiedenis van Nederland*, edited by J. H. Stuijvenberg, 79–118. Groningen: Wolters-Noordhoff, 1979.

———. "De Tonkinees-Japanse Zijdehandel van de Vereenigde Oost-Indische Compagnie en et Inter-Aziatische Verkeer in de 17de Eeuw." In *Bewogen en Bewegen. De Historicus in het Spanningsveld Tussen Economie en Cultuur.* Tilburg: J. J. Voskuil, 1986.

Kobata Atsushi. *Nihon Kahei Ryūtsūshi.* Tokyo: Tōkō Shoin, 1969.

———. "The Production and Uses of Gold and Silver in Sixteenth and Seventeenth Century Japan." *The Economic History Review* 18: 2 (1965): 245–266.

———. *Kōzan no Rekishi.* Tokyo: Nihon Rekishi Shinsho, 1959.

———. "Edo Shoki ni okeru Kaigai Kōeki." In *Nihon Keizai no Kenkyū*, edited by Kobata Atsushi. Tokyo: Shibunkaku Shuppan, 1978.

Kodama Kōta. *Shiryō ni yoru: Nihon no Ayumi, Vol. 3: Kinsei Hen.* Tokyo: Yoshikawa Kōbunkan, 1972.

Kokushi Daijiten, 15 Volumes. Tokyo: Yoshikawa Kōbunkan, 1979–1997.

Kuiper, J. Fenstra. *Japan en de Buitenwereld in de Achtiende Eeuw.* 's-Gravenhage: Martinus Nijhoff, 1921.

Kuno Yoshio. *Japanese Expansion on the Asiatic Continent.* Berkeley: University of California Press, 1937.

Lach, Donald, and Edwin van Kley. *Asia in the Making of Europe: Volume 3, A Century of Advance.* Chicago: The University of Chicago Press, 1993.

Lee, John. "Trade and Economy in Pre-Industrial East Asia, c.1500–1800." *The Journal of Asian Studies* 58: 1 (1999): 2–26.

Lewis, James. *Frontier Contact between Chosŏn Korea and Tokugawa Japan.* London: RoutledgeCurzon, 2003.

Lockwood, William. "Adam Smith and Asia." *The Journal of Asian Studies* 23: 3 (1964): 345–355.

Lunsford, Virginia. *Piracy and Privateering in the Golden Age Netherlands.* New York: Palgrave, 2005.

Maehira Fusaaki. "Bōeki no Tenkai." In *Shintaikei Nihon Shi 12: Ryūtsū Keisai Shi*, edited by Sakurai Eiji and Nakanishi Satoru Tokyo: Yamakawa Shuppansha, 2002.

Marshall, P. J. "Western Arms in Maritime Asia in the Early Phases of Expansion." *Modern Asian Studies* 14: 1 (1980): 13–28.

Massarella, Derek, and Izumi Tyler. "The Japonian Charters. The English and Dutch Shuinjō." *Monumenta Nipponica* 45: 2 (1990): 189–205.

———. "Ticklish Points: The East India Company and Japan, 1621." *The Journal of the Royal Asiatic Society* 11 (2001): 43–50.

———. *A World Elsewhere: Europe's Encounter with Japan in the Sixteenth and Seventeenth Centuries.* New Haven: Yale University press, 1990.

McClain, James. "Castle Towns and Daimyo Authority: Kanazawa in the Years 1583–1630." *Journal of Japanese Studies* 6: 2 (1980): 267–299.

Meilink-Roelofsz, M. A. P. *Asian Trade and European Influnce in the Indonesian Archipelago Between 1500 and About 1630.* The Hague: Martinus Nijhoff, 1962.

———. "Een Vergelijkend Onderzoek van Bestuur en Handel der Nederlandse en Engelse Handelscompagnieën op Azië en de Eerste Helft van de Zeventiende Eeuw." *Bijdragen en Mededelingen Betreffende de Geschiedenis der Nederlanden* 91 (1976): 196–217.

Moer, A van der. *Een Zestiende Eeuwse Hollander in het Verre Oosten en het Hoge Noorden: Leven en Werken, Reizen en Avonturen van Jan Huygen van Linschoten.* 's-Gravenhage: Martinus Nijhoff, 1979.

Montanus, Arnoldus. *Gedenkwaerdige Gesantschappen der Oost-Indische Maetschappy in't Vereenigde Nederland, aen de Kaisaren van Japan: Vervaetende Wonderlijke Voorvallen op de Togt der Nederlandsche Gesanten: Beschryvinge van de Dorpen, Sterkten, Steden, Landschappen, Tempels, Gods-Diensten, Dragten... Vereeuwde en Niewe Oorlogs-Daeden der Japanners: Verciert met een Groot Getal Afbeeldsels in Japan Geteikent: Getrokken uit de Geschriften en Reis-Aentekeningen Derselve Gesanten.* 't Amsterdam: Jacob Meurs, 1669.

Morris-Suzuki, Tessa. *The Technological Transformation of Japan: From the Seventeenth Century to the Twenty-first Century.* Cambridge: Cambridge University Press, 1994.

Murakami Naojirō. *Bōeki Shijō no Hirado*. Tokyo: Nihon Gakujutsu Fūkyūkai, 1917.

———, ed. *Ikoku Ōfuku Shōkan Shū.* Tokyo: Omatsu-dō Shoten, 1966.

Murdoch, James, and Iso Yamagata. *A History of Japan, Vol. I.* London: Routledge and K. Paul, 1949.

Nachod, Oskar. *Niederländishen Ostindischen Kompagnie zu Japan in Siebzehnten Jahrhundert.* Leipzig: Rob. Friese Sep.-Cto., 1897.

Nagahara Keiji and Yamamura Kozo. "Shaping the Process of Unification: Technological Progress in Sixteenth- and Seventeenth-Century Japan." *Journal of Japanese Studies* 14: 1 (1988): 77–109.

Nagazumi Yoko. *Hirado Oranda Shōkan no Nikki, Volume 1,3.* Tokyo: Iwanami Shoten, 1969.

——— and Takeda Mariko. *Hirado Oranda Shōkan Igirisu Shōkan Nikki: Nihon to no Sakoku e no Michi.* Tokyo: Soshiete, 1981.

———. "Yamada Nagamasa—Shijitsu to Densetsu." in *Nihon Rekishi 9: Shuinsen to Minami e no Senkishi*, edited by Ōishi, 48–61. Tokyo: Gyōsei, 1986.

———. *Nihon Rekishi Sōsho 60: Shuinsen.* Tokyo: Yoshikawa Kōbunkan, 2001.

———. "17 Seiki no Higashi Ajia Bōeki." In *Ajia Kōekihen to Nihon Kōgyōka, 1500–1900*, edited by Hamashita Takeshi and Kawakatsu Heita. Tokyo: Liburo, 1991.

Nakada Yasunao. "Itowappu no Seiritsu." In *Ronshu Bakuhan Taisei Shi 8: Taigai Kankei to Sakoku*, edited by Tamotsu Fujino Tokyo: Yūzankaku, 1995.

Nakai, Kate Wildman. *Shogunal Politics: Arai Hakuseki and the Premises of Tokugawa Rule.* Cambridge: Harvard University Press, 1988.

Nakamura Hidetaka. *Nissen Kankei Shi no Kenkyū, Volume II.* Tokyo: Yoshikawa Kōbunkan, 1967.

Nakamura Tadashi, ed. *Ikoku Nikki: Konchi-in Sūden Gaikō Bunsho Shūsei: Eiinbon.*Tokyo: Tokyo Bijutsu, 1989.

———. *Kinsei Nagasaki Bōekishi no Kenkyū.* Tokyo: Yoshikawa Kōbunkan, 1988.

———, ed. *Sakoku to Kokusai Kankei.* Tokyo: Yoshikawa Kōbunkan, 1997.

———. "Taiwan wo Meguru Nichi-Ran Kankei." In *Shuinsen to Minami e no Senkisha.* Tokyo: Gyōsei, 1986.

Nakane, Chie, and Shinzaburō Ōishi, *Tokugawa Japan: The Social and Economic Antecedents of Modern Japan.* Translated by Conrad Totman (Tokyo: Univeristy of Tokyo Press, 1991).

Narushima Motonao. *Kokushi Taikei: Tokugawa Jikki, Vol. 38–41.* Edited by Kuroita Katsumi. Tokyo: Yoshikawa Kōbunkan, 1981.

Negotie Journalen 1636–1666. Het Archief van de Nederlandse Factorij in Japan, 1609–1860. Folios 836–860. Den Hague: Algemene Rijksarchief.

Nihon Gakushi-in. *Meiji-zen Nihon Kōgyō Gijitsu Hattatsu Shi*. Tokyo: Nihon Gakushi-in.

Nihon Kagaku Gijitsushi Taikei, 25 Volumes, Vol. 20. Tokyo: Nihon Kagakushi Gakkai, 1965.

Numata Jirō. "Edo Jidai no Bōeki to Taigai Kankei." In *Iwanami Kōza Nihon Rekishi*, *Vol. XIII*, edited by Ienaga Saburō. Tokyo: Iwanami Shoten, 1963.

Okumura Shōji. *Hinawajū kara Kurofune made: Edo Jidai Gijitsu Shi.* Tokyo: Iwanami Shoten, 1970.

Opstall, M. E. van, ed. *De Reis van de Vloot van Pieter Willemsz. Verhoef naar Azië, 1607–1612.* 's-Gravenshage: Martinus Nijhoff, 1972.

Ota Katsuya. *Sakoku Jidai Nagasaki Bōeki Shi no Kenkyū.* Kyoto: Shibunkaku, 1992.

Pacheco, Diego. "The Founding of the Port of Nagasaki and Its Cession to the Society of Jesus." *Monumenta Nipponica* 25 (1970), 303-323.

Pamuk, Sevket. "In the Absence of Domestic Currency: Debased European Coinage in the Seventeenth-Century Ottoman Empire." *The Journal of Economic History* 57: 2 (1997): 345–366.

Paske-Smith, M. *Western Barbarians in Japan and Formosa in Tokugawa Days.* New York: Paragon Books, 1968.

Patterson, C. C. "Silver Stocks and Losses in Ancient and Medieval Times." *The Economic History Review* 25: 2 (1972): 205–235.

Placatten, Ordonnanties, Instructies, Resoluties van de Staten Generaal en de Staten van Holland. Den Hague: Algemeine Rijksarchief.

Pombejra, Dhiravat. *Court, Company, and Campong: Essays on the VOC Presence in Ayutthaya.* Phra Nakhon Sri Ayutthaya: Ayutthaya Hisorical Study Center, 1992.

Prakash, Om, ed. *Precious Metals and Commerce: The Dutch East India Company in the Indian Ocean Trade.* Hampshire: Variorum, 1994.

———. "The Dutch East India Company in the Trade of the Indian Ocean." In *India and the Indian Ocean, 1500–1800*, edited by Ashin Das Gupta and M. N. Pearson. Oxford: Oxford University Press, 1977.

———. "Trade in a Culturally Hostile Environment: Europeans in the Japan Trade, 1550–1700." In *Clashes of Culture: Essays in Honor of Niels Steensgard*, edited by Jens Christian, et al., 50–79. Odense, Odense University Press 1992.

Purchas, Samuel. *Hakluytus Posthumus or Purchas his Pilgrimes: Contayning a History of the World, in Sea Voyages, & Lande-Trauells, by Englishmen and Others. ...Some Left Written by Mr. Hakluyt at his Death more since added, his also Perused, & Perfected. All Examined, Abreuiated, Illustrated w[i]th Notes, Enlarged w[i]th Discourses, Adorned w[i]th Pictures, and Expressed in Mapps. : In Fower Parts, each Containing Fiue Bookes. [Compiled] By Samuel Purchas, B.D.* London: H. Fetherston, 1625.

Purnell, C. J. *The Log-Book of William Adams, 1614–19*. London: The Eastern press, 1915.

Ravina, Mark. *Land and Lordship in Early Modern Japan*. Stanford: Stanford University Press, 1999.

Realia: Register op de Generale Resolutiën van het Kasteel Batavia, 1632–1805. Batavia: Bataviaasch Genootshap van Kunsten en Wetenschappen, 1885.

Reid, Anthony. "An 'Age of Commerce' in Southeast Asian History." *Modern Asian Studies* 24: 1 (1990): 1–30.

Richards, J. F., ed. *Precious Metals in the Later Medieval and Early Modern Worlds.* Durham: Carolina Academic Press, 1983.

Rietbergen, Peter. *Japan Verwoord: Nihon door Nederlandse Ogen, 1600–1799.* Amsterdam: Hotei Publishing, 2003.

Roeper, Vibeke, and Roelof van Gelder, eds. *In Dienst van de Compagnie: Leven bij De VOC in Honderd Getuigenissen, 1602–1799.* Amsterdam: Athenaeum, 2002.

Roessingh, M. P. H. *Het Archief van de Nederlandse Factorij in Japan.* 's-Gravenhage: National Archive, 1964.

———. "Nederlandse Betrekkingen met de Phillipijnen, 1600–1800." *Bijdragen tot de Taal, Land, en Volkenkunde* 124: 4 (1968), 482–504.

Roover, Raymond de. "Monopoly Theory Prior to Adam Smith." *The Quarterly Journal of Economics* 65: 4 (1951): 492–524.

Roy, Denny. *Taiwan: A Political History.* Ithaca: Cornell University Press, 2003.

Rundall, Thomas, ed. *Memorials of the Empire of Japon in the XVI and XVII Centuries.* London: The Hakluyt Society, 1963.

Saar, Johann Jacob. *Verhaal van Drie Voorname Reizen naar Oostindiën; te Weten van Johan Jacobsz. Saar, Volkert Evertsz, en Albrecht Herport: Daarin, Beneffens de Bezondere Voorvallen, hen Overkomen, de Historie en de Voornamste Dingen, die Sedert Vijventwintig Jaren Herwaarts, tot het Jaar Achtenzestig toe, in de Gewesten Geschied Zijn, Voorgestelt Worden.* Amsterdam: Jan Rieuwertsz en Pieter Arentsz, 1671.

Sado-gun Kyōikukai. *Sado Nendai-Ki.* Kanazawa: Sado-gun Kyōikukan, 1938.

Saito Yoshiyuki, ed. *Atarashii Kinsei Shi 3: Shijo to Minkan Shakai.* Tokyo: Shin Jinbutsu Oraisha, 1996.

Sakai, Robert. "The Satsuma-Ryūkyū Trade and the Tokugawa Seclusion Policy." *The Journal of Asian Studies* 23: 3 (1964): 391–403.

Sakuma Shigeo. "Mindai Kaigaishi Bōeki no Rekishiteki Haikai." *Shigaku Zasshi* 63: 1 (1953): 19–21.

Sakurai Eiji and Nakanishi Satoru, eds. *Shintaikei Nihon-Shi 12: Ryūtsū Keizai Shi.* Tokyo: Yamakawa Shuppansha, 2002.

Sanjōnishi Kinkōsa. *Kōdō: Rekishi to Bungaku.* Kyoto: Tankōsha, 1985.

Satow, Ernest, ed. *The Voyage of Captain John Saris, 1613.* London: The Hakluyt Society, Second Series, 1967.

———. "Notes on the Intercourse Between Japan and Siam in the Seventeenth Century." *Transactions of the Asiatic Society of Japan* 13 (1885): 139–210.

Scammell, G. V. "European Exiles, Renegades, and Outlaws and the Maritime Economy of Asia, c.1500–1750." *Modern Asian Studies* 26: 4 (1992): 641–661.

Shepherd, John. *Statecraft and Political Economy on the Taiwan Frontier, 1600–1800.* Stanford: Stanford University Press, 1993.

Shiryō Hensanjo. *Nihon Kankei Kaigai Shiryō. Dagregisters Gehouden bij de Opperhoofden van het Nederlandsche Factorij in Japan, Vols. 1–5.* Tokyo: Tokyo Daigaku Shiryō Hensanjo Kankō, 1974.

Shiryō Hensanjo. *Nihon Kankei Kaigai Shiryō. Igirisu Shōkanchō Nikki.* Tokyo: Tokyo Daigaku Shiryō Hensanjo Kankō, 1974.

Simpkin, C. G. F. *The Traditional Trade of Asia.* London: Oxford University Press, 1968.

Smith, Alan. *Creating a World Economy: Merchant Capital, Colonialism, and World Trade, 1400–1825.* Boulder: Westview Press, 1991.

Smith, George Vinal. *The Dutch in Seventeenth Century Thailand.* Dekalb: Northern Illinois University Special Report No. 16, 1977.

Smith, Woodruff. "The Function of Commercial Centers in the Modernization of European Capitalism: Amsterdam as an Information Exchange in the Seventeenth Century." *The Journal of Economic History* 44: 4 (1984): 985–1005.

Spence, Jonathan, and John Wills, eds. *From Ming to Ch'ing: Conquest, Region, and Continuity in Seventeenth-Century China.* New Haven: Yale University Press, 1979.

Stapel, F. W. *De Vereenigde Oostindische Compagnie in de Groote Oorlogen der 17de Eeuw.* Groningen: Wolters, 1932.

———. ed. *Geschiedenis van Nederlandsche Indië, Vol. II.* Amsterdam: Joost van den Vondel, 1938.

Steensgaard, Niels. "The Seventeenth-Century Crisis and the Unity of Eurasian History." *Modern Asian Studies* 24: 4 (1990): 683–697.

———. *The Asian Trade Revolution of the Seventeenth Century: The East India Companies and the Decline of the Caravan Trade.* Chicago: University of Chicago Press, 1973.

———. "The Dutch East India Company as an Institutional Innovation." In *Dutch Capitalism and World Capitalism*, edited by Maurice Aymard, 235–257. Cambridge: Cambridge University Press, 1982.

Stohls, Eric. "De Zuidelijk Nederlanden en de Oprchting ven de Oost en Westindische Compagnieën." *Bijdragen en Mededelingen Betreffende de Geschiedenis der Nederlanden* 88 (1973): 1–18.

Sugimoto Masayoshi and David Swain. *Science and Culture in Traditional Japan: A.D. 600–1854.* Cambridge: The MIT Press, 1978.

Sugiyama Hiroshi. *Nihon no Rekishi 11: Sengoku Daimyō.* Tokyo: Chūo Kōronsha, 1974.

Suzuki Yasuko. *Kinsei Nichi-Ran Bōeki Shi no Kenkyū.* Tokyo: Shibunkaku, 2004.

Swinhoe, Robert. "Notes on the Island of Formosa." *Journal of the Royal Geographical Society of London* 34 (1864): 6–18.

Takeno Toshi. "Sappan Ryūkyū Bōeki to Shōnin Ishimoto-ke no Kankei." *Kyūshū Keizai Shi Ronshū* 2 (May 1956).

Takeo Itazawa. *Nihon to Oranda: Kinsei no Gaikō, Bōeki, Gakumon.* Tokyo: Nohon Rekishi Shinsho, 1955.

Tanaka Takeo. "Sakoku ni tsuite." In *Nihon Rekishi 14: Kaikin to Sakoku,* edited by Kamiya Nobuyuki and Kimura Naoya, 37–40. Tokyo: Tokyo-dō Shuppan, 2002.

Tex, Jan den. *Oldenbarnevelt.* Haarlem: Tjeenk Willink, 1960–72.

Thompson, Edward, ed. *Diary of Richard Cocks, Cape-Merchant in the English Factory in Japan, 1615–1622: With Correspondences.* London: Hakluyt Society, 1883.

Toby, Ronald. *State and Diplomacy in Early Modern Japan: Asia in the Development of the Tokugawa Bakufu.* Princeton: Princeton University Press, 1984.

———. "Reopening the Question of Sakoku: Diplomacy in the Legitimation of the Tokugawa Bakufu." *Journal of Japanese Studies* 3: 2 (1977): 323–363.

Tomimura Shinen. "Ryūkyū ni okeru Min Nihon to no Kankei." *Rekishi Kyōiku* 8 (1960), 12–18.

Tokugawa Yoshinobu. "Luzon no Tsubo no Imi-suru Mono." In *Nihon Rekishi 9: Shuinsen to Minami e no Senkisha,* edited by Ōishi, 62–75. Tokyo: Gyōsei, 1986.

Tokutomi Ichirō. *Yoyaku Kinsei: Nihon Kokumin Shi, Vol. III: Tokugawa-shi Jidai.* Tokyo: Jiji Press, 1967.

Totman, Conrad. *Politics in the Tokugawa Bakufu, 1600–1843.* Cambridge: Harvard University Press, 1967.

Tracy, James, ed. *The Political Economy of Merchant Empires.* Cambridge: Cambridge University Press, 1991.

Ts'ao Yung-Ho. "Chinese Overseas Trade in the Late Ming Period." *Proceedings, International Association of Historians of Asia, Second Biennial Conference*, 429–457. Taipei: Chinese Historical Association, 1962.

Tsūji Tatsuya. *Nihon no Rekishi 13: Edo Kaibaku.* Tokyo: Chūo Kōronsha, 1966.

Tsukahira Toshio. *Feudal Control in Tokugawa Japan: The Sankin Kōtai System.* Cambridge: Harvard University Press, 1966.

Uehara. *Buhansei Keiseki no Ryūkyū Shihai.* Tokyo: Yoshikawa Kōbunkan, 2001.

Valentyn, Francois. *Oud en Niew Oost-Indiën, Vervattende een Naaukeurige en Uitvoerige Verhandelinge van Nederlands Mofentheyd in die Gewesten, Benevens eene Wydlustige Beschryvinge der Moluccas, Amboina, Banda, Timor, en Solor, Java, en alle de Eylanden onder Deselve Landbestieringen Behoorende; het Nederlands Comptoir op Suratte, en de Levens der Groote Moguls; als ook een Keurlyke Verhandeling van 'tWezentlyskste, dat men Behoort te Weten van Choromandel, Pegu, Arracan, Bengale, Mocha, Persien, Malacca, Sumatra, Ceylon, Malabar, Celebes, of Macassar, China, Japan, Tayouan, of Formosa, Tonkin, Cambodia, Siam, Borneo, Bali, Kaap der Goede Hoop en van Mauritius.* Te Dordrecht: Joannes van Braam te Amsterdam, 1724.

Verhoeven, F. R. J. *Bijdragen tot de Oudere Koloniale Geschiedenis van het Eiland Formosa.* 's-Gravenhage: J. C. van Langen, 1930.

Viraphol, Sarasin. *Tribute and Profit: Sino-Siamese Trade, 1652–1853.* Cambridge: Council for East Asian Studies, Harvard University and Harvard University Press, 1977.

Volker, Tijs. *Porcelain and the Dutch East India Company, as Recorded in the DaghRegisters of Batavia Castle, Those of Hirado and Deshima and Other Contemporary Papers, 1602–1682.* Leiden: Brill, 1954.

Volskuil-Groenewegen, J. H. J. Leeuwrik, and Titus Eliens. *Zilver uit de Tijd van de Vereenigde Oostindische Compagnie.* Zwolle: Waanders Uitgevers, 1998.

De Vries, Jan. "The Population and Economy of the Preindustrial Netherlands." *Journal of Interdisciplinary History* 15: 4 (1985): 661–682.

Wakita Haruko. "Towards a Wider Perspective on Medieval Commerce." *Journal of Japanese Studies* 1: 2 (1975): 321–345.

Wakita Osamu. "The Emergence of the State in 16th Century Japan: From Oda to Tokugawa." *The Journal of Japanese Studies* 8: 2 (1982): 343–367.

Walker, Brett. *The Conquest of Ainu lands: Ecology and Culture in Japanese Expansion, 1590–1800.* Berkeley: University of California Press, 2001.

Watanabe Yogorō. *Kinsei Nihon Bōeki-ron no Tenkai, 1600–1866.* Tokyo: Bunka Shobō Hakubun-sha, 1978.

Wätjen, Hermann. *Die Niederländer im Mittelmeergebiet zur Zeit Ihrer Höchsten Machtstellung.* Berlin: Curtius, 1909.

Wennekes, Wim. *Gouden Handel: De Eerst Nederlanders Overzee, en wat zij daar Haalden.* Amsterdam: Uitgeverij Atlas, 1996.

Whiteway, Richard. *The Rise of Portuguese Power in India, 1497–1550.* London: Santiago de Compostela, Susil Gupta, 1967.

Wills, John E. *Pepper, Guns and Parlays: The Dutch East India Company and China, 1622–1681.* Cambridge: Harvard University Press, 1974.

———. "Maritime China from Wang Chih to Shih Lang: Themes in Peripheral History." In *From Ming to Ch'ing: Conquest, Region, and Continuity in Seventeenth-Century China*, edited by Jonathan Spence and John Wills. New Haven: Yale University Press, 1979.

———. *Embassies and Illusions: Dutch and Portuguese Envoys to K'ang-hsi, 1666–1687.* Cambridge: Council on East Asian Studies, Harvard University, 1984.

Wilson, Charles. "Treasure and Trade Balances: Further Evidence." *The Economic History Review, New Series* 4: 2 (1951): 231–242.

Yamaguchi Keiji. "Kinginzan no Gijitsu to Shakai." In *Kōza Nihon Gijitsu no Shakaishi*, Tokyo: Hyōronsha, 1983.

Yamamoto Hirofumi. *Sakoku to Kaikin no Jidai.* Tokyo: Azekura Shobō, 1995.

Yamamura Kozo and Susan Hanley. "A Quiet Transformation in Tokugawa Economic History." *The Journal of Asian Studies* 30: 2 (1971): 373–384.

Yamawaki Teijirō. *Nagasaki no Oranda Shōkan: Sekai no Naka Sakoku Nihon.* Tokyo: Chūo Shinsho, 1980.

———. *Nagasaki no Tōjin Bōeki (Nihon Rekishi Gakkai Henshū 6).* Tokyo: Yoshikawa Kōbunkan, 1964.

———. "Kinu to Shihaisha-tachi." In *Nihon no Rekishi 10: Shōgun no Kuni to Ihenjin*, edited by Ōishi Shinzaburō. Tokyo: Gyōsei, 1986.

Yanai Kenji. *Nagasaki.* Tokyo: Shibundō, 1959.

——— and Numata Jirō. *Kaigai Kōshōshi no Shiten*, edited by Iwao Seiichi. Tokyo: Nihon Shoseki, 1975.

Yao Keisuke. *Kinsei Oranda Bōeki to Sakoku*. Tokyo: Yoshikawa Kōbunkan, 1998.

Yokoi Tokifuyu. *Nihon Kōgyō Shiyō*. Tokyo: Yoshikawa Hanshichi, 1900.

Yoshida Bonshun. *Shunkyūki, 3 Vols.* Tokyo: Zoku Gunsho Ruijū Kansei-Kai, 1970.

Zandtfleet, Kees. *The Dutch Encounter with Asia, 1600–1950.* Amsterdam: Rijksmuseum, 2002.

Zoku Gunsho Ruijū Kanseikai. *Todaiki/Sunpuki.* Tokyo: Zoku Gunsho Ruijū Kanseikai, 1995.

Index

www.ingramcontent.com/pod-product-compliance
Lightning Source LLC
Chambersburg PA
CBHW051254200926
51612CB00001B/45
* 9 7 8 1 6 0 4 9 7 5 0 0 0 *